With Malice
Toward All?

6/16/00

With Malice Toward All?

The Media and
Public Confidence in
Democratic Institutions

Patricia Moy and Michael Pfau

Praeger Series in Political Communication

Westport, Connecticut
London

Library of Congress Cataloging-in-Publication Data

Moy, Patricia.
    With malice toward all? : the media and public confidence in democratic institutions / Patricia Moy and Michael Pfau.
        p. cm.—(Praeger series in political communication, ISSN 1062–5623)
    Includes bibliographical references and index.
    ISBN 0–275–96433–7 (alk. paper)—ISBN 0–275–96434–5 (pbk. : alk. paper)
    1. Mass media—Political aspects—United States. 2. Mass media—Public opinion. 3. Mass media—Influence. 4. Public opinion—United States.
5. Democracy—United States. 6. United States—Politics and government—1993–
I. Pfau, Michael. II. Title. III. Series.
P95.82.U5 M69   2000
302.23'0973—dc21   99–046408

British Library Cataloguing in Publication Data is available.

Library of Congress Catalog Card Number: 99–046408
ISBN: 0–275–96433–7
      0–275–96434–5 (pbk.)
ISSN: 1062–5623

First published in 2000

Praeger Publishers, 88 Post Road West, Westport, CT 06881
An imprint of Greenwood Publishing Group, Inc.
www.praeger.com

Printed in the United States of America

The paper used in this book complies with the Permanent Paper Standard issued by the National Information Standards Organization (Z39.48–1984).

10 9 8 7 6 5 4 3 2 1

To our parents

Contents

CONTENTS

Series Foreword

Those of us from the discipline of communication studies have long believed that communication is prior to all other fields of inquiry. In several other forums I have argued that the essence of politics is "talk" or human interaction.[1] Such interaction may be formal or informal, verbal or nonverbal, public or private but it is always persuasive, forcing us consciously or subconsciously to interpret, to evaluate, and to act. Communication is the vehicle for human action.

From this perspective, it is not surprising that Aristotle recognized the natural kinship of politics and communication in his writings *Politics* and *Rhetoric*. In the former, he establishes that humans are "political beings [who] alone of the animals [are] furnished with the faculty of language."[2] And in the latter, he begins his systematic analysis of discourse by proclaiming that "rhetorical study, in its strict sense, is concerned with the modes of persuasion."[3] Thus, it was recognized over 2,300 years ago that politics and communication go hand in hand because they are essential parts of human nature.

Back in 1981, Dan Nimmo and Keith Sanders proclaimed that political communication was an emerging field.[4] Although its origin, as noted, dates back centuries, a "self-consciously cross-disciplinary" focus began in the late 1950s. Thousands of books and articles later, colleges and universities offer a variety of graduate and undergraduate coursework in the area in such diverse departments as communication, mass communication, journalism, political science, and sociology.[5] In Nimmo and Sanders' early assessment, the "key areas of inquiry" included rhetorical analysis, propaganda analysis, attitude change studies, voting studies, government and the news media, functional and systems analyses, tech-

nological changes, media technologies, campaign techniques, and research techniques.[6] In a survey of the state of the field in 1983, the same
authors and Lynda Kaid found additional, more specific areas of concerns such as the presidency, political polls, public opinion, debates, and
advertising to name a few.[7] Since the first study, they also noted a shift
away from the rather strict behavioral approach.

A decade later, Dan Nimmo and David Swanson argued that "political
communication has developed some identity as a more or less distinct
domain of scholarly work."[8] The scope and concerns of the area have
further expanded to include critical theories and cultural studies. While
there is no precise definition, method, or disciplinary home of the area
of inquiry, its primary domain is the role, processes, and effects of communication within the context of politics broadly defined.

In 1985, the editors of *Political Communication Yearbook: 1984* noted that
"more things are happening in the study, teaching, and practice of political communication than can be captured within the space limitations
of the relatively few publications available."[9] In addition, they argued
that the backgrounds of "those involved in the field [are] so varied and
pluralist in outlook and approach. . . . it [is] a mistake to adhere slavishly
to any set format in shaping the content."[10] And more recently, Nimmo
and Swanson called for "ways of overcoming the unhappy consequences
of fragmentation within a framework that respects, encourages, and benefits from diverse scholarly commitments, agendas, and approaches."[11]

In agreement with these assessments of the area and with gentle encouragement, Praeger established the Praeger Series in Political Communication. The series is open to all qualitative and quantitative
methodologies as well as contemporary and historical studies. The key
to characterizing the studies in the series is the focus on communication
variables or activities within a political context or dimension. As of this
writing, over seventy volumes have been published and there are numerous impressive works forthcoming. Scholars from the disciplines of
communication, history, journalism, political science, and sociology have
participated in the series.

I am, without shame or modesty, a fan of the series. The joy of serving
as its editor is in participating in the dialogue of the field of political
communication and in reading the contributors' works. I invite you to
join me.

                                              Robert E. Denton, Jr.

NOTES

1. See Robert E. Denton, Jr., *The Symbolic Dimensions of the American Presidency*
(Prospect Heights, Ill.: Waveland Press, 1982); Robert E. Denton, Jr., and Gary
Woodward, *Political Communication in America* (New York: Praeger, 1985; 2nd

ed., 1990); Robert E. Denton, Jr., and Dan Han, *Presidential Communication* (New York: Praeger, 1986); and Robert E. Denton, Jr., *The Primetime Presidency of Ronald Reagan* (New York: Praeger, 1988).

2. Aristotle, *The Politics of Aristotle*, trans. Ernest Barker (New York: Oxford University Press, 1970), p. 5.

3. Aristotle, *Rhetoric*, trans. W. Rhys Roberts (New York: The Modern Library, 1954), p. 22.

4. Dan Nimmo and Keith Sanders, "Introduction: The Emergence of Political Communication as a Field," in *Handbook of Political Communication*, ed. Dan Nimmo and Keith Sanders (Beverly Hills, Calif.: Sage, 1981), pp. 11–36.

5. Ibid., p. 15.

6. Ibid., pp. 17–27.

7. Keith Sanders, Lynda Kaid, and Dan Nimmo, eds., *Political Communication Yearbook: 1984* (Carbondale: Southern Illinois University, 1985), pp. 283–308.

8. Dan Nimmo and David Swanson, "The Field of Political Communication: Beyond the Voter Persuasion Paradigm," in *New Directions in Political Communication*, ed. David Swanson and Dan Nimmo (Beverly Hills, Calif.: Sage, 1990), p. 8.

9. Sanders, Kaid, and Nimmo, *Political Communication Yearbook: 1984*, p. xiv.

10. Ibid.

11. Nimmo and Swanson, "The Field of Political Communication," p. 11.

Preface

> The great problem for American democracy . . . is that people barely trust elected leaders or the entire legislative system to accomplish anything of value.
>
> Journalist James Fallows (1996, p. 7)

> When skepticism gives way to cynicism, a self-destructive dynamic is created.
>
> Communication scholars Joseph Cappella
> and Kathleen Hall Jamieson (1997, p. 237)

Beginning in the late 1960s and early 1970s, American confidence in key democratic institutions plummeted. A synthesis of public opinion polls points to a pattern of declining confidence in the presidency, Congress, state governments, public schools, the court system, the news media, and a host of other institutions. This pattern accelerated during the 1970s, abated somewhat in the early 1980s, then resumed its downward spiral in the late 1980s, and has continued into the 1990s. The problem appears pervasive in nature, crossing most all population cohorts and impacting virtually all democratic institutions. This pervasiveness led Joseph Nye to conclude, "Cynicism about government has become the new conventional wisdom" (1997, p. 6).

This development is not without consequences that can be dangerous in a democratic society. Nye, Philip Zelikow, and David King predict that cynicism may reduce participation, thereby undermining democratic values. Michael Robinson warns: "In the long run, democratic systems do not—cannot—survive monetary or social crisis with institutions that lack the public's trust and respect" (1975, p. 97).

This is a book about distrust of and cynicism toward democratic institutions and the causes behind this lack of confidence. The causes of declining confidence are complex and multifaceted. One commonly accepted explanation among public opinion scholars is that declining confidence is the direct result of the substantive failings of the institutions themselves and of the people who lead them. Proponents of this position hold that public disaffection toward democratic institutions is a perfectly rational response to "real events" (Lipset & Schneider, 1987, p. 375).

However, most people have no direct contact with public institutions and limited awareness, interest, and knowledge about institutions. As a result, they have no choice but to base their assessment of the institutions' performances on bits and pieces of information collected from the mass media. This raises an alternative explanation for this nation's crisis of confidence: that the negative tone of the mass media undermines public confidence in institutions. Following on the heels of Vietnam and Watergate, news reporting, particularly on television, began to stress "what's wrong with institutions" (Robinson, 1976, 1977). Larry Sabato characterized this "junkyard dog" era of journalism as "harsh, regressive, and intrusive" (1991, p. 26). Contemporary media coverage continues to focus on the shortcomings of public figures and institutions. The media's critical tone has become a normative feature of today's news reporting. Modern-day media coverage paints the American political scene as "a race to the bottom," as James Fallows (1996, p. 7) describes it; this tone has decidedly destructive results in terms of public trust and confidence.

We believe that both the substantive and mass media explanations for declining public confidence carry an element of truth. In addition, both explanations are grounded on a common assumption: that it is public *perceptions* of institutional performance that causes dissatisfaction. They differ primarily on the question of whether these perceptions are an accurate or inaccurate reflection of reality.

This book examines the influence of sociodemographic factors, political expertise—which embodies a combination of awareness and knowledge about institutions—and use of communication media on people's confidence in democratic institutions. The book's conclusions are based on two years of data collection. Between 1995 and 1997, we conducted a series of content analyses of media depictions of democratic institutions, including the presidency, Congress, the court system, public schools, and the news media themselves. In conjunction with these analyses, we conducted four public opinion surveys, which examined people's sociodemographics, political expertise, use of a variety of communication media, and their perceptions of the democratic institutions previously noted.

The investigation presented in this book constitutes one of the most comprehensive examinations ever conducted on media effects on public confidence. The combination of content analyses and public opinion surveys was designed to assess the contribution of specific communication sources to public confidence in democratic institutions. This is after accounting for the influence of sociodemographic factors and political expertise. The use of content analysis in conjunction with survey data was designed to offer two levels of proof: evidence that a particular medium's coverage of an institution is negative, coupled with evidence that people who rely more on that medium perceive the institution in much the same manner as it is depicted.

Most previous research on the media's influence on confidence has relied singularly on content analysis or opinion surveys and does not take "an interconnected approach," which Arthur Miller and colleagues (1979) argue is necessary in order to determine the influence of the media on confidence. Few studies examine the influence of multiple media simultaneously, which is essential in order to accommodate differing media use patterns. Our work compares the relative contributions of seven communication modalities on public perceptions of confidence: newspapers, news magazines, network television news, local television news, television news magazines, television entertainment talk shows, and political talk radio.

In addition to the "interconnected data approach" and analysis of multiple communication modalities, this study features a unique approach to data analysis. The results reported in this book are based on a combination of approaches, including multivariate analysis of variance (MANOVA) to assess differences in media depictions of each institution and structural equation modeling to track the path of media influence on perceptions of confidence.

Part I of the book lays the foundation for subsequent chapters, examining the erosion of confidence in democratic institutions over the past 30 years. Part II of the book focuses on factors influencing public confidence. Chapter 3 describes the design of our studies. Chapter 4 presents the results of our content analyses, which compare communication media depictions of each of five institutions featured in the study. Chapters 5, 6, 7, and 8 report on the patterns of influence for specific communication media sources: the print media, traditional television news, other television programming, and political talk radio.

The pattern of results indicates, and the book will demonstrate, that communication modalities contribute to perceptions of confidence, but that *the story is a good deal more intricate* than was previously assumed. Certain sociodemographics affect media use, and media use—often indirectly through political expertise, and sometimes directly—influences confidence and trust in democratic institutions. Some communication media exert an overall positive influence on confidence (e.g., the print media), and some exert a persistent negative impact (e.g., political talk radio). The net influence of other communication media (e.g., network television news) is mixed. This book explores the implications of these findings for America's crisis of confidence.

Acknowledgments

As with most undertakings, this study reflects the efforts of many. We would first like to thank a number of graduate students in the School of Journalism and Mass Communication at the University of Wisconsin–Madison who helped to collect and code the data reported in this book: Satoko Adachi, Sirathorn Balakula, Qiujing Bu, Wan Chien, Martha Cusick, Maria Domellof, Jessica Genova, Prathana Kannaovakun, Wenche Nilsen, Shannon Payette, Jason Powless, Bret Shaw, Tom Springer, Gemma Tarlach, Dawn Tijerina, Chia-chen Wu, Gi Woong Yun, and Stephen Zubric. Other students collected, coded, and entered data: Michael Bridgeman, Lance Holbert, LeeAnn Kahlor, Erin Kock, Wai-Peng Lee, Debra Levy, Jia-Jiun Lin, Wei-Kuo Lin, Barry Radler, and Weiwu Zhang. Robert H. Lee of the University of Wisconsin Survey Research Center supervised the telephone survey operations and was assisted by senior undergraduate students.

We also owe a debt of gratitude to our respective institutions. The School of Communications at the University of Washington provided support to the first author from its Test Trust Fund, and the University of Wisconsin's Vilas Associate Appointment was awarded to the second author. Both sources provided support for data collection and writing of the manuscript.

Finally, this manuscript would not be in its current form if not for several individuals who, knowingly or not, have helped to shape it: Dietram Scheufele, Jack McLeod, and Diana Mutz, whose feedback and support at various stages of this long-term project were invaluable. Rich Morin provided some insights into an early version of what eventually evolved into Chapter 7. Meredith Li-Vollmer and Melissa Wall read and commented on specific chapters, and Jennifer Krivosha made endless electronic changes to the manuscript. We especially appreciate the diligent efforts of Alex Credgington and Samara Wolcott, who played a great role in the preparation of the manuscript. Carol Blumentritt and Nicole Cournoyer, our copy and production editors at Greenwood, took the manuscript to its final form, and we thank them for their patience and eye for detail. Last but certainly not least, we are indebted to our editor Lori Packer, who was instrumental in merging our two voices.

As with most multi-phase research projects, the results of individual phases of this study have appeared in a variety of venues. Results of the spring 1995 phase were presented at a 1996 colloquium sponsored by the School of Journalism at the University of Wisconsin–Madison and at the 1996 meeting of the International Communication Association in Chicago, Illinois, and appeared in the Winter 1998 issue of *The Southern Communication Journal* (Vol. 63, No. 2, pp. 91–112). The results of the fall 1995 phase were presented at the 1996 meeting of the American Association for Public Opinion Research in Salt Lake City, Utah, and appeared in the Spring 1999 issue of *Journalism of Broadcasting & Electronic Media* (Vol. 43, No. 2, pp. 137–158). Results of the spring 1997 phase were presented at a 1998 symposium, which was sponsored by the School of Journalism at the University of Wisconsin–Madison, at the 1997 meeting of the Association for Education in Journalism and Mass Communication in Chicago, Illinois, and appeared in the winter 1998 issue of *Journalism & Mass Communication Quarterly* (Vol. 75, No. 4, pp. 730–745). Finally, the preliminary results of the survey concerning the influence of network television programming and public confidence in institutions, which are reported as exploratory findings in Chapter 7, were presented at the 1998 annual meeting of the International Communication Association in Jerusalem, Israel. However, the aggregate results, including the models of effects based on the combined survey data, are reported for the first time in this book.

Part I

Crisis of Confidence

Chapter 1

Erosion of Confidence

Over time, the confidence gap clearly has become pervasive in American society. . . . [I]t is unlikely that any level, any branch, or any major institution of government has managed to totally escape the wrath of citizens during this tumultuous period.
  Political scientist Stephen C. Craig (1996, pp. 49 & 54)

It becomes problematic . . . when a majority of the electorate distrusts the government over an extended period of time. Prolonged discontent and alienation from the political system may challenge its legitimacy and, ultimately, its very existence.
  Political scientists Ralph Erber and Richard R. Lau (1990, p. 236)

Although there is some disagreement on how exactly to define and measure the concept of "confidence," most experts agree that public confidence in democratic institutions experienced a steep decline in the late 1960s and early 1970s, a decline from which it has yet to recover. Public opinion polls have documented this overwhelming drop in confidence, motivating Joseph Cappella and Kathleen Hall Jamieson to characterize it as "an epidemic" (1996, p. 72). Similarly, Gordon and Benjamin Black argue that "the American people no longer believe in their government" (1994, p. 108). Although Black and Black may overstate the breadth and depth of public cynicism toward government, we believe that the current lack of public support for key democratic institutions is a serious issue, one that motivated our interest in its causes, especially in the role the mass media may play in suppressing confidence levels. Research into this question is the primary focus of this book.

This first chapter focuses on the erosion of confidence. We begin with a discussion of the term "confidence." What does it mean? How has it been defined and operationalized in the past? We then examine the fluctuating levels of confidence over time, as evidenced in survey reports. We will pay particular attention to the free fall in public confidence that occurred in the late 1960s and the early 1970s, before turning our attention to confidence patterns in the 1990s. In our analyses, we will focus not just on public confidence in the critical institutions of national government—including the presidency and Congress—but also on such integral institutions as the court system, public schools, and the mass media, which serve as the primary source of information about the performance of these institutions. Finally, we examine the potential consequences of this lack of public confidence. When a majority of people living under a democratic government believe they no longer have a voice in the political process, and no longer take part in the process, then that democracy ultimately may lose its legitimacy and, perhaps, even its existence (Erber & Lau, 1990; Verba, Schlozman, & Brady, 1995).

THE NOTION OF CONFIDENCE

The concept of confidence has been used in a variety of ways in the political communication literature. Public confidence long has been a slippery term to define, and some scholars have resorted to defining what it is not. This lack of confidence has been termed "cynicism" (Cappella & Jamieson, 1997; Erber & Lau, 1990), "disaffection" (Pinkleton, Austin, & Fortman, 1998), "lack of trust" (Miller, 1974a), "alienation" (Finifter, 1970), "discontent" (Craig, 1993), and "negativism" (Citrin, 1974). Despite the different terms employed, the concept of public confidence is used generally to characterize attitudes toward the political system, including its institutions and their leaders. Public confidence is in part a manifestation of the system's performance and in part an indication of the system's responsiveness to people's concerns.

Although this characterization of public confidence reflects current and past usage of the concept, it also can lead to theoretical confusion. First, this characterization can involve multiple points of reference. For example, is confidence a judgment of the political system and its individual institutions as a whole? Or is it more an assessment of the current leaders of those institutions? Bernard Barber criticizes the term "confidence" on the basis of this ambiguity (1983, p. 86). Sometimes the term encompasses what Barber calls "specific spheres," such as the political sphere. Sometimes it refers to specific institutions such as the presidency. At other times it characterizes the occupants or leaders of institutions. Second, this characterization of public confidence can involve various assessment criteria. Is the assessment of confidence based on the system's performance or on its responsiveness to the public? If a judgment is grounded in performance, is this judgment absolute or is it relative, perhaps based on people's current expectations or on the system or institution's recent performance?

The theoretical fuzziness surrounding the concept of confidence fore-shadows difficulties in its operationalization in research. The problem is compounded by an understandable preference for longitudinal data that enable researchers to compare relative confidence levels over time. However, this type of data can only be attained by perpetuating survey questionnaire items that have their origins in the 1950s and that predate careful deliberation concerning the exact nature of the confidence concept and how to assess it most effectively.

The most established measure of the public's confidence in the federal government is the "trust-in-government" scales employed in the National Election Studies (NES), which were conducted initially by the Survey Research Center (SRC) and more recently by the Center for Political Studies (CPS) at the University of Michigan. The SRC first employed the "trust-in-government" questions in its 1958 NES survey. The "trust-in-government" measure consists of the following four items:

Do you think that people in the government waste a lot of money we pay in taxes, waste some of it, or don't waste very much of it?

Do you think that quite a few of the people running the government are a little crooked, not very many are, or do you think that hardly any of them are crooked at all?

How much of the time do you think you can trust the government in Washington to do what is right—just about always, most of the time, or only some of the time?

Would you say that the government is pretty much run by a few big interests looking out for themselves or that it is run for the benefit of all the people? (Lipset & Schneider, 1983, p. 17)

These items have been asked regularly in NES biennial surveys since 1958 and constitute the core of the SRC/CPS political trust measure. However, the SRC/CPS measures two additional concepts, both of which are related to public confidence: political efficacy and government responsiveness (or internal and external efficacy, respectively).

Political efficacy concerns an individual's perception of his or her ability to understand and influence political outcomes. The first political efficacy items were employed by the SRC in the 1952 NES. The four items took the form of "people-like-me" statements to which respondents were asked to agree or disagree:

People like me don't have any say about what the government does.

Voting is the only way that *people like me* can have any say about how the government runs things.

I don't think public officials care much about what *people like me* think.

Sometimes politics and government seem so complicated that a *person like me* can't really understand what's going on. (Lipset & Schneider, 1987, p. 19)

Two additional personal efficacy agree/disagree items were added in 1968: "Generally speaking, those we elect to Congress in Washington lose touch with the people pretty quickly," and "Parties are only interested in people's votes, but not in their opinions."

The SRC added "responsiveness-of-government" questions in 1964. These items were designed to assess institutions' responsiveness to "what people think" (Lipset & Schneider, 1987, p. 24). The items asked people to respond to each of the following questions by indicating "a good deal," "some," or "not much":

Over the years, how much attention do you feel the government pays to what the people think when it decides what to do?

How much do you feel that having elections makes the government pay attention to what the people think?

How much do you feel that political parties help to make the government pay attention to what the people think?

How much attention do you think most Congressmen pay to the people who elect them when they decide what to do in Congress. (Lipset & Schneider, 1987, p. 25).

The NES's public confidence measure, in part because of its long use, has become the most popular measure of political trust and cynicism, and many of its specific items have found their way into other survey instruments (Feldman, 1983). Nonetheless, the NES measure has received its share of criticism. The first, and most debated, of its alleged shortcomings concerns the interpretation of the term government in the survey questions. Do respondents think of government more in broad terms, therefore rendering a holistic judgment concerning the general performance of government institutions? Or, do most respondents tend to interpret government in terms of the specific occupants of those institutions, thus offering an assessment of the Clinton presidency or the Republican-controlled Congress? This constitutes a fundamental question of validity. Do NES "trust-in-government" items assess overall trust in government, as they purport to, or do they measure trust in current leaders (Hill, 1981)?

Arthur Miller (1974a, b) and Jack Citrin (1974) have led the debate on this question. Both parties to the exchange marshaled formidable arguments and evidence for their respective positions. They utilized the same data set but came to opposite conclusions. Miller maintains that the NES's political trust items assess general "hostility toward political and social leaders, the institutions of government, and the regime as a whole" (1974a, p. 951). Citrin counters that the items designed to gauge political trust instead "largely reflect their [Americans'] feelings about the incumbent national administration" (Citrin & Green, 1986, p. 432). If Citrin is right, periodic dissatisfaction with government is normal—indeed, inevitable and healthy—and results in the removal of an incumbent regime. But if Miller is correct, dissatisfaction is more endemic, and the act of " 'throwing the rascals out' will have little, if any, effect on restoring confidence in government or the political system" (1974a, p. 951).

The underlying point of dispute is the focus of the NES measure. Unfortunately, this issue cannot be resolved to most experts' satisfaction without "a more precise understanding of forces which shape the public's responses to the trust questions" (Hill, 1981, p. 261). Nonetheless, the debate is important when we consider the causes behind low confidence levels, which will be explored systematically in Chapter 2. In truth, the NES measure of "trust-in-government" undoubtedly taps *both* systemwide dissatisfaction with institutions as well as a more temporary dissatisfaction with current political leaders (Abramson, 1983; Erber & Lau, 1990).

A second criticism of the NES "trust-in-government" index concerns its lack of focus. Barber characterizes the NES index as "jumbled," encompassing two distinct notions: the people's perception of government's fiduciary responsibilities and of its overall competence (1983, pp. 77–78). John Hibbing and Elizabeth Theiss-Morse (1995) concur, describing the NES items as "somewhat tired" (p. 22). One item, "Would you say the government is pretty much run by a few big interests looking out for themselves or that it is run for the benefit of all the people?" is singled out as virtually unanswerable for those respondents who believe that special interests control some, but not most, members of an institution, or that they control some, but not most, institutions. As a consequence of this semantic and conceptual confusion, Barber (1983) maintains that the NES "trust-in-government" items are at best a relatively crude measure of public confidence. Barber, like Paul Abramson (1983), calls for improved conceptualization and operationalizations of trust.

Questionnaire items developed and administered by the National Opinion Research Center (NORC) at the University of Chicago and Louis Harris and Associates provide alternative measures of confidence in democratic institutions. Both organizations utilized wording designed to assess people's relative confidence in the leaders of a variety of institutions. These institutions were political in nature, including the executive branch, Congress, and the Supreme Court. Other, more general institutions included the military, the medical community, organized religion, educational institutions, corporations, labor unions, and the press. NORC and Harris posed the following overarching question: "As far as the people running [various institutions] are concerned, would you say you have a great deal of confidence, only some confidence, or hardly any confidence at all in them" (Lipset & Schneider, 1987, p. 41). Harris first posed this question in national surveys conducted in 1966 and 1967 and began using it on a regular basis in 1971. NORC asked the question in numerous national surveys starting in 1973.

Whereas the NES "trust-in-government" index received considerable criticism for failing to provide greater precision about the meaning of government, NORC and Harris confidence measures force this issue out into the open by referring specifically to the "leaders" of various institutions. However, Hibbing and Theiss-Morse are still not satisfied with this measure, criticizing the Harris poll confidence questions as "narrow" (1995, p. 22).

By contrast, both Gallup and the Opinion Research Center (ORC) ask respondents about their confidence in the institutions. In short, the Gallup and ORC confidence items are system-oriented, while the Harris and NORC items are people-oriented. This difference lies at the heart of the confidence construct and makes it difficult to compare NORC/Harris and Gallup/ORC data. Not surprisingly, Seymour Martin Lipset and William Schneider (1983) report that system-based wording tends to yield confidence levels that are "substantially higher than those reported by Harris and NORC" (p. 42).

In addition, Gallup and ORC confidence items offer a wider range of options to respondents. Whereas the NORC and Harris responses feature only one positive option ("a great deal"), Gallup offers two positive choices. The Gallup wording features this blanket question,

I am going to read you a list of institutions in American society. Would you tell me how much confidence you, yourself, have in each one—a great deal, quite a lot, some, or very little.

The list of institutions that follows includes the Congress, Supreme Court, church (or organized religion), the public schools, banks and banking, organized labor, big business, the military, the medical community, free enterprise, newspapers, and television (Lipset & Schneider, 1987, p. 57). ORC response options went even further than Gallup's. Respondents are presented with seven-interval scales ranging from "no trust and confidence at all" to "complete trust and confidence."

Figure 1.1
Declining Trust in Government

Year

Note: Figures represent proportions of respondents who trust the government in Washington "just about always" or "most of the time."

Source: American National Election Studies, 1958–1996, in Pew Research Center (1998).

DOWNWARD SPIRAL IN CONFIDENCE

The late 1950s and early 1960s may well represent a high-water mark in terms of public confidence in democratic institutions, what Robert Blendon and colleagues characterize as "a golden age of public support for the government" (1997, p. 206). In 1958, when the SRC first employed the trust-in-government items in the NES, 73 percent—nearly three of every four American adults—indicated that they trusted the government in Washington to do the right thing "most of the time" or "just about always." But by 1994, responses to the NES "trust-in-government measures" had reversed completely with three out of four respondents now claiming to mistrust the government.

This collapse in public support actually occurred in the 1960s and early 1970s, when levels of distrust in government tripled (Orren, 1997). As Figure 1.1 reveals, the positive responses to NES "trust-in-government" items dropped from 76 percent in 1964 to 61 percent in 1968, and 54 percent in 1970. By 1974, only 36 percent of respondents said they trusted the government (Pew Research Center, 1998). Lipset and Schneider comment on the "virtual explosion" in negative sentiment toward government and other societal institutions during this period (1987, p. 16). Hibbing and Theiss-Morse point to a "steep drop in confidence in [the presidency, Congress, and the courts] occurring between 1966 and 1971," adding that "confidence never recovered from this drop" (1995, p. 33). The NES data support this claim. After 1974, NES trust-in-government scores hovered at around 30 percent through the first half of the 1980s before beginning a steady ascent, to 44 percent in 1984. The index then resumed its downward trajectory, settling in the upper twenties throughout most of the 1990s before increasing slightly in 1998. Available Harris Poll data on confidence in institutional leaders tend to parallel recent NES trends.

If, as the NES data suggest, the critical period in the collapse of public opinion is from ,1964 to 1974, it would be useful to have other polling data to provide additional nuance. Unfortunately, this is not possible. As indicated earlier, Harris and Associates did not regularly administer confidence questions until 1971, while Gallup and NORC did not initiate their confidence questions until 1973. Thus, the NES "trust-in-government" index is the only continuous confidence data for this tumultuous period, and specific people-oriented or system-oriented data are just not available.

When we examine more recent trends, we find a variety of data supporting the conclusion that public confidence has continued to erode during the 1990s. Although the NES data reveal that public trust in government increased between 1994 and 1996, 62 percent of Americans trust the government only "some of the time" or "never." The Pew Research Center for the People and the Press (1998) put this recent increase in public confidence in historical perspective: "The direction of the trend notwithstanding, distrust of government remains substantial" (p. 4). In comparing recent data to that of the early 1960s, it concludes that public trust in government can only be described as "low" (p. 14).

Indeed, prior to the most recent upturn in public trust, some journalists and pollsters stood ready to declare a full-blown "crisis of confidence" in democratic institutions. A 1995 poll by Americans Talk Issues Foundation revealed that 76 percent of respondents "rarely or never trust government to do what is right," the highest negative rating ever recorded (Myers, 1995). Joe Klein commented that "frustration . . . has been building, steadily, for a quarter century, but seems to have reached a critical mass in the 1990s. The disgust is ecumenical, bipartisan" (1995, p. 34). Perhaps, pollsters Black and Black (1994) put it best:

For the past four years, practically every poll has displayed a near collapse in public confidence and support for the president, Congress, both political parties, and nearly everyone else involved in the political system. The American people no longer believe in their government. (pp. 101, 108)

PERVASIVENESS OF THE PROBLEM OF CONFIDENCE

It is the pervasiveness of the so-called crisis of confidence that makes it hard to dismiss. This pervasiveness is in part a function of the depth of public cynicism across the public and in part a function of its breadth across institutions. Evidence indicates that mistrust of government crosses most sociodemographic lines. Cynicism is not simply the purview of a minority of citizens. It affects all segments of society without regard for race, socioeconomic status, ethnicity, or other demographic factors. Frank Luntz and Ron Dermer describe this collapse of public confidence in institutions as so complete that cynicism "has become a long-term national mindset" (1994, p. 13).

A recent study by the Pew Research Center for the People and the Press (1998) asked 1,762 Americans this question: "How much of the time do you think you can trust the government in Washington to do what is right?" Table 1.1 reveals that a majority of Americans, 61 percent, replied "only sometimes" or "never." This figure remained constant across a number of sociodemographic lines—sex, ethnicity, age, education, and household income. The proportion responding with "only sometimes" or "never" varied slightly across party affiliation, with Democrats, perhaps indicating some identification with President Bill Clinton, expressing slightly less negativity.

Although cynicism levels appear most pronounced in middle-aged males—"people who came of age during Vietnam and Watergate" (Toedtman, 1995, p. A11)—cynicism among younger cohorts also has increased over time, a trend that does not bode well for the future. *Who's Who Among American High School Students* surveys of high-achieving students, using the same confidence items in 1971 and in 1995, reveal a sharp decline in the proportion of young people expressing "a great deal of confidence" in various institutions: the presidency, from 31 to 11 percent; Congress, from 26 to 9 percent; and the media, from 20 to 5 percent (Sanchez, 1995).

Besides its pervasiveness across segments of society, there is compelling evidence that the erosion of public confidence is also visible across a wide range of societal institutions. Ronald Inglehart reports "a substantial decline in confidence" touching on virtually all major institutions during the past quarter century (1997, p. 226). Darrell West, in analyzing the increasing popularity of "conspiracy theories" in America, refers to "a deep-seated distrust, not just of government but of all kinds of institutions that people once had a great deal of confidence in" (Spayd, 1995, p. C1). In assessing public opinion survey data over time and across institutions, Stephen Craig concludes that "it is unlikely that any level, any branch, or any major institution of government has managed to totally escape the wrath of citizens during this tumultuous period" (1996, p. 49).

Table 1.1
Trust in Government

	Trust the government in Washington . . .	
	"just about always" or "most of the time"	"only sometimes" or "never"
Sex		
Male	37	63
Female	40	60
Age		
Under 30	38	61
30-49	38	62
50-64	36	64
Over 64	43	56
Education		
High school graduate	37	63
Some college	39	60
College graduate	41	59
Income		
Under $20,000	40	59
$20,000 to $29,999	41	59
$30,000 to $49,999	36	64
$50,000 to $74,999	42	58
$75,000 or more	36	64
Race		
White	39	61
Black	39	61
Hispanic	44	56
Political Party Affiliation		
Democrat	48	52
Republican	33	67
Independent	35	65
Total	39	61

Source: Pew Research Center (1998).

In their seminal book *The Confidence Gap* (1987), Lipset and Schneider highlight the evidence, supporting what they describe as "disturbing signs of deep and serious discontent" concerning all major democratic institutions (p. 412). Although confidence levels vary somewhat between institutions and fluctuate over short periods of time, syntheses of Harris/ NORC surveys from 1966 to 1986 (Lipset & Schneider 1987) and Gallup polls from 1973 to 1995 (Gallup, 1987; Moore & Newport, 1993) document a sustained pattern of declining public confidence in the presidency, Congress, the Supreme Court, the press, state government, public education, and other institutions.

The pattern of confidence across institutions reveals far more similarities than differences. Figure 1.2 depicts the proportion of Americans expressing "a great deal of confidence" in the leaders of the executive branch, Congress, Supreme Court, educational institutions, and the press between 1966 and 1992. The Harris poll data illustrate that public confidence in governmental and nongovernmental leaders plummeted between the pre-Watergate years of 1966 and 1971, and then settled into this newly established, and decidedly lower, range. This pattern bears a striking resemblance to the NES measure of overall trust in government, as depicted in Figure 1.1. A closer examination of confidence in specific institutions will further illustrate the problem.

The Executive Branch

Opinion polls from 1974 to 1996 suggest a profound and consistent lack of confidence in the executive branch of the federal government (GSS News, 1997). Table 1.2 depicts the proportion of American adults expressing "a great deal of," "some," or "hardly any" confidence in the leaders of the executive branch. Typically, no more than two in ten Americans express "a great deal of confidence" in the presidency. In 1974, at the height of Watergate, there was a particularly negative shift from those who reported "some confidence" in the presidency to those who reported "hardly any." A similar downward spike occurred again in 1996, with over 40 percent of Americans expressing "hardly any confidence" in the executive branch. In fact in most years, the proportion of respondents expressing "hardly any confidence" easily exceeds those reporting "a great deal of confidence."

Obviously, partisan leanings influence people's opinion of the executive branch of the federal government to a greater degree than any other democratic institution. The president, the embodiment of the executive branch to most people, is elected as a representative of a political party. Nonetheless, partisanship alone does not explain the negative sentiment toward the executive branch. First, stronger partisan leanings often engender greater feelings of attachment to democratic institutions (King, 1997; Lipset & Schneider, 1987). Although Lipset and Schneider go on to

Figure 1.2
Confidence in Leaders of Institutions

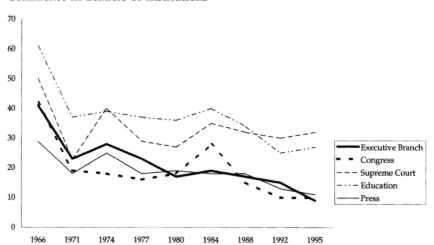

Note: Figures represent proportions of people expressing "a great deal of confidence" in each institution.

Source: Taylor (1993).

caution that extreme ideological disposition carries with it "anti-institutional connotations" (1987, p. 107), David King makes the essential point that "the more professed affinity one has for a party, the more likely one is to trust the government—even when the government is run by the other party" (1997, p. 175).

Second—as Figure 1.2 suggests—with the exception of the upward surge in public confidence in the executive branch registered in 1984, for nearly three decades Americans have been disenchanted with the executive branch, regardless of whether the sitting president is a Democrat or a Republican. Indeed, recent evidence reveals that people are extremely frustrated with *both* major parties, expressing as much negativity toward the parties as they do toward government. A 1992 poll conducted by Black and Black reported that 59 percent of the voters expressed "anger" or "dissatisfaction" with the Democratic Party, but "60 percent said the same thing about the Republican Party" (1994, p. 149).

Congress

If anything, Americans are even more negative in their recent assessment of Congress. As Table 1.2 illustrates, less than two in ten—sometimes, less than one in ten—indicate "a great deal of confidence" in Congress. From 1974 to 1996, the number of respondents voicing "hardly any confidence" has always exceeded those indicating "a great deal of

Table 1.2
Confidence in the Federal Government

	Confidence in People Running these Institutions		
	"Great Deal of"	"Some"	"Hardly Any"
The Executive Branch			
1974	13.9	43.2	42.9
1976	13.4	61.2	25.4
1980	12.3	52.4	35.3
1984	19.2	52.0	28.8
1988	17.1	55.4	27.5
1991	27.2	51.0	21.8
1996	10.2	46.2	43.6
Congress			
1974	17.5	61.0	21.5
1976	13.6	59.7	26.7
1980	9.2	56.1	34.7
1984	13.0	65.3	21.7
1988	16.5	63.7	19.9
1991	18.1	55.6	26.3
1996	7.4	48.5	44.1

Source: GSS News (1997).

confidence." In 1980, the ratio of those reporting "hardly any confidence" to those reporting "a great deal of confidence" approached four to one; in 1996, it approached six to one. In the early 1990s, at the same time that the proportion of Americans voicing "hardly any confidence" in Congress was skyrocketing, an ABC News/Washington Post poll revealed a congressional disapproval rating of 78 percent (Black & Black, 1994). To put this number in perspective, Roger Davidson and colleagues summarize survey data from the American Institute for Public Opinion during the 1940s and 1950s. The institute regularly asked Americans to evaluate the performance of Congress as "good," "fair," or "poor." The proportion of adults who gave Congress a "poor" rating in the 1950s never exceeded 16 percent (1966, p. 53).

Although research indicates that public opinion of Congress is associated with opinion of the executive branch (Davidson & Parker, 1972; Parker, 1977; Patterson & Caldeira, 1990), Congress typically fares worse than the presidency, a tendency that has grown much more pronounced in recent years. Indeed to many Americans, Congress is the "broken branch" of the federal government (Patterson & Caldeira, 1990, p. 26), and attitudes toward Congress have "degenerated into corrosive cynicism" (Mann & Ornstein, 1994, p. 1). A 1993 survey by the Americans Talk Issues Foundation found widespread public contempt toward Congress. One-third of the sample agreed that congressional seats "might as well be auctioned to the highest bidder" (Phillips, 1994, p. 6).

John Hibbing and Elizabeth Theiss-Morse have presented the most recent synopsis of public opinion about Congress. For their book, *Congress as Public Enemy* (1995), they conducted two national surveys during the summer and fall of 1992. They reported that 75 percent of respondents rated Congress as "poor" in its handling of important problems facing the nation (as compared to a 62 percent "poor" rating for the presidency and 46 percent for the Supreme Court). Their questionnaires also featured emotional response items, and the results of these items are particularly revealing. When asked a closed-ended question about how they felt about the federal government, 60 percent of respondents chose the word "angry," and 61 percent used the term "disgusted" to describe their reaction to Congress (the same figures for the presidency were 33 and 32 percent, respectively, and for the Supreme Court, 7 percent) (1995, p. 58).

Hibbing and Theiss-Morse (1995) agreed with the Kettering Foundation's (1991) report, which placed the primary blame for public contempt of Congress on the perception that it is run by special interest groups that block the input of ordinary citizens. The results of Roper polls conducted in 1964 and 1990 offer some support for this position. When asked, "How much attention do you think most congressmen pay to the people who elect them when they decide what to do in Congress?" 42 percent responded affirmatively in 1964; only 12 percent did so in 1990 (Black & Black, 1994). Ultimately, the perception that special interests control Congress is rooted in the present campaign finance morass. As long as average Americans see their representatives running for office on money from political action groups or what David Magleby and Kelly Patterson call "interested money" (1994, p. 422), then this lack of public confidence in Congress is likely to continue.

The Courts

Public opinion surveys seldom inquire about the court system in general, preferring to focus on specific institutions, particularly the Supreme Court. Figure 1.2 illustrates that, following a rather precipitous drop in public attitudes toward the Supreme Court during the late 1960s, public opinion settled at relatively positive levels compared to the executive and legislative branches of the federal government. Harris data indicate that in 1984, 1988, and 1992 about one-third of respondents expressed "a great deal of confidence" in leaders of the Supreme Court. NORC opinion surveys suggest a similar pattern. With the exception of the period from the late 1970s through the early 1980s, when the courts were involved in extending the rights of the accused, mandating forced busing and other acts of judicial activism (Caldeira, 1986), about one third of NORC respondents in annual polls from 1973 to 1993 voiced "a great deal of confidence" in those running the Supreme Court (NORC, 1993). Finally, Gallup polls conducted during the 1970s and 1980s reported the Supreme Court to be the "highest ranked government institution," with a positive rating between 44 and 52 percent (Lipset & Schneider, 1987, p. 71).

The 1997 Pew Research Center (1998) survey places the public's attitude toward the Supreme Court in an even more positive light. Pew respondents were offered four choices describing their opinion of public institutions: "very unfavorable," "mostly unfavorable," "mostly favorable," or "very favorable." All together, 77 percent of respondents viewed the Supreme Court as either mostly or very favorable.

Given this nation's fundamental emphasis on the rule of law, public confidence in the court system is very important. This is especially true in the late 1990s, with the televised gavel-to-gavel coverage of the O. J. Simpson trial and other high-profile cases, the media circuses that often surround these trials, and the emergence of reality-based television shows such as *Burden of Proof*, that address legal issues and strategies. Therefore, we consciously and specifically asked about "the court system" for each of the four surveys reported in Part II of this book.

Unfortunately, traditional polls do not offer comparable data about the nation's courts. The closest they come is to evaluate public attitudes toward law enforcement agencies—but only sporadically—or the criminal justice system overall. During the 1980s, Roper assessed attitudes toward the Justice Department, in each instance finding that more than half of all respondents had a "mostly favorable" or "very favorable" opinion of the department (Pew Research Center, 1998). In addition, Harris examined attitudes toward federal, state, and local law enforcement officials between 1967 and 1981, asking respondents to rate them as "excellent," "pretty good," "only fair," or "poor." Positive ratings (either "excellent" or "pretty good") ranged from 47 percent for federal law enforcement officials to 59 percent for local officials (Lipset & Schneider, 1987). Finally, beginning in 1993, Gallup added the criminal justice system to the list of institutions it regularly evaluates. In 1993, 1994, 1995, and 1996, Gallup respondents rated the criminal justice system even lower than Congress, with only 15 to 20 percent expressing "a great deal" or "quite a lot" of confidence in the system as a whole (Gallup, 1996).

The Press

The press has long been one of the most reviled of institutions, typically scoring lower confidence ratings than most others. As reflected in Figure 1.2, Harris data from 1966 to 1992 reveal that no more than 29 percent of Americans have ever voiced "a great deal of confidence" in the press. This is even prior to the precipitous drop in public confidence in all major institutions that occurred during the late 1960s. Roper surveys indicate that after the early 1980s, the proportion of Americans expressing "a great deal of confidence" in leading media figures never exceeded 18 percent (NORC, 1993).

However, the use of the term "press" in the Harris and Roper surveys may lead to exaggerated negative figures. The word "press" conjures up an image of the impersonal national media, which consistently receives lower ratings from the public than local media (Kohut & Toth, 1998). As they do in rating Congress, people seem to distinguish between their media outlet and the generic institution. A recent Electronic Media/Bullet Poll survey of 1,500 viewers nationwide asked respondents to grade local television news using letter grades of "A" through "F." Overall, assessments were quite positive: 66 percent graded local newscasts with an "A" or "B," and only 6 percent assigned a failing grade (*Electronic Media*, 1995).

Other polling organizations employ terms other than "press," and produce more positive responses than the Harris surveys. The Pew Research Center, for example, uses "news media" instead of "press." It reported that 50 percent of its 1997 respondents expressed either a "very favorable" or "mostly favorable" opinion of the "news media" (1998). Gallup goes further, measuring responses to two categories of media: television news and newspapers. During the 1990s, the proportion of respondents voicing either "a great deal" or "quite a lot" of confidence in newspapers remained relatively steady, hovering at just beyond 30 percent (1996). In contrast, those expressing either "a great deal" or "quite a lot" of confidence in television news dropped from 46 percent in 1993 to 36 percent by 1996. However, it is important to remember that Gallup data are based on people's perception of institutions as opposed to those who represent them. Hence, Gallup's confidence results tend to be more positive than those of the "people-oriented" Harris/NORC.

The 10-point drop in public support for television news after 1993 is interesting. The decline may reflect the country's weakening reliance on traditional television news. The mid-1990s have witnessed a dramatic erosion in television news viewing. Pew Research Center data (1996) indicates that the proportion of people claiming to have watched television news in any form during the previous day has declined from 74 percent in 1994 to just 59 percent in 1996. While there is no evidence to suggest that reduced confidence in television news has triggered reduced viewership, recent research suggests that, in comparison with Democrats or independents, Republicans are much more distrustful of traditional news media, particularly network television news (Moy, Pfau, & Kahlor, 1999). Perhaps not coincidentally, this group also comprises the nucleus of the audience that has fueled the growth of political talk radio in the 1990s (Times Mirror Center for the People and the Press, 1993).

Also troubling is the decline in the public's perception of the press's credibility, which portends further erosion of confidence in the news media in the years to come. Compared to the spokespersons who represent other American institutions (e.g., the executive branch, Congress, churches, etc.), news sources continue to receive high credibility ratings (Kohut & Toth, 1998). Nonetheless, from the mid-1980s to the mid-1990s, believability ratings for the major television networks (ABC, CBS, and NBC) declined from between 86 and 87 percent to between 76 and 77 percent, and the ratings for familiar daily newspaper correspondents dropped from 84 to 65 percent (Times Mirror Center for the People and the Press, 1995).

Still, we need to place public negativity toward the news media in some perspective. Laurence Parisot compared 1987 Harris survey data to similar expressions of public confidence from select European countries. The results indicated that Americans were far more confident in their institutions generally, and in their news media in particular, than citizens of France, Germany, Britain, or Spain were in theirs (Parisot, 1988). This implies that the conventional wisdom about the public's negativity toward the national media—Stephen Budiansky went so far as to exclaim, "The public these days does not merely dislike the press—it hates it!" (1995, p. 45)—may actually overstate the breadth and depth of public hostility toward the news media.

Education

The Harris polling data depicted in Figure 1.2 show that the pattern of public support for leaders of the public school system tends to follow roughly the same pattern as other institutions. Confidence in the public schools initially plunged between 1966 and 1971, but until 1984, confidence levels remained above those of the executive branch, Congress, the Supreme Court, and the press. The Gallup poll, which measures attitudes toward the schools as opposed to their leaders, reports a similar trend but with higher aggregate support levels. The proportion of respondents voicing either "a great deal" or "quite a lot" of confidence in the public schools dropped from 58 percent in 1973 to 42 percent in 1981, regained some of this loss in the mid-1980s, but then declined again to 40 percent in 1995 (Gallup, 1987, 1995). Roper surveys reveal a similar pattern, finding that the proportion of respondents voicing "a great deal of confidence" in the people running the public schools declining to about 25 percent in the mid-1990s, the lowest level since NORC first posed the question of public confidence in the schools in 1973 (Hochschild & Scott, 1998).

Robert Hagerty, whose book *The Crisis of Confidence in American Education* was published in 1995, at the same time that confidence in the schools bottomed out, declared, "Support for the public schools in America is at a low ebb" (p. 3). Hagerty places most of the blame for this lack of confidence on substantive failings within public education. He argues that "by many accounts, the American education system is not working well" (1995, p. 7). He also argues that major reform is the only way to reverse the downward spiral of confidence, concluding that the "public schools can and must improve" (p. 160) if public confidence is to fully rebound.

Another way of measuring people's attitudes toward the public schools is to ask them to grade their performance. Gallup has used this method since 1974, and the results corroborate previous data on declining confidence in the schools. The median grade given to the schools in each administration of the Gallup survey is "C," but the ratio of "A/B" to "D/F" grades has changed over time. Throughout the 1980s, between 20 and 28 percent of those surveyed graded the schools nationally with an "A" or a "B," and 13 to 22 percent rated them with a "D" or an "F," and in every year from 1984 to 1989, respondents awarded more "A/B" grades than "D/F" grades (Gallup/PDK, 1997). During the 1990s, however, public opinion turned more critical. In every year from 1992 to 1997, respondents awarded more "D/F" than "A/B" grades. By 1997, only 18 percent of people surveyed graded the schools with an "A" or a "B," whereas 28 percent rated them with a "D" or an "F" (Gallup/PDK, 1997).

In a detailed examination of confidence in the public schools, Jennifer Hochschild and Bridget Scott express a more guarded view of trends in public confidence in the schools. Although they acknowledge a modest decline in confidence toward public education generally, they do not see this development as significant. For one thing, public opinion toward the school system has been relatively stable over time. For the past 25 years, most people have graded the schools' performance a "C," and until recently, most others did not venture an opinion. Further, they argue that the distribution between those who assign the schools an "A/B" grade and those who grade them "D/F" has been relatively even over time. Hochschild and Scott conclude that "none of this has changed in almost 20 years" (1998, p. 80).

Additionally, as was the case with both Congress and the press, there is a sizable discrepancy in people's perceptions about national institu-

Table 1.3
Grading the Public Schools

	Grade					
	"A"	"B"	"C"	"D"	"F"	Don't Know
Public Schools Nationally						
1981	2	18	43	15	6	16
1983	1	17	38	16	6	21
1985	3	24	43	12	3	15
1987	4	22	44	11	2	17
1989	2	20	47	15	4	12
1993	2	17	48	17	4	12
1995	2	18	50	17	4	9
1997	1	17	48	22	6	6
Public Schools Here ("in this community")						
1981	9	27	34	13	7	10
1983	6	25	32	13	7	17
1985	9	34	30	10	4	13
1987	12	31	30	9	4	14
1989	8	35	33	11	4	9
1993	10	37	31	11	4	7
1995	8	33	37	12	5	5
1997	9	30	33	14	9	5

Source: Gallup/Phi Delta Kappan, 1981–1997.

tions and those they are able to observe firsthand. Hence, when people are asked specifically to grade the schools "here" ("in their community"), their assessment is much more positive. As Table 1.3 reveals, the proportion of respondents who assign an "A/B" grade to their local schools has exceeded those dispensing "Cs" or "D/Fs" in almost every year since 1981. Furthermore, even accounting for the decline in positive ratings after 1993, approximately 40 percent of those surveyed continue to assess their local schools with an "A" or "B" (Gallup/PDK, 1997). Generally, the more familiar people are with an institution, including the public schools, the more positively they perceive it (Cannon & Barham, 1993; Loveless, 1997). Thus, it should come as no surprise to learn that people are even more enthusiastic about their own child's school. About two-thirds of respondents give that school an "A" or a "B," and almost none consider it a failure (Hochschild & Scott, 1998).

The discrepancy in attitudes toward local school and public education in general, when coupled with declining numbers of school-age children,

has been used as an explanation for the downturn in confidence toward
the public schools as a whole, as documented by Harris, Gallup, and
Roper. The proportion of school-age children in the population declined
sharply between the mid-1970s and 1980s. Since those adults with children attending the public schools tend to be more supportive of at least
their own local schools, Stanley Elam, Lowell Rose, and Alec Gallup
(1995) argue that this demographic shift has had the effect of distancing
more adults from the public school system and "could explain" the decline in overall confidence expressed in the mid-1990s. However, Tom
Loveless (1997) disputes this claim, arguing that "from 1983 and 1994,
the school-age percentage of the population was basically flat," and
therefore, the demographic changes "might explain some of the fall before 1983 but not later shifts in public opinion" (p. 132).

Loveless (1997) discerns "a paradox" in the public's response to the
public schools. In contrast to Hagerty's position that declining confidence
in the public schools is a response to substantive failings in education,
Loveless documents positive trends in education, including improving
retention and graduation rates, increasing enrollment in public schools
over private schools, and increasing financial support for public education. Yet despite these developments, he acknowledges the polling data
pointing to declining public confidence in the public schools.

He also looks to the discrepancy between local and institutional attitudes for an explanation, albeit a different one than posited by Elam,
Rose, and Gallup. Loveless points to Gallup data indicating that, in those
instances when people rate their local schools more positively than
schools in general, they most often explain this discrepancy by claiming
that their local schools place much more emphasis on academic achieve-
ment. Loveless maintains that the "educational maladies" the public is
most critical of in schools nationwide, such as drug abuse, lack of discipline, and violence, "are general rather than specific, disconnected from
teaching and learning, and blamed on schools in the aggregate rather
than on any school in particular" (1997, p. 154).

So is it fair to say that there is a problem of confidence in the public
schools? The answer remains complex. Available polls document an erosion of confidence in the schools in general, a pattern that was most
evident in the late 1960s and early 1970s and continued in the mid-1990s.
These disappointing aggregate ratings may primarily reflect deep-rooted
societal problems, as Loveless maintains, but they are nonetheless an
enduring element of public opinion toward the public schools and carry
undeniable implications for educational policy. However, survey data
also indicate that nearly 40 percent of people continue to give high marks
to their own local schools. This seeming inconsistency in survey data
prompted Hochschild and Scott to characterize the available evidence as
"fascinating but incomplete," concluding that "the issue of how to pro-

Table 1.4
Confidence in Other Institutions

	Military	Banks	Organized Religion	Medicine/ Med. System	Organized Labor	Big Business
1973	--	--	66	--	30	26
1975	58	--	68	80	38	34
1977	57	--	64	73	39	33
1979	54	60	65	--	36	32
1981	53	51	57	--	28	37
1984	58	51	54	--	30	29
1986	63	49	57	--	29	28
1988	58	49	59	--	26	25
1991	69	30	56	--	22	22
1993	68	37	53	34	26	22
1996	66	44	57	--	25	24

Note: Entries represent proportions of respondents expressing either "a great deal" or "quite a lot" of confidence in each institution.

Source: McAnery (1996); McAnery & Moore (1995).

vide public education is extremely complicated *politically* as well as substantively" (1998, p. 89, emphasis added).

Other Institutions

Harris, NORC, Gallup, ORC, and other polling organizations have provided a wealth of data on other institutions outside the scope of those covered in this book. Public confidence in other institutions is reported in Tables 1.4 and 1.5. The tables feature Gallup and NORC polling results dating from 1973, when both organizations began systematic confidence assessments on the military, banks, organized religion, medicine, labor unions, and big business. The Gallup results in Table 1.4 report the proportion of those surveyed indicating either "a great deal" or "quite a lot" of confidence in each institution. The Roper results in Table 1.5 indicate respondents expressing "a great deal" of confidence in "the people running" the institutions listed.

Confidence levels appear higher in the Gallup results for two reasons: Gallup features two positive response options whereas Roper employs just one, and Gallup asks those surveyed about their confidence in the institution itself, while Roper assesses confidence in the people running the institutions.

The patterns of results are somewhat predictable. Both polls, but especially Roper, reflect a surge of confidence in the U.S. military in 1991

Table 1.5
Confidence in People Running Other Institutions

	Military	Banks	Organized Religion	Medicine	Organized Labor	Major Companies
1973	32	--	35	54	16	29
1975	35	32	24	51	10	19
1977	36	42	40	52	15	27
1980	28	32	35	52	15	27
1982	31	27	32	45	12	23
1984	36	32	31	51	9	31
1986	31	21	25	46	8	24
1988	34	27	20	51	10	25
1991	60	12	25	47	11	20
1993	42	15	23	39	8	21

Note: Entries represent proportions of respondents expressing "a great deal" of confidence in the people running each institution.

Source: General Social Survey (GSS) data, National Opinion Research Center, 1996.

following the Gulf War, and both mirror a loss of confidence in the banking system in 1991 following the savings and loan debacle. Both indicate some softening of confidence in organized religion over time and a further erosion in confidence in organized labor starting in the 1980s.

SERIOUSNESS OF THE PROBLEM OF CONFIDENCE

Does the available evidence indicate that America is experiencing a full-blown crisis of confidence? This is a difficult question to answer. Experts disagree, and the research we will report in this book was never intended to directly address this overarching question.

We believe there is a problem involving lack of confidence in, distrust of, and cynicism toward democratic institutions. The weight of evidence supports this conclusion but is equivocal as to whether or not this problem has reached crisis proportions. In this section, we will synthesize this evidence and explore potential consequences.

Evidence of an Intrinsic Problem

Certainly, one could provide a strong case for the position that this nation is in the throes of a crisis of confidence in democratic institutions. Black and Black (1994), Luntz and Dermer (1994), Craig (1996), Gary

Orren (1997), and other academics and professional pollsters have depicted this disaffection as "pervasive." We find the evidence compelling that the erosion of confidence is widespread, affecting a wide range of societal institutions and cutting across demographic groups. Survey results fluctuate somewhat between institutions and over short intervals, but they tend to point to a persistent pattern of declining public confidence in democratic institutions. Although cautious about precisely what the survey data signify, Joseph Nye and Philip Zelikow conclude their edited volume on the causes of distrust in government with the statement that "what cannot be dismissed ... is the consistent and quite dramatic downward shift in answers to the *same* questions" (1997, p. 255).

In addition to the apparent pervasiveness of public distrust in government, the persistence and severity of these attitudes point toward a crisis of confidence. To say that the nation's institutions have never recovered from the sudden and dramatic plummet in trust levels that occurred in the late 1960s and early 1970s would be an understatement. If anything, public confidence levels have resumed a generally downward trend during the 1990s, marking nearly three decades of unparalleled cynicism toward public institutions. Richard Neustadt maintains that "present levels of mistrust are ... historically unusual," both with regard to length and severity (1997, p. 200). Orren argues:

Today's cynicism is much more than the public's long-standing suspicion of government or its current disfavor with particular leaders or policies. It is a deeper disillusionment with government in general.... [It] is ... not just a temporary slump.... The ensuing cynicism has lasted for three decades, during which time mild discontent for many citizens turned to outrage and loathing. (1997, p. 79)

Despite these arguments, there are those who dispute the claim of public outrage. To back their position, they point to abundant survey data indicating that Americans feel very positive about their own lives, even as they express concern for the nation. The 1997 Pew Research Center poll found nearly half of Americans "highly contented with their lives," a sharp increase over 1996. The survey reported considerable distrust of government but concluded that "there is no indication that these attitudes are near a crisis stage" (1998, p. 3). Further, the report argues that public discontent does not necessarily translate to anger. The survey reported that while 56 percent of respondents expressed "frustration" with government, only 12 percent voiced "anger" (p. 4). We tend to view this data with greater alarm. When more than half of all citizens are "frustrated" with their government, and more than one in ten are "angry," it strikes us as a cause for genuine concern.

Potential Consequences

Perhaps the most fundamental, and yet vexing, component of the debate over the so-called crisis of confidence is the consequences that might stem from such low levels of confidence in democratic institutions. In the concluding chapter of *Why People Don't Trust Government*, Nye and Zelikow acknowledge that the consequences of distrust remain elusive. They conclude:

We feel a bit like doctors who have encountered a patient with an irregular heartbeat. We do not know if the problem is really threatening. We do not know if it will be self-correcting, will require medication, or will require more serious intervention. *We do know* that the symptom commands attention, and that we ought to investigate possible causes more before we prescribe a remedy. (1997, pp. 278–279, emphasis added)

The consequences of political cynicism are, on the one hand, speculative, based on circumstances that are typically hypothetical. Discussion of potential consequences often involves some future "trip wire," or threshold such as a further drop in confidence levels, or an unanticipated crisis. Since it is impossible to identify these "trip wires," all discussions of consequences are inherently speculative. On the other hand, consequences involve the most serious of costs, such as this nation's potential to survive a crisis or the very survival of our democratic system.

The consequences have not yet occurred as the thresholds have yet to be reached. However, this does not mean that current levels of distrust and cynicism should not be of concern. The present problem of confidence may not, as yet, constitute "a crisis of confidence." The problem is that we may not reach a "crisis of confidence" until it is too late: until after we have surpassed a critical threshold and can no longer avert the consequences.

All potential consequences detract from the health and viability of our democratic system. Democracy requires willing participation from its citizens; political cynicism and distrust undermines this. According to the Pew Research Center (1998), the most common response to distrust is apathy, which translates into withdrawal from the political process. Disenchantment with institutions may depress people's perception that they can influence decision makers (Goel, 1980). This notion of political efficacy is intertwined with the notion of political participation, the "mechanism by which citizens can communicate information about their interests, preferences, and needs and generate pressure to respond" (Verba, Schlozman, & Brady, 1995, p. 1). In support of this position, one recent study reported political cynicism to be "negatively related to voting efficacy" (Pinkleton et al., 1998, p. 45). Clearly, voting in presidential elections—perhaps the most minimal participatory act—has declined from levels exceeding 60 percent in the 1950s and 1960s to just above 50 percent during the 1980s and 1990s, and to below 50 percent in 1996 (Black & Black, 1994). Black and Black voice particular concern with the declining voting rate among 18- to 34-year-olds which, they argue, "raises a troubling specter for the future rate of voting participation" (1994, p. 98). William Crotty and Gary Jacobson add, "American voters appear turned off to virtually everything associated with politics" (1980, p. 22). The result may be a further erosion of political participation.

At another level, political distrust may diminish social capital, recently defined as "features of social life—networks, norms, and trust—that enable participants to act together more effectively to pursue shared objectives . . . in short . . . social connections" (Putnam, 1995b, pp. 664–665). Stemming in part from Hannah Arendt's (1958, 1961) notion of "human connectedness," a condition "in which humans share turf and therefore jointly confront problems" (Jaffe, 1994, p. 16), social capital is a crucial component of any democratic system.

Declining trust and confidence in institutions erodes the stock of available social capital. In his essay "Bowling Alone," Robert Putnam advances the thesis that "the vibrancy of American civil society—the magic variable—has notably declined over the past several decades" (1995). The result is a society less able to resolve problems or to respond to crises. In fact, the Kettering Foundation has reported widespread and deep public anger grounded in people's perception that "the system often is incapable . . . of resolving major issues" (1991, p. 1). Based on their exhaustive examination of trust and confidence more than a decade ago, Lipset and Schneider reached the grave conclusion that

the United States enters the 1980s . . . with a lower reserve of confidence in the ability of its institutional leaders to deal with the problems of the polity, the society, and the economy than at any time in this century. Our institutional structure is less resilient than in the past. (1987, pp. 411–412)

During lengthy periods of peace and prosperity, such as America has experienced in the 1990s, present trust and confidence levels may not appear to exert an impact—perhaps simply precluding action on issues that have yet to reach critical mass, such as ensuring adequate health care, rescuing Social Security, or addressing racial divisiveness. Virginia Chanley and Wendy Rahn found that trust in government "affects citizens' desires for government activity" (1996, p. 5), thus suggesting support for this position. Jean Elshtain argues that cynicism promotes gridlock, and the resulting gridlock results in further cynicism, triggering a potential "spiral of deligitimation" (1995, p. 24). Even more disturbing is the prospect that the present levels of trust and confidence may not prove sufficient in the face of the serious domestic or international crises that occur from time to time.

Finally, cynicism may undermine legitimate authority to the point that it fosters increasing disrespect for the rule of law. Chanley and Rahn put forth this prospect, arguing that trust in government is important because "it directly shapes people's willingness to comply with government decisions in the absence of coercion" (1996, p. 5). They acknowledge that the issue of noncompliance with the law—and the resulting problems of disorder and instability—is more common to newer nations, but they warn that "even settled countries may need to confront [it] with renewed urgency if confidence in the institutions of democracy continues to erode" (p. 18).

Orren also maintains that cynicism undermines governance and goes on to argue that it fosters extremism. He explains that cynicism "hampers governing in a constitutional structure. . . . It is the oxygen that fuels the incendiary tone and negativity of today's political discourse" (1997, p. 79). One manifestation of extremism is violent action against government, as exemplified in the growing militia movement and by the bombing of the Oklahoma City Federal Building in 1995. While concluding that present levels of distrust are not linked to the tendency to disobey laws, the Pew Research Center survey did indicate that a surprisingly large number of Americans—38 percent of respondents—"could see justifications for violent acts against the federal government" (1998, p. 5).

If negativity resulted in action to "throw the rascals out," then the system would contain a fail-safe mechanism to prevent discontent from spiraling out of control. This was the intent of the Founders; in a system where the ruling elite may be corrupt or untrustworthy, a healthy dose of public skepticism is a good and necessary thing (Barber, 1983). But Anne Macke maintains that "the self-corrective function hypothesized is only indirect at best" (1979, p. 86). Her investigation of NES confidence data and voting records from 1952 to 1972 revealed that, when public dissatisfaction is high, voters are much more likely to reelect—rather than unseat—incumbents. She speculates that this could unleash a vicious spiral in which government performance deteriorates, public trust and efficacy plummet, and political participation drops (1979). This scenario is consistent with Erber and Lau's warning that "prolonged discontent and alienation from the political system may challenge its legitimacy and, ultimately, its very existence" (1990, p. 236).

Are we in the midst of a crisis of confidence, a crisis that bodes ill for the future? The evidence suggests we *are* experiencing a problem of confidence, but less clear are its severity and consequences. Nye, Zelikow, and King echo our position: "A clear assessment lies somewhere between Chicken Little and Pollyanna" (1997, p. 5).

This book is based on the assumption that there is a problem of lack of confidence in, distrust of, and cynicism toward democratic institutions. The question we investigate and report on in Part II concerns the relative contribution of communication sources to public confidence and trust levels. Do the media influence public confidence? Previous research reported here shows there is an impact. If so, which media are most influential? What is the process by which this influence takes place? Because we were interested in the effects of mass media on public perceptions of *democratic* institutions, we concentrated on institutions that play a direct or indirect role in the American *democratic* process: the presidency, Congress, and the court system, which are central to our political process; the news media, which serve as an information conduit in that process; and the public schools, which prepare future citizens to play a role in the process. In the next chapter, we examine the broad range of possible causes for the public's lack of confidence in democratic institutions, including the role of the mass media.

Chapter 2

The Question of Causality

Citizens' beliefs about the competency and sincerity of government actors are probably not derived from direct experience. Instead, people are informed about their qualities by journalists.
  Political scientists Virginia Chanley and Wendy Rahn (1996, p. 17)

Most complex social phenomena have multiple causes, and it would be surprising if this one did not.
                  Political scientists Joseph S. Nye, Jr., and Philip Zelikow
                                                    (1997, p. 269)

Researchers have offered a number of rival explanations for the problem of lack of confidence in, distrust of, and cynicism toward democratic institutions. This chapter systematically examines a number of plausible explanations for the confidence problem. We group these rival explanations under three broad categories: substantive failings of institutions and/or their leaders; citizens' sociodemographic factors; and the negativity of the mass media. Although this book is particularly interested in the influence of the mass media—and to a lesser extent, sociodemographic variables—we must make the caveat that all three classes of explanations may partially contribute to the confidence problem.

THE SUBSTANTIVE EXPLANATION

When scholars in the early 1970s first focused their attention on the problem of public confidence levels following their initial collapse, a debate developed as to the meaning of the National Election Studies (NES) "trust-in-government" items: do they measure overall trust in government, or do they assess trust in incumbent leaders, which is more a reflection of a regime's performance?

As we explained in Chapter 1, Arthur Miller (1974a, b) and Jack Citrin (1974) led the debate on this question with Miller arguing that the trust items assess general "hostility toward political and social leaders, the institutions of government, and the regime as a whole" (1974a, p. 951), and Citrin responding that the NES items instead "largely reflect Americans' feelings about the incumbent national administration" (Citrin & Green, 1986, p. 432).

This early debate between Miller and Citrin constituted the first major exchange in what has now become a long-standing dispute over the potential causes of low confidence levels. In essence, Citrin had advanced the first salvo for substantive failings as an explanation for the confidence problem, and eventually, two camps emerged: one blaming failings in leadership (Citrin, 1974; Citrin & Green, 1986; Citrin, Green, & Reingold, 1987; Horowitz, 1987; Ladd, 1981), the other maintaining that institutions had failed to respond effectively to America's substantive problems (Converse, 1972; Kernall, 1978; Kinder, 1981; Lipset & Schneider, 1983, 1987; Miller, 1974a, 1974b). In time, both camps—each pointing to poor government performance as the force behind falling confidence levels— would stand together in stark contrast to those who would later argue that it is the mass media that distort and undermine public perceptions of institutions. Seymour Martin Lipset and William Schneider (1987) summarize the former position, explaining that the confidence problem "is not primarily attitudinal. It is essentially substantive" (p. 351). In this view, public disaffection with institutions is a perfectly rational response to "real events" (p. 375).

If the substantive explanation is valid, then there should be a strong correlation between institutional performance—as gauged by various indices—and public confidence levels. We will explore this position, first by examining indices that are relevant to the performance of the national government, and then scrutinizing those pertinent to the performance of the court system and public education. We rely on a series of studies reported in Joseph Nye, Jr., Philip Zelikow, and David King's (1997) recent edited volume *Why People Don't Trust Government*.

Can the intense hostility toward the federal government, which manifests itself in terms of negativity toward the presidency and Congress, be explained as a rational response to events? Some researchers believe so. Vivian Hart is among those who view distrust as a result of a substantive failing of democratic institutions as a whole. She argues that the cause of people's frustration lies in "the failure of the political process" (1978, p. xi). She adds, "The lack of public confidence is in fact . . . a realistic assessment of actual government performance" (p. 87). Kevin Phillips concurs and refers to "the increasing ineffectiveness of American government," adding that, "it would be surprising if the sad state of Washington and the ineffectiveness of national politics were not making voters indignant" (1994, p. xii). Others place the blame for the public's lack of confidence in institutions on a variety of specific events and issues, such as the Vietnam War, deteriorating race relations, Watergate, the AIDS epidemic, and long-standing federal budget and trade deficits, (Abramson, 1983; Braun, 1994; Craig, 1993; Lipset & Schneider, 1987; Markus, 1979; Miller, 1974a).

Scholars have systematically examined the influence of specific events on the erosion of confidence. John Hibbing and Elizabeth Theiss-Morse (1995), for example, examined the "steep drop" in the NES trust-in-government index, pointing out that the bulk of this drop occurred between 1966 and 1972. Confidence levels have fluctuated within a relatively narrow range ever since. The NES data, they believe, rule out Watergate as a cause of the sharp drop in public confidence in the presidency and Congress, since the events underpinning Watergate took place in 1972, and the subsequent inquiry into those events occurred in 1973 and 1974 (1995, pp. 33–34).

By contrast, Robert Lawrence (1997) believes that Vietnam and Watergate are the primary causes behind this major drop in confidence. He examines economics as the potential cause of dissatisfaction with institutions and concludes that "the links between economic performance and satisfaction with government are uncertain" (p. 111). Citrin and Donald Green had maintained over a decade earlier that economic performance affects presidential approval ratings, "which in turn [affect] more generalized feelings of confidence in government" (1986, pp. 440–441). But Lawrence completely dismisses economics as the cause of the 16-point drop in the NES index between 1966 and 1968, for the simple reason that this period was one of economic prosperity. He acknowledges the possibility that the additional 10-point drop from 1972 to 1974 could be attributed to economics, since it took place during "the OPEC oil shock" and the resulting upturn in the rate of inflation. But Lawrence asserts that this drop in public confidence is more closely linked to Watergate than to the economy. Furthermore, although he admits that income inequality has increased sharply since the 1960s, his analysis indicates that political dissatisfaction was not much greater among those Americans who were left at the economic starting gates—particularly unskilled, blue-collar workers.

Derek Bok dismisses the theory that national government performance and specific events explain low confidence levels. He offers two compelling reasons. First, public malaise seems to transcend the presidency and Congress. Bok maintains that "the fact that trust and confidence have dropped substantially in the past thirty years for almost all institutions in our society suggests that something more far reaching than poor performance in Washington must be responsible" (1997, p. 56). Second, Bok asserts that any systematic and objective examination of relevant performance indices refutes the notion that the federal government has somehow failed. As he explains, "On the basis of some sixty to seventy specific objectives of importance to most Americans, the United States has made definitive progress over the past few decades in the vast majority of cases" (p. 61). During the last four decades, economic output has tripled, the stock market has multiplied tenfold, and "unemployment and inflation have come down to levels only slightly above those of the early 1960s" (p. 61). In addition, opportunities for Americans have significantly expanded in terms of college attendance, professional access, and home ownership. Americans are "more secure through wider coverage of Social Security, the advent of Medicare and Medicaid, and stricter safeguards for consumers" (p. 61). Our air and water are cleaner, the arts are flourishing, crime has fallen sharply during the 1990s, and "the federal courts have greatly expanded the scope of individual freedom" (p. 61).

While acknowledging some shortcomings—such as race relations, poverty, access to health care, and government waste—Bok concludes that, even in these areas, there has been far more forward movement than most realize over the past four decades. He argues that, based on objective indices, there is a much stronger case for public optimism about the performance of the national government than pessimism and that there is certainly nothing to support the widespread and deep cynicism reflected in public opinion polls. Virginia Chanley and Wendy Rahn support Bok's position, concluding that "America's beliefs about government do not seem to be related to government performance, at least . . . in terms of economic optimism and presidential approval" (1996, p. 17).

So is there *any* substantive basis for the erosion of confidence? The public certainly does not perceive the performance of the federal government as Bok does. A 1997 *Washington Post* survey of 1,514 Americans found that the main reason people give for unhappiness with government is that "the federal government has failed in its efforts to solve many of the nation's most serious problems." In six main areas identified in the survey, under 20 percent of respondents believed things had improved over the past 20 years (Blendon et al., 1997).

Bok's alternative interpretation of these perceptions is that the public is quite simply wrong. He concedes that lack of confidence may stem from rising expectations of government, coupled with the fact that, since the 1960s, the federal government has addressed an array of more controversial, and possibly intractable, social and cultural issues. Bok goes on to argue that "the public may have a jaundiced view of government because many people are in error about the facts" (p. 56). This conclusion offers support for a position that Bok never directly advances in his essay: that the media may be responsible for public cynicism. If people's perceptions about the performance of the federal government are at odds with most objective indices, then what could be the basis of the public's disaffection toward the government? If reality supports a positive assessment of government's performance, are the mass media responsible for the breadth and depth of public negativity toward government? Bok does not examine this important question, but we will begin to address it later in this chapter.

Jane Mansbridge (1997) systematically examined Bok's position that a combination of rising public expectations for government and a changing social agenda is partly responsible for falling confidence levels. She observes that sociocultural changes have led to a greater demand for government services and have enhanced "expectations for government action" (p. 133). Both of these trends contribute to the perception that the federal government is inept. She identifies a number of sociocultural trends. A new host of issues has emerged, including rising homicide rates, the decline of two-parent families, poverty, and growing drug use. The public expects government to address these issues, yet these issues may simply be beyond the capability of government to solve. Even if they could be addressed by government, this would require a much more activist public sector and higher levels of taxation than most Americans are willing to tolerate. Mansbridge argues that this "government overload" (p. 152) is responsible for the most of the decline in confidence levels. As for the rest of the explanation? She blames broader trends, such as declining respect for authority, "growing normative divisions within the country," and the increasing negativism of the mass media (p. 152).

Still another potential cause for lack of confidence in democratic institutions is found in the political process. David King and others place the blame for rising public cynicism on the growing polarization in politics; the public has remained centrist in its attitudes while political elites have grown more extreme. While acknowledging that the nation has edged slightly toward conservatism over the past 30 years, King (1997) maintains that most Americans remain centrist; this is evident in their unchanging responses to such polling items as "Government is getting too powerful," and "Government should provide fewer services in order to reduce spending." The proportion of Americans who feel that "government is getting too powerful" was 39 percent in 1966 and 40 percent as late as 1994. The ratio of people who favor and oppose cuts in government spending has held steady at about 20 and 15 percent, respectively, since the NES first began asking this question in 1982.

While the majority of Americans remain centrist, the attitudes of political party elites have changed, shifting to the left in the Democratic

Party and to the right in the Republican Party. This change results in rhetoric and policy agendas increasingly out of touch with mainstream Americans. In *Why Americans Hate Politics*, E. J. Dionne, Jr. (1991) advances the position that political parties have grown extremist and fail to represent the interests of most Americans. This development has produced extreme and shrill ideological debates that ignore possible solutions to real problems:

Democratic politics is supposed to be about making public arguments and persuading fellow citizens. Instead, . . . over the past thirty years of political polarization, politics has stopped being a deliberative process through which people resolved disputes, found remedies, and moved forward. . . . Politics these days is . . . about discovering postures that offer short-term political benefits. . . . Thus, when Americans say that politics has nothing to do with what really matters, they are largely right. (p. 332)

The net result of this polarization is political communication that invites cynicism among those people who are less inclined to strongly identify with a political party. This was the conclusion of Stephen Ansolabehere and Shanto Iyengar (1995), who examined voter turnout and the tone of rhetoric in 1992 U.S. Senate campaigns and conducted experiments featuring positive and negative candidate spots in a variety of California races. Ansolabehere and Iyengar found that negative ads do work, with a single showing producing a shift in candidate preference of about 5 percent. However, negative ads also turn voters away, reducing total voter turnout by a similar amount (4.6 percent). Of particular relevance to King's position on polarization is the fact that the effect on voter turnout was uneven. Negative ads reduced turnout among nonpartisan voters by as much as 11 percent, producing an increasingly polarized electorate.

Ansolabehere and Iyengar's finding suggests that strident, hostile, negative campaign ads—what Dionne calls " 'killer' television spots" (1991, p. 15)—fuel cynicism and distrust, especially in less partisan citizens who are most at risk for disaffection with government. Lipset and Schneider's analysis of confidence a decade ago found that nonpartisans hold the lowest confidence levels (1987, p. 104). King's own data, which featured 11,756 respondents, also found distrust greatest among those "who were most distant from the major political parties" (1997, p. 175).

King argues that the widening gap in the attitudes of Democratic and Republican Party elites, and the resulting polarization with mainstream public attitudes, "covers the same period during which mistrust grew" (1997, p. 174). King concludes that "mistrust seems to follow from polarization" (p. 175), and the relationship between polarization and mistrust held after controlling for the effects of variables such as education, age, gender, unemployment, income, partisan strength, and place of residence.

Samuel Huntington's (1975) analysis of the decline of confidence consists of elements of both Mansbridge's "government overload" and King's polarization theories. In the 1950s and early 1960s, the most salient issue of the day was defense; after the late 1960s, it was social welfare. This shift produced two effects. First, it resulted in the polarization, not just of elites as King argues, but of the entire electorate. Just as defense policy during the Cold War era was largely the nonpartisan product of elite and public consensus, social welfare policy since the late 1960s has been heavily partisan and tinged with divisiveness. The result was that "public opinion on major issues of public policy tended to become more polarized and ideologically structured" (p. 76). Second, social welfare issues, by their very nature, are much more intractable, as Mansbridge argues. Barring a "cataclysmic crisis" in which the government would dare to impose the sacrifices that would be required to address these issues effectively (Huntington, 1975, p. 105), the public is destined to be disappointed. The inevitable result of this shift in issue salience has been rising public frustration with the performance of federal government.

When we turn our attention from the federal government to the courts and public schools, we also find disagreement as to whether the decline in confidence is substantively warranted. For both institutions, current confidence levels appear to reflect some combination of reality and distorted perceptions.

As we indicated in Chapter 1, tangible evidence of the public's perceptions of the court system is circumstantial at best. We argued that people's attitudes toward the Supreme Court tend to be much more positive than their view of the criminal justice system. This is, perhaps, most clearly revealed in the discrepancy in public assessment of the Supreme Court versus the criminal justice system. Since the 1970s, public perceptions of the former have been quite positive compared to other institutions (Lipset & Schneider, 1987; Pew Research Center, 1998). By contrast, Gallup poll data on public attitudes toward the criminal justice system suggest the opposite. In fact, the criminal justice system typically has scored even lower than Congress since 1993, with only 15 to 20 percent expressing "a great deal" or "quite a lot" of confidence in the system (Gallup, 1996).

Low ratings for the criminal justice system may reflect the public's frustration with crime—a substantive matter. Bok's (1997) assessment of relevant performances indices does identify violent crime—including crime rates, the failure of law enforcement to solve crimes, and fear for personal safety—as one of the relatively few categories in which actual circumstances have deteriorated since the 1960s. However, research also documents the public's tendency to misperceive crime. For example, a Time/CNN poll (Shannon, 1995) revealed that, despite the indisputable evidence that crime rates have decreased in the 1990s, a staggering 89 percent of respondents believed they were increasing. Studies have attributed this misperception to the overemphasis by local television news on violent crime reporting, as manifested in the maxim "If it bleeds, it leads" (Edwards, 1995; McLeod et al., 1995, p. 1; O'Keefe & Reid-Nash, 1987).

Researchers also disagree as to whether declining confidence in public schools is based on substantive failings. As we indicated in Chapter 1, Robert Hagerty points to substantive failings as the cause, commenting that "by many accounts, the American education system is not working well" (1995, p. 7). But Tom Loveless (1997) disputes this contention, citing positive developments in education such as improving retention and graduation rates, and increased willingness to support revenue growth for education at rates far exceeding inflation. It may be that people's attitudes toward the public schools are a reflection of broader social changes, similar to the sociocultural problems that Mansbridge maintains are responsible for declining confidence in the national government. If so, the public is blaming the schools for problems—such as drugs, lack of discipline, and violence—that are beyond the capacity of the schools to solve.

As we observed at the outset, there is undoubtedly some validity to substantive explanations for eroding confidence in democratic institutions. We do not deny that specific events and issues—especially America's involvement in Vietnam, racial discord, and, to some degree, Watergate—contributed to the dramatic decline in public confidence in democratic institutions during the late 1960s and early 1970s. Further, we accept a number of the substantive explanations described previously as initially contributing to rising levels of distrust and cynicism and as subsequently precluding their reversal in this era of unprecedented economic expansion. The most plausible of these include the emergence of seemingly intractable "sociocultural problems," such as drug use and violent crime; the profound change in the issue agenda since the late 1960s; and the growing polarization between partisan elites and the mainstream public, which has spawned growing dissatisfaction with politics. These substantive explanations, however, do not tell the complete story behind public cynicism.

THE SOCIODEMOGRAPHIC EXPLANATION

Individual and social factors are possible alternative explanations for the confidence problem. These fall under the broad rubric of sociodemographics.

Philip Converse (1972) originally posited that rising education levels contribute to reduced confidence levels. Converse argued that education leads to greater general awareness, which in turn, leads to greater awareness of government shortcomings. If Converse is right, those individuals with more education should be more cynical toward government institutions. Some support for Converse's position is found in Herb Asher and Mike Barr's examination (in Mann & Ornstein, 1994) of NES data during the period of 1978 to 1992. Their analysis of education levels and attitudes toward Congress indicated that the most negativity is found among the most educated respondents.

On balance, however, the data in support of this explanation are underwhelming. Donald Stokes (1962) initially reported a positive, but weak, relationship between education levels and trust, but Paul Abramson's (1983) analysis of NES data from the 1960s to 1980s disputes the strength of the relationship between education and cynicism. Abramson concludes that "what is more striking is the weakness of the relationship between education and feelings of political trust," especially in light of the robust relationship between education levels and feelings of political efficacy (p. 232). Michael Delli Carpini and Scott Keeter (1996) also reported a weak association between education and trust. Seymour Martin Lipset and William Schneider (1987) are even more emphatic. They deny any relationship whatsoever between education and trust levels, concluding, "The correlations between the general index of confidence and education . . . turn out to be approximately zero." Across five samples, the proportion of respondents voicing high confidence ranged from 28 to 31 percent across all education levels (1987, p. 100).

The relationship between education and confidence levels is slightly different when we consider specific knowledge of government activities—whether gained indirectly through the mass media or directly through contact with government—as opposed to general education levels. Delli Carpini and Keeter's examination of 1988 NES data and their own 1989 survey of political knowledge reported negative, albeit weak, associations between political knowledge and trust (1996, p. 183). This finding received further support in a recent study that found slightly less confidence in people who knew more about current issues and politics (Morin & Balz, 1996).

Another survey reported few significant differences in confidence levels between respondents with and without "direct experience" with government (Pew Research Center, 1998). People on the receiving end of such federal benefits as Social Security, Medicare, and college aid displayed no more trust and confidence in the federal government than nonrecipients. However, poverty recipients and government employees reported somewhat greater confidence levels.

In our own research, we accounted for something we refer to as "institutional expertise," described in detail in Chapter 3. We are interested in the possible relationship between "institutional expertise" and public trust and confidence, particularly as such relationships are influenced by people's media use patterns.

When we look at age and confidence, we find the research results are mixed. Miller (1974a), James Wright (1976), and Abramson (1983) report that aging is negatively associated with trust and confidence in institutions, whereas the Pew Research Center (1998) finds that aging is positively related to confidence levels. Lipset and Schneider (1987) predicted a positive relationship, reasoning that "older people tend to identify more strongly with institutions simply because they have been tied to them for a longer period of time"; nonetheless, they found no significant relationship between aging and confidence one way or the other (p. 101).

To provide some perspective on claims of a relationship between aging and trust, regardless of its purported direction, Abramson reports that the strength of his finding of a negative association is weak when compared to "historical forces that erode trust among persons of all ages" (1983, p. 236). He further reports that people's trust in government has declined in all age cohorts since the 1950s and 1960s. However, as we noted in Chapter 1, cynicism among younger age cohorts in particular has increased dramatically from the early 1970s to the 1990s (Sanchez, 1995), a particularly troubling development.

Indeed, it is the absence of differences across most sociodemographic categories that is most striking, which motivated us in Chapter 1 to characterize confidence as a pervasive problem. Current trust levels are relatively consistent across such categories as gender, race, age, education, and family income (Pew Research Center, 1998). This pattern of consistency has changed very little through the years (Citrin & Green, 1986; Lipset & Schneider, 1987).

People's own interpersonal trust is another factor that drives their trust in institutions (Lane, 1959). Citing evidence from a nationwide study, Rich Morin and Dan Balz conclude that "the collapse of trust in human nature has fueled the erosion of trust in government and virtually every other institution" (1996, p. A6). Surveys and focus groups—sponsored by the *Washington Post*, Harvard University, and the Kaiser Family Foundation—revealed a sharp decline in interpersonal trust. In the 1960s, most Americans thought that most other people could be trusted; today, only 35 percent believe that most people can be trusted, a cynicism that is the most pronounced among young adults, victims of crime, and "economically anxious Americans" (Morin & Balz, 1996).

This finding is relevant to the issue of confidence in democratic institutions only if interpersonal distrust is a potential cause of institutional distrust. Unfortunately, research findings have proven to be ambiguous. The *Washington Post*/Harvard/Kaiser Foundation study found a significant positive relationship between people's trust in others and their trust in government (Morin & Balz, 1996). This result prompted Wendy Rahn to observe that "mistrust of one another breeds suspicion towards government, and sometimes outright fear" (Morin & Balz, 1996).

Other experts, while conceding a sharp decline in interpersonal trust over the past three decades, question whether it has indeed contributed to the erosion of institutional trust (Craig, 1996; Lipset & Schneider, 1987). Gary Orren contends that "most academic studies have found only a modest relationship between interpersonal trust and trust in government" (1997, p. 85). Ronald Inglehart's findings capture this position: "The decline in confidence in established institutions and of trust in government does not represent a broad withdrawal of trust concerning people in general; it is specifically a withdrawal of confidence from authoritative institutions" (1997, p. 231).

THE MASS MEDIA EXPLANATION

As we noted at the outset of this chapter, the problem of public confidence in democratic institutions is a complex one and undoubtedly involves multiple causes. Substantive issues are, without question, one part of the puzzle. Specific calamitous events, coupled with subtle social and political changes, have contributed to the erosion of public confidence since the 1960s. Sociodemographics, by contrast, appear to exert very little impact on confidence. The impact of individual difference variables on public confidence, at least when viewed alone, is minimal.

Another explanation for public distrust and cynicism is the mass media. The mass media as an explanation for low levels of public confidence does not rule out substantive issues as a cause of the problem. Specific events and the mass media both may have contributed to the erosion of public confidence, sometimes exercising their influence on confidence independently and at other times exerting their influence in concert with each other, with the media inflaming the impact of events. The melding of substantive and media explanations for the problem of confidence is a form of blended causation, which we argue constitutes the most plausible causal rationale.

The Case for Blended Causation

The possibility of this blended causation prompted some of the most ardent proponents of the substantive explanation to hedge their bets, acknowledging the prospect that the mass media *also* may have contributed to the confidence problem. For example, Citrin and Green (1986) admit that the public obtains most of its information about government from the media and that media are often critical of government. Donald

Horowitz (1987) acknowledges the role of the media in shaping public opinion about the president. Huntington concedes that "television news ... functions as a 'dispatriating' agency—one which portrays the conditions in society as undesirable and as getting worse" (1975, p. 99). Lipset and Schneider recognize that "perhaps the major source ... of information concerning the condition of the country is ... the mass media" (1987, p. 403), and they unflinchingly grant that "... research has found strong and direct links between political cynicism and exposure to negative information from the media." Mansbridge identifies the "increasing negativism in the media" (1997, p. 152) as an integral component of a comprehensive explanation for declining public confidence. Nye and Zelikow explain:

The media do more than hold up a mirror to the actual behavior of government officials. . . . It is always a mistake to kill the messenger bringing bad news, but it is also important to ask if the messenger is reporting faithfully or having an independent distorting effect. While the media are holding up a mirror to political reality, some analysts have shown that their mirrors used since the 1960s are more often like those found in carnivals. The figures are recognizable, but they appear in strange, entertaining shapes. (1997, p. 274)

We believe that both the substantive and mass media explanations for declining public confidence carry an element of truth. After all, both explanations are grounded on a common assumption: that it is the public's *perception* of institutional performance that causes dissatisfaction. They differ primarily on the question of whether these perceptions are an accurate or inaccurate reflection of reality.

The Media as "Fun House" Mirror

Does the media's negative tone simply reflect reality? Does it simply mirror the substantive failings of the nation's institutions and leaders? There is no question that bad news permeated the 1970s: stagflation, Watergate, the energy crisis, and the Iran hostage crisis. Media coverage certainly reflected these substantive events.

However, economic conditions improved in the 1980s and then shot further upward during the 1990s. Also, the early 1990s brought such international events as the collapse of communism, the end of the Cold War, and a decisive U.S. victory in the Gulf War. Yet, news coverage continued to express negativity toward institutions and leaders, providing a distorted view rather than reflecting substantive events. Perhaps news coverage had changed, resulting in reporting that increasingly bore very little resemblance to reality.

Michael Robinson (1975, 1976, 1977) advanced the position that news coverage of institutions and leaders changed during the 1970s. Others have also chronicled the pattern of changes in reporting in the wake of Vietnam and Watergate, which taught reporters to approach government officials and their pronouncements with skepticism. Soon a new press emerged, one with an aggressive and cynical mindset. Their reports took on an increasingly hostile tone toward institutions and their leaders (Weaver, 1972). Reporting, especially on television, began to place greater emphasis on "what's wrong with institutions" (Robinson, 1976, 1977).

The new journalism fixates on the foibles, follies, and failings of public figures and institutions. This more critical tone became a normative feature of news reporting, a trend that, if anything, has accelerated over the years. In examining the roots of today's critical journalism, Thomas Patterson observes that "the antipolitics bias of the press that came out of the closet two decades ago has stayed out" (1993, p. 19). Orren describes contemporary journalism as "adversarial," noting that the news media has shifted "to a more interpretive, evaluative type of reporting," which stresses political strategy and tactics (what Orren calls "inside baseball"), the leader's foul-ups (what he and others term "gotcha journalism"), or "what the news really means" (1997, p. 98). The Kettering Foundation notes that the news media "too often focus their coverage . . . on scandals, gossip, and 'insiders' talk' about politics" (1991, p. 59), and one reporter cast political journalism in the 1990s as "a perpetual sneer" (Harwood, 1996, p. A21).

These trends are exacerbated by growing nontraditional outlets for news. Darrell West observes that more and more Americans derive their news from a wider array of outlets, including tabloids such as *The National Enquirer*, television news magazines, political talk radio, and even late-night talk shows such as *The Tonight Show with Jay Leno*. "Unfortunately," laments West, "that leaves people—already over-anxious and alienated—with a distorted view of reality" (Spayd, 1995, p. C1). This critical media bias, whether it originates in traditional or nontraditional media, has resulted in an increasingly negative, harsh, and cynical treatment of institutions, a trend that is documented in greater detail in Chapter 4. The unique influence of nontraditional media outlets, and political talk radio in particular, is treated in Chapters 7 and 8, respectively.

The Media as Conduit of Perceptions

Whether or not the media accurately reflect events, the point is that the mass media function as the critical conduit of perceptions of democratic institutions. How do people form perceptions concerning the performance of democratic institutions? Some people form informed judgments based on considerable knowledge about specific institutions

(Fiske, Lau, & Smith, 1990), in some cases based on their own direct observation of institutions and in other instances based on fairly extensive utilization of multiple media. For informed people, media depictions alone are likely to exert only a modest influence. Indeed, past research indicates that people's knowledge of political objects (e.g., persons, issues, or institutions) exerts greater influence on their perceptions than their sociodemographic status or media use (Fiske, Lau, & Smith, 1990; Moy, Pfau, & Kaylor, 1999; Pfau et al., 1998a; Price & Zaller, 1993).

However, most people have no direct contact with institutions and possess limited awareness, interest, and knowledge about institutions. Their beliefs about the performance of institutions probably do not stem from direct experience. Such individuals base their perceptions of institutions on the bits and pieces of information that they glean from mass media reports. For the majority of Americans, the media *are* their link to the real world—their window to the condition of the country and the performance of its institutions. Moreover, people with less awareness, interest, and knowledge of institutions are not in a position to assess the probity of mediated claims. As a result, they are likely to view institutions and leaders much as they are depicted in media reports, and where media coverage is slanted negatively, Orren is correct in his conclusion that mass media coverage "fuels the cynicism of an already cynical public" (1997, p. 98).

OUR APPROACH TO ASSESSING THE MEDIA'S IMPACT ON CONFIDENCE

If mass media coverage influences public perceptions about the performance of democratic institutions, how can we explain its impact? We require a macro theoretical rationale, one that is consistent with the approach to our study. This investigation employs content analyses to detail media depictions of democratic institutions in conjunction with surveys to examine people's media use habits and their perceptions of institutions. We employ a broad interconnected approach, as Miller and colleagues (1979) urged in research examining the media's impact on confidence.

Our data do not permit us to address micro-level questions, such as what draws particular individuals to certain communication sources? Why do people process some media content while ignoring other content? How does media content elicit information processing? What kind of processing does it elicit? How does mass media content exert an influence on people? Furthermore, attempts to answer these questions require specific theoretical rationales appropriate to each. These are, without a doubt, interesting and important issues, but they lie outside the scope of this investigation.

A useful macro explanation for the way that mass media communication influences public perceptions is a modified version of the cultivation paradigm. The cultivation paradigm, with its Cultural Indicators approach, is widely used to explain the influence of television programming on perceptions of reality. It posits that the mass media, especially television—the most pervasive medium—serves as a powerful source of perceptions (Gerbner, et al., 1986). In time, television, through repetition of patterns, alters one's images and/or perceptions of "the ways of the world" (Gerbner & Gross, 1976, p. 178). The effects are most pronounced among heavier users (Signorielli, 1987) and in those circumstances in which people have more limited direct experience, as they are not able to confirm or deny television's images by means of direct experience (Gerbner & Gross, 1976). Most early cultivation research dealt with television programming and its impact on people's views of crime and victimization, race, gender, and professional roles (for a review, see Potter, 1993). More recent studies, however, have applied a modified version of cultivation in examining the influence of mass media news depictions on public perceptions about the incidence and severity of crime (Gebotys, Roberts, & DasGupta, 1988; McLeod et al., 1995, O'Keefe, 1984; O'Keefe & Reid-Nash, 1987; Perse, 1990) and a variety of other national and local issues (Neuendorf, Jeffres, & Atkin, 1995).

Despite its heuristic value, cultivation has been the focus of extensive criticism, both on theoretical and methodological grounds (see Hirsch, 1980, 1981; Potter, 1993). Critics of the Cultural Indicators approach focusing on its methodology claim that most cultivation research fails to adequately document television world images (Hirsch, 1980; Potter, 1993). Critics of the "uniform message" assumption proposed by George Gerbner and colleagues (1986) contest its suggestion that television messages are homogeneous across program types (Hawkins & Pingree, 1981; Potter, 1988, 1993; Potter & Chang, 1990; Rubin, Perse, & Taylor, 1988). At the heart of the criticism are the measures of only total television viewing time used to classify people as either light or heavy consumers of television programming.

Critics further maintain that the relationship between viewing levels and cultivation effects is not linear and that use of forced-choice items in most cultivation research suppresses correlation coefficients (Hirsch, 1980, 1981). Finally, critics charge that television's effect is spurious: The reported correlations are small, and when studies control for relevant sociodemographic variables, such as gender and education, relationships between television viewing and perceptions of reality became nonsignificant (Hawkins & Pingree, 1982; Hirsch, 1980; Potter, 1986, 1988, 1993; Rubin, Perse, & Taylor, 1988), especially in those circumstances when controls are applied simultaneously (Hawkins & Pingree, 1982; Shrum, O'Guinn, & Faber, 1993).

Perhaps the most serious theoretical shortcoming of cultivation theory is that the approach offers no explanation as to how the media distort perceptions (Potter, 1993). This investigation posits that the concept of internalization, in conjunction with the notions of primary and secondary socialization (Berger & Luckmann, 1967), provides a good explanatory mechanism for the influence of mass media coverage on perceptions of democratic institutions. Primary socialization occurs during childhood whereas secondary socialization occurs later and is the focus of this study. Secondary socialization offers people a frame of reference for evaluating institutions. Peter Berger and Thomas Luckmann explain that secondary socialization involves "internalization of semantic fields structuring routine interpretations and conduct within an institutional arena" (1967, p. 138). Together these concepts serve to enrich cultivation theory and explain how mass media communication influences people's perceptions of democratic institutions.

Both direct and mediated experiences are sources of secondary socialization. Cultivation explains that whenever real and mediated reality converge they act to "resonate and amplify" each other (Morgan & Signorielli, 1990), producing a reinforcing effect (Gerbner et al., 1980). But, absent direct experience, people tend to accept mediated depictions of reality and, in those instances when mediated depictions are inaccurate, develop distorted perceptions. We previously noted that most people, by necessity, are forced to rely more heavily on mediated depictions than direct experience about public affairs content. Most people find themselves "at the mercy of the media" for most of their information about public institutions and, ever more importantly, for interpretations of this information (Graber, 1980, p. 123). The likelihood of accepting mass mediated depictions of reality is the most pronounced for heavier media users. This process of mass media influence is termed "mainstreaming," which explains how heavy media use can "reduce or override differences in perspectives and behavior" from other sources, such as experiences or interpersonal exchanges (Pfau et al., 1995), resulting in "shared meanings in people" (Signorielli & Morgan, 1996, p. 118). As a result, people who share common media experiences eventually come to view the world much as the media depict it.

The mass media's mainstreaming effect is further magnified with regard to democratic institutions because most people's direct experience with institutions is limited in scope and confined to what Erving Goffman (1973) calls "front regions" and "back regions." If front regions are the public sphere and back regions represent a nonpublic, or private, domain, then trust in institutions may be contingent on restricting public access to front regions. Trust rests on "vague and partial understandings" (Giddens, 1990, p. 27). Similarly, respect for elevated people and institutions depends on restricting the public's access to backstage behaviors. Television, by inviting viewers into more private back regions, has unwittingly eroded confidence in all societal institutions (Meyrowitz, 1985).

A recent illustration of the media's foray into the back regions of democratic institutions can be found in their coverage of the Monica Lewinsky scandal, when the media learned of sexual relations between President Bill Clinton and a former White House intern. As Independent Council Kenneth Starr investigated allegations of perjury and obstruction of justice allegations against Clinton, Americans were treated to sensational media coverage. Not only did this scandal spawn heavy coverage by traditional news media, but also it was almost the exclusive focus of a number of cable programs. Shows such as *Geraldo Rivera Live, Hardball,* and *Charles Grodin* featured little else. The scandal also did not escape the attention of television late night talk shows and political talk radio. Coverage of the president's troubles even exceeded the amount of coverage devoted to the death of Princess Diana during August 1997. In the first week after the story of Clinton's affair with Lewinsky broke, coverage of the three major television networks exceeded 120 stories, ranking it as among the three most-covered stories of the 1990s. Coverage of the affair has proven a bonanza to media. The data indicate that newspaper single-copy sales are up, and audiences for nontraditional media, including radio and television talk shows, are sizable (Moore, 1998).

However, typically lacking in hard evidence, the media's coverage was often grounded on nothing more than hearsay and rife speculation. Martha Moore notes that media coverage of Clinton's alleged affair has accelerated two trends in contemporary journalism: "anonymously leaked information and explicit language" (1998, p. 7A). She sees both as partly responsible for the sizable majorities in opinion polls who express criticism of the media's coverage of this story.

Three decades ago, in a more genteel era, media preoccupation with a president's extramarital sex life would have been deemed inappropriate by media decision makers as well as the general public. The mainstream media, which totally dominated the dissemination of news during this period, confined itself to reporting on the public front stage behaviors of presidents, even in those circumstances when some journalists were aware of such activity (e.g., in the Kennedy administration). Today, by contrast, the media routinely cover the private back regions of public figures, which further magnifies the media's mainstreaming impact.

So far, our description of cultivation implies that use of all media, in aggregate, influences perceptions of confidence. Indeed, the cultivation paradigm assumes that mass media content provides a coherent homogeneous message for all users (Tapper, 1995). Robert Hawkins and Suzanne Pingree (1981) and W. James Potter (1993) reject this assumption, maintaining that cultivation of perceptions should be unique to specific media genres. The limited research on this issue provides support for the more specific operationalization of cultivation (Hawkins & Pingree, 1981; Pfau et al., 1995a, b; Potter & Chang, 1990; Rubin, Perse, & Taylor, 1988).

Applying this criticism to the realm of media news influence on confidence in institutions, Lee Becker and D. Charles Whitney argued nearly two decades ago that people "differ not only in terms of their dependence on the media as a whole but also in terms of their dependence on specific media" (1980, p. 95); therefore, their reliance on "specific media sources for news is a critical variable in understanding media effects" (p. 96). Becker and Whitney hypothesized that greater use of television news, as opposed to newspapers, would be more likely to fuel negative perceptions of government. They found support for this position but modest effect sizes.

We fully anticipated that specific communication sources would vary in terms of their relative negativity and thus are interested in how individual communication modalities differ—not only in their depictions of specific democratic institutions, but also in the nature of their influence on trust in these institutions. Indeed, the results reported in Part II of this book confirm that media forms vary in their depictions of democratic institutions and, therefore, in their patterns of influence on people's perceptions of institutions. In the next chapter, we explain in greater detail the methods employed in our study.

Media Influences on Confidence

Chapter 3

Design of the Studies

Only an interconnected data set of survey responses and media content allows one to move beyond analysis based on measures of media exposure or media message alone to consider the actual media content to which people have been exposed.

Political scientists Arthur Miller, Edie Goldenberg, and Lutz Erbring (1979, p. 68)

This investigation is a difficult undertaking, and our approach differs from most past research in two basic respects. First, we examine the impact of *multiple communication sources* on public confidence in a variety of democratic institutions. Past research typically stressed one, or perhaps two, communication sources in isolation from others (Miller, Goldenberg, & Erbring, 1979). This past line of research began in the 1970s, focusing primarily on the traditional news media, particularly newspapers and network television news.

However, today's media environment embodies a complex mosaic of communication sources, most of which have gone unexplored in terms of their impact on perceptions of confidence. Montague Kern, Marion Just, and Ann Crigler (1997) maintain that we are in the midst of "a sea change" in mass media use, in which traditional media—including newspapers and network television news—are declining in use and, by implication, in influence, while nontraditional outlets—such as television magazines, television talk shows, political talk radio, and the World Wide Web—are growing in use and influence. James Chesebro and Dale Bertelsen call the implications of these changes "transformational" (1996, pp. 134–135).

There is no question that use of traditional news media has fallen. Daily newspaper readership has been declining for nearly a decade, and the precipitous drop in newspaper use among younger age cohorts suggests that readership levels are likely to decline even further in the future (Fallows, 1996; Hulin-Salkin, 1987). The erosion of network television news viewership has been more recent and dramatic. A survey conducted by the Pew Research Center for the People & the Press (1996) reported that the proportion of Americans who said they watched television news "yesterday" dropped sharply from 74 percent in as recently as 1994 to just 59 percent in 1996. Various nontraditional media have moved in to fill this void, increasingly serving as alternative sources of information about public affairs for many people (Just et al., 1996; Kern, Just, & Crigler, 1997; Rehm, 1996). Yet, there has been little research on the influence of these nontraditional sources, or what Barry Hollander terms "new news" (1995, p. 787).

Research that stresses the impact of one or two traditional communication sources on public confidence is unable to capture all the nuances involving media influence, especially in the midst of the ongoing "sea changes" in media use. As a consequence, this investigation paints a broad stroke, featuring a comprehensive examination of communication media. We do this based on two assumptions: that individual communication sources vary in terms of their depictions of specific democratic institutions, and that people vary in terms of their reliance on particular communication sources. In other words, individual media will depict some institutions positively and others negatively, and those depictions may change over time. In addition, some people rely primarily on newspapers whereas others prefer political talk radio in order to monitor public affairs, and the difference may determine perceptions of institutions. The latter assumption prompted Lee Becker and D. Charles Whitney (1980) to speculate that people's preference for a communication source shapes attitudes. In comparing people who rely primarily on newspapers as opposed to television news for information about public affairs, they concluded that "audience members dependent on a given medium for their information about the world about them may well end up viewing the world quite differently from persons dependent on another medium" (p. 118).

In order to capture all the nuances in this changing media environment, we examine the simultaneous influence of multiple communication sources, traditional and nontraditional, on public perceptions of confidence in a variety of institutions. The communication media featured in the investigation include network and local television news, national and local newspapers, news magazines, television talk shows, television news magazines, and political talk radio.

Second, our approach differs from past research in that it employs multiple, interconnected data sets. Most past research on public confidence featured single data points, usually surveys, conducted at a fixed point in time. This approach is fraught with difficulty. The results of a single survey may simply reflect an anomaly or a methodological artifact. By contrast, a consistent pattern of results gleaned from multiple surveys conducted over a period of time enhances confidence in one's conclusions.

In addition, use of content analysis or surveys alone is inappropriate in gauging the influence of media communication on public confidence in institutions. Arthur Miller, Edie Goldenberg, and Lutz Erbring (1979), in a classic article nearly two decades ago, warned of the inadequacy of content analysis or surveys alone. As they cautioned:

No analysis of the relationship between media exposure (or reliance) and political attitude can really answer questions about media impact on political efficacy or trust, because such an analysis can only assume, without empirical evidence, that there is something about the media content to which people have been exposed that affects individual attitudes.... On the other hand, case studies of media content are not adequate either.... Determining whether ... coverage [affects] attitudes ... requires information on both individual attitudes and exposure to particular media messages. (p. 68)

What is required is an interconnected data set: a content analysis of media depictions of institutions and opinion surveys to determine whether those people who rely on a given communication source perceive the institution in much the same manner as the source depicted it.

One notable exception to the research approach of the past is Miller and colleagues' study of the influence of newspapers on public confidence. Although it featured an interconnected data set with both content analysis and opinion surveys, it focused only on one medium at a single point in time. It found that readers of more critical newspapers felt greater distrust toward politicians and institutions (Miller, Goldenberg, & Erbring, 1979). Unfortunately, this was not a robust test of media influence on public confidence, which Miller and his colleagues conceded. They called for more research to confirm their preliminary findings.

Our investigation employed two extensive content analyses of individual communication sources' depictions of specific institutions. These content analyses were conducted in conjunction with four surveys conducted over a two-year period; the surveys assessed respondents' confidence in specific democratic institutions, their media use patterns, and their sociodemographic profile. This chapter describes the content analysis and survey phases of the investigation and the variables and instruments used.

CONTENT ANALYSIS PHASE

The content analyses were designed to assess the quantity and tone of communication media depictions of specific democratic institutions at two distinct points, both in advance of and during the administration of the opinion surveys. In all, two extensive content analyses were conducted: the first between April 3 and 23, 1995; the second nearly a year and a half later, from October 21 to November 10, 1996.

General Procedures

In all cases, content analyses were conducted with the most widely used media products from within the individual genres, according to official statistics. As a result, the specific sources examined varied some across the two content analyses. A list of all media sources included in the content analyses is presented in Table 3.1.

Twelve graduate students content-analyzed the communication media. Inter-coder reliabilities were computed for depictions of the tone of coverage of an institution as operationalized across three dependent measures: global attitude, trust, and confidence. In all cases, assessment of media depictions was done using the same scales as those used in the telephone surveys. These scales, which are detailed in the "Variables and Instruments" section of this chapter, featured measures used in numerous past studies of public confidence. The sample frame and the unit of observation for each of the various communication genres, and the effective inter-coder reliability ratings (Rosenthal, 1984, 1987) for the coder pairs, are noted as follows.

Media Categories

Network Television News. Because audience data indicated that all three prime time network news shows had similar viewer distribution in the region on weekdays (Mediamark Research, 1993), ABC, CBS, and NBC were weighted equally in the 1995 content analysis. A systematic random sample of 15 news programs was selected. The unit of observation was each news story. In all, we analyzed 180 stories that made reference to one or more of the democratic institutions covered in the study. The respective effective inter-coder reliability ratings in the 1995 content analysis for the three dependent measures of global attitude, trust, and confidence were .92, .94, and .96.

Viewership of network evening newscasts in the area did not remain stable. Audience data from Nielsen Media Research (Nielsen, 1996) indicated that by late 1995 *CBS Evening News* enjoyed nearly twice the viewing audience of either *ABC World News Tonight* or *NBC Nightly News*

Table 3.1
Summary of Media Content Analyzed

	1995	1996
Network television news	ABC World News CBS Evening News NBC Nightly News	ABC World News CBS Evening News NBC Nightly News
Local television news (6 and 10 pm)	ABC, CBS, and NBC affiliates	ABC, CBS, and NBC affiliates
Other television news	CNN Prime News The News Hour	
National newspapers	New York Times USA Today Wall Street Journal	New York Times USA Today
Local newspapers	Wisconsin State Journal Wisconsin Times	Wisconsin State Journal Wisconsin Times
National magazines	Newsweek Time People Life Saturday Evening Post	Newsweek Time U.S. News & World Report
Television entertainment talk shows	Donahue Oprah Winfrey Late Night with David Letterman The Tonight Show with Jay Leno	Oprah Winfrey Late Night with David Letterman The Tonight Show with Jay Leno
Political talk radio	The Rush Limbaugh Show The G. Gordon Liddy Show	The Rush Limbaugh Show The Ken Hamblin Show
Television news magazines		60 Minutes 20/20 Dateline NBC

in the sample area. Thus, in the 1996 content analysis *CBS Evening News* was weighted proportionately. A random sample of 16 weekday programs was selected: 8 for *CBS Evening News* and 4 each for *ABC World News* and *NBC Nightly News*. A total of 195 stories were coded. Respective effective inter-coder reliabilities in the 1996 content analysis for the three measures were .86, .76, and .92.

Other Television News. The *CNN Prime News* and *The MacNeil/Lehrer News Hour* on PBS were selected in the 1995 content analysis, since they constituted prime time alternatives to network news. A systematic random sample of 15 news programs was selected: The unit of observation was each news story, and 146 stories were coded. The respective effective reliability ratings of other television news across the three dependent measures were .93, .94, and .98. Because of low market ratings in comparison to the network newscasts (Nielsen, 1996), this category was dropped in the 1996 content analysis.

Local Television News. A total of 23 local television news shows were selected for inclusion in the 1995 content analysis. In the 6 P.M. time slot, the ratings for the local news shows of the three major networks were similar (Nielsen, 1993). Therefore, one local news show was analyzed on each weeknight, alternating across the three stations, for a total of five programs for each station for this time slot. However, at the 10 P.M. slot, the CBS local news attracted nearly half of all viewers (Nielsen, 1993) and therefore was the only program selected for analysis in this time slot. It was analyzed on alternating weeknights during the three weeks of the study, for a total of eight additional programs. The unit of observation was each news story, and 247 stories were coded. Respective inter-coder reliabilities in the 1995 content analysis for each of the dependent measures were .59, .66, and .75.

In the 1996 content analysis, 12 weekday local television news programs were selected. Once again, Nielsen (1996) ratings indicated that in the 10 P.M. time slot the CBS affiliate commanded nearly twice the audience share of either the NBC or ABC affiliate. A random sample of 12 weekday news programs was selected from this time slot, with distribution of programs across stations reflecting audience shares. The respective inter-coder reliabilities for the 1996 content analysis across the three dependent measures were .78, .78, and .81.

Newspapers. There are two local dominant newspapers in the local area with combined circulations exceeding 100,000 on Monday through Saturday (Editor & Publisher International Year Book, 1995). Only one of the papers published a Sunday edition with a circulation of 163,808 (1995, p. I-441). Three national papers with sizable and similar circulations in the area were the *New York Times, USA Today,* and the *Wall Street Journal* (Audit Report, 1995). Because the *New York Times* and *Wall Street Journal* have similar readership figures in the region, only the former was selected for content analysis given its role as "newspaper of record" in setting the agendas of other newspapers (Trumbo, 1995). *USA Today* also was included in the analysis because of unique readership compared to the other two national newspapers. In the 1995 content analysis two of four papers were examined each day, alternating between the four. A systematic sampling procedure was used to determine the content analyzed. The six most prominent articles, based on column inches, were selected from each paper. The articles were selected from the front page of the two national and two local newspapers, the next two pages in the national newspapers, the next single page dealing with national news in the local newspapers, and the first page dealing with state and local news in the two local newspapers. This sampling procedure was based on the premise that the most prominent articles would be representative of each newspaper's treatment of public affairs content. The unit of observation was each article, and 180 articles were coded that made reference to one or more of the five democratic institutions examined in this study. Respective inter-coder reliability ratings for the 1995 content analysis across the three dependent measures were .60, .64, and .70.

The Monday through Saturday combined circulations of the two dominant local newspapers in the community increased to 120,000 in 1996 (Editor & Publisher International Year Book, 1996). The *New York Times* and *USA Today* continued to enjoy sizeable circulations in the area (Audit Report, 1996). In the three weeks of the 1996 content analysis, the larger local paper was coded seven days a week, the smaller local paper four days each week, and the two national papers one day each week. The unit of observation was each article. In the 1996 content analysis, the four most prominent articles, based on column inches, were selected from the same set of pages as in 1995. The respective inter-coder reliabilities in the 1996 content analysis for newspapers were .66, .65, and .75.

National Magazines. In the 1995 content analysis, two types of magazines were featured: hard news magazines and "softer" magazines of general interest. The two hard news magazines with the highest readership—*Newsweek,* with an area circulation of 10,473, and *Time,* area circulation 6,352 (Supplemental Data Report, 1994, p. 16)—were included in the analysis. Two issues of each weekly magazine were analyzed. Also included in the analyses were three general-interest magazines with modest coverage of public affairs and sizable circulation in the area (Supplemental Data Report, 1994, p. 16)—*People,* published weekly, and *Life* and *Saturday Evening Post,* both published monthly. Two editions of *People* and one issue each of *Life* and *Saturday Evening Post* were analyzed. For all magazines, eight articles with the most column inches were included in the content analysis, again based on the assumption that the most prominent articles would be representative of a publication's coverage. The unit of observation was each article, and a total of 64 articles were coded. Effective inter-coder reliability ratings were unacceptably low (.58, .29, and .40, respectively), in part, due to the limited number of articles that made reference to democratic institutions.

In the 1996 content analysis, only the three news magazines with the most readership—*Newsweek,* with an area circulation of 10,705, *Time,* area circulation 9,666, and *U.S. News & World Report,* area circulation 4,858 (Simmons Study, 1996)—were included for study. They were analyzed weekly. For *Newsweek* and *Time,* eight articles on national affairs with the most column inches were included in the content analysis; four articles were included from *U.S. News & World Report,* reflecting its smaller circulation. The unit of observation was each article. Respective inter-coder reliability ratings in the 1996 content analysis for magazines were .70, .71, and .76.

Television Entertainment Talk Shows. The 1995 study featured the two most-watched daytime television talk shows—*Donahue* and *Oprah Winfrey*—and the two most-watched late-night television entertainment talk shows, *Late Night with David Letterman* and *The Tonight Show with Jay Leno* (Nielsen, 1995, pp. 40–45). All together, eight installments of the four programs were examined on alternate days over a three-week period. The unit of observation was each five-minute segment (excluding openings and commercial breaks) that aired during the first half hour of each show. The remainder of these shows was not included due to evidence indicating that viewership of late-night talk shows falls sharply after the first half-hour (Nielsen, 1995). All together, 177 segments were coded that made reference to democratic institutions. The respective inter-coder reliability ratings in the 1995 content analysis were .80, .84, and .94.

The approach taken in the 1996 content analysis was similar, although *Donahue* was no longer on the air. The 1996 study included the three most viewed television talk shows (Nielsen, 1996), *Oprah Winfrey*, *The Late Show with David Letterman*, and *The Tonight Show*. Five installments of each of the three shows, viewed on a rotating schedule, were analyzed during the three-week period. The unit of observation was each five-minute segment, excluding program openings and commercial breaks, that aired during the first 20 minutes of each show. Respective reliability ratings in the 1996 content analysis across dependent measures were .95, .93, and .98.

Political Talk Radio. The two most highly rated political talk radio programs—*The Rush Limbaugh Show*, with a 7.2 share in this market, and *The G. Gordon Liddy Show*, with a 4.9 share—were included in the 1995 content analysis (Arbitron, 1994). No other political talk radio program had an audience share of more than 2.0, suggesting that these two programs were representative of this genre. Both shows run for three hours each day, Mondays through Fridays. The first hour was analyzed, alternating every other weekday. The unit of observation was each program segment between commercial breaks. A total of 53 segments were analyzed. The respective inter-coder reliability ratings in the 1995 content analysis were .87, .92, and .91.

The demise of the *G. Gordon Liddy Show* after the initial study prompted changes in the configuration of the political talk radio genre for the 1996 content analysis. The two most highly rated political talk radio programs in 1996—*The Rush Limbaugh Show*, with a 7.3 audience share in this market, and *The Ken Hamblin Show*, with a 4.6 share—were included in the content analysis (Arbitron, 1996). No other political talk radio program had an audience share of more than 1.0. To reflect the disparity in audience share, *The Rush Limbaugh Show* was analyzed Mondays, Wednesdays, and Fridays; *The Ken Hamblin Show* was analyzed on Tuesdays and Thursdays. Again, the first hour of each show was analyzed. The unit of observation was each six-minute block of programming, excluding commercial breaks, for a total of ten units per hour. Respective effective inter-coder reliabilities in the 1996 content analysis across the three measures were .95, .93, and .94.

Television News Magazines. The category of television news magazines was added for the 1996 content analysis. The three most watched television news magazines (Nielsen, 1996)—*60 Minutes, 20/20,* and *Dateline NBC*—were selected for analysis. The first two shows air weekly; the latter, four times a week. One edition of each of the three shows was analyzed in its entirety each week for three weeks. Selection of *Dateline* was rotated so that one Tuesday, Wednesday, and Friday edition was included. The unit of observation was each individual story. The respective inter-coder reliabilities for television news magazines were .94, .97, and .99.

PUBLIC SURVEY PHASE

This investigation featured four telephone surveys conducted over a two-year period. The surveys were conducted under the direct supervision of the University of Wisconsin Survey Center on a probability sample of households using the center's Computer-Assisted Telephone Interviewing (CATI) system. All four samples were drawn from Dane County, Wisconsin, telephone numbers. Dane County is home to Madison, Wisconsin, the state's capital and second-largest city.

Respondents were selected based on random-digit dialing. In all cases, one adult from each eligible household was chosen as respondent. The survey instruments were pilot-tested before actual fieldwork commenced; details of fieldwork are noted in Table 3.2. The four surveys featured basically the same scales, which are described in detail in the "Variables and Instruments" section of this chapter.

Sample Characteristics

The use of local samples may generate concern over the extent to which they represent the populations from which they were drawn, as well as the extent to which they represent the U.S. population as a whole. These concerns are somewhat subdued in this investigation for two reasons. First, the focus of this research is not simply people's attitudes. If it were, the local samples would need to perfectly mirror the national population in order to justify any generalizations. Instead, the focus of

Table 3.2
Fieldwork of Public Opinion Surveys

Dates of Fieldwork	N	Cooperation Rate
April 11 to May 10, 1995	235	49.5%
November 14 to December 4, 1995	318	47.0%
October 21 to November 10, 1996	357	55.3%
October 20 to November 10, 1997	368	46.6%

Note: The cooperation rate is defined as the number of completed interviews divided by
the number of completed interviews plus refusals.

this study is on the *linkages* between individual media depictions of specific democratic institutions, people's use of those media, and people's
perceptions of those institutions.

Second, the samples are reasonably representative and thus mitigate
concerns over external validity. Whenever sample respondents reasonably reflect the population from which they are drawn, generalizability
is usually ensured even when cooperation rates are less than ideal (Merkle, 1996). This investigation set stringent standards to ensure external
validity. The pooled samples had to be reasonably representative of sociodemographic features in the local population from which they were
drawn and in the U.S. population, and the local population's media use
patterns had to reasonably reflect the media use tendencies of the nation
as a whole.

As shown in Table 3.3, the composite or pooled samples are reasonably
representative of the population of Dane County, Wisconsin, and the
United States as a whole. Compared to the county from which the samples were drawn, the pooled sample respondents were similar in terms
of sex, racial composition, and age but were somewhat better educated
and more affluent. Compared to participants in the 1996 National Election Study, residents of the county from which the samples were drawn
were similar in income and education but were more likely to be Cau-
casian and were somewhat younger. Compared to the NES national sample, respondents in the pooled samples were as likely to be Democrat
but were much more likely to classify themselves as an independent as
opposed to Republican. Party identification data from the county from
which the samples were drawn are unavailable because Wisconsin does
not require partisan voter registration.

Table 3.3
Characteristics of Survey Samples versus Benchmarks

	SAMPLES						
	Spring 1995	Fall 1995	Fall 1996	Fall 1997	Pooled Sample	Dane Co., Wisconsin	National Sample
Sex							
Male	43.7	44.3	50.7	45.4	46.3	49.3	44.8
Female	56.3	55.7	49.3	54.6	53.7	50.7	55.1
Age							
18-24	13.2	18.6	15.1	13.4	15.1	20.4	6.8
25-34	31.2	29.8	19.8	19.9	24.5	25.7	19.4
35-44	23.9	18.6	22.5	18.3	20.6	21.3	24.5
45-54	17.1	14.1	21.2	24.9	19.7	12.1	15.9
55-64	6.0	8.8	9.1	9.3	8.5	8.7	13.0
65+	8.5	10.0	12.3	14.2	11.6	11.9	20.4
Education							
No HS degree	2.5	5.1	3.9	4.9	3.9	10.5	13.4
HS degree only	21.8	20.3	20.7	16.3	19.6	25.6	32.0
Some college	23.1	27.8	24.1	23.4	24.7	34.2	27.0
College degree	34.9	31.6	32.2	33.2	33.0	18.9	17.9
Post-graduate	17.6	15.2	19.0	22.0	18.8	10.8	9.6
Income							
Under $20,000	11.4	18.3	14.2	16.6	15.3	27.1	30.0
$20,000-$39,999	35.0	28.5	25.6	27.5	28.7	33.7	28.8
$40,000-$59,999	27.3	30.6	26.9	24.3	27.2	22.6	18.9
$60,000-$99,999	20.4	16.9	25.0	21.1	21.0	12.7	17.3
$100,000+	5.9	5.6	8.2	10.8	7.9	3.9	4.9
Race							
White	--	94.6	92.4	93.9	93.7	93.9	84.8
Non-white	--	5.4	7.6	6.1	6.3	6.1	15.2
Political party affiliation							
Democrat	35.7	38.1	35.9	36.7	36.6		38.7
Republican	22.3	21.4	20.2	14.3	19.0		27.5
Independent	40.3	37.4	42.0	46.0	41.8		26.0
Other	1.7	3.2	2.0	3.0	2.5		7.8

Note: Data in the fifth and sixth columns are from the 1990 Census data for Dane County, Wisconsin, and the 1996 National Election Study, respectively. The last two income categories for 1996 NES data differ slightly ($60–105,000 and more than $105,000). Because the state of Wisconsin does not require partisan voter registration, political party identification data are not available for Dane County.

As illustrated in Table 3.4, the local population's media use habits reasonably reflect those of the nation. Dane County residents view slightly more television each day (International Demographics, 1996), including more network and local television news (Audience Research & Development, 1997; Center for Political Studies, 1996; Newspaper Association of America, 1997). They are about as likely as people across the country to read a newspaper or listen to radio news/talk radio (Audi-

Table 3.4
Media Use in Dane County versus the Nation

	Dane Co.	Nation
Percentage of adults using at least once a week[1]		
Newspaper	80	76
Network television news	87	73
Local television news	94	88
Radio news/Talk radio	69	68
Average weekly newspaper readership[2]	52.3%	58.8%
Magazine readership per week[3]		
Newsweek	6.9%	3.7%/4.1%[4]
Time	6.6%	5.3%/5.2%
U.S. News & World Report	3.1%	2.5%/2.2%
Total television viewing per day (in hours)[5]	7.62	7.22
Days per week watching television news[6]	4.11	3.54
Television program ratings, May 1996[7]		
ABC World News Tonight	7	8
CBS Evening News	14	6
NBC Nightly News	6	7
60 Minutes	18	12
20/20	16	13
Dateline NBC (Tuesdays)	13	10
The Tonight Show with Jay Leno	4	5
The Late Show with David Letterman	7	4
Oprah Winfrey	7	8
Donahue (May 1995)	5	3

Notes:
1. Audience Research & Development, 1997; Newspaper Association of America, 1997.
2. Simmons Study of Media and Markets, 1996.
3. SRDS, 1996.
4. Figures are based on Chicago and Los Angeles readership, respectively.
5. International Demographics, 1996.
6. Center for Political Studies, 1996.
7. Nielsen Media Research, 1996.

ence Research & Development, 1997; Newspaper Association of America, 1997; Simmons Study of Media and Markets, 1996), and somewhat more inclined to read national news magazines compared to residents of Chicago or Los Angeles (SRDS, 1996). Dane County residents' tastes in television entertainment talk shows, news, and television magazines are comparable to the nation as a whole, except that they are more inclined to watch the CBS Evening News and 60 Minutes (Nielsen, 1996).

VARIABLES AND INSTRUMENTS

All of the scales employed in this study of the media's influence on public confidence are measures that have established impressive track records. In addition, measures were pilot-tested prior to use in each of the four opinion surveys. Internal consistency of multiple-item scales used in this investigation was gauged using Cronbach's alpha (Cronbach, 1951). The specific measures, and their reliabilities in each of the four surveys, are described as follows.

Measures of Confidence in Institutions

Media depictions of confidence in each democratic institution functioned as the dependent variable in the content analysis phase of the investigation. Similarly, public perceptions of confidence in each institution, as revealed in the telephone interviews, served as the dependent variable in the survey phase of the investigation. The same measures were employed in both phases.

As discussed in Chapter 1, public confidence in institutions has been conceptualized in various ways. It has been called "confidence" (Craig, 1993; Lipset & Schneider, 1987), "trust" (Miller, 1974a), absence of "cynicism" (Cappella & Jamieson, 1997; Erber & Lau, 1990), "discontent" (Craig, 1993), and "disaffection/disenchantment" (Sniderman, 1981). Lipset and Schneider (1987) indicate that the different conceptualizations of confidence result in different outcomes in research. Civen this backdrop, this investigation employed multiple measures, drawn from past research on either public opinion in general or public confidence in particular.

Measures were employed to tap three depictions/perceptions: global attitude toward institutions, trust in institutions, and confidence in institutions. Global depictions/perceptions toward institutions were evaluated using six semantic differentials: foolish/wise, unfavorable/favorable, wrong/right, negative/positive, unacceptable/acceptable, and bad/good. The scales were developed and refined in several past studies (Miller & Burgoon, 1979; Pfau & Burgoon, 1988; Pfau et al., 1990, 1998). The global perceptions measure has achieved excellent reliability ratings in past research and performed very well in this investigation. Reliabilities of the global perceptions measure for each of the democratic institutions across the four studies were as follows: presidency, .97, .90, .88, and .91; Congress, .96, .93, .91, and .93; court system, .94, .93, .93, and .94; the news media, .98, .93, .92, and .94; and the public schools, .96, .95, .93, and .94.

Depictions/perceptions of trust in institutions were gauged using a single semantic differential item with anchors of untrustworthy/trustworthy. Public trust has been a staple in past assessments of confidence in institutions (Lipset & Schneider, 1987; Miller, 1974a). However, the standard measures of trust (e.g., "How much of the time do you think you can trust the government in Washington to do what is right?") leave some room for improvement. First, "people vary in terms of how they interpret trust-in-government items," which have been used in most surveys of confidence (Erber & Lau, 1990, p. 237). Second, the trust items employed in past assessments are more applicable to the national government, whereas this investigation is interested in trust in multiple institutions, some national (e.g., presidency and Congress), but others not (e.g., the court system, which is national, state, and local; the public schools, which are local; and the news media, which are commercial). The trust item used in the investigation was adapted from a measure developed and used in past research by Lynda Lee Kaid and Keith Sanders (1978) and Gina Garramone (1983, 1985) to assess perceptions of trust in political candidates.

Finally, depictions/perceptions of confidence were assessed by a 0–100 point measure asking, "Taken as a whole, on a scale from 0 to 100, where 0 represents complete lack of confidence, and 100 signifies utmost confidence, how much confidence would you place in [the institution]?" The wording of this item was patterned after an item used in past studies of public confidence conducted by, among others, the Institute for Social Research/Center for Political Studies (Asher, 1988) and Harris, Gallup, and NORC (see Lipset & Schneider, 1987).

Measures of Institutional Expertise

The concept of expertise captures people's knowledge of and their interest in political objects (Fiske, Lau, & Smith, 1990). Recent research indicates that people's expertise concerning political objects (e.g., persons, issues, or institutions) exerts greater influence on their perceptions of confidence than their sociodemographic status or mass media use (Fiske, Lau, & Smith 1990; Moy, Pfau, & Kahlor, 1999; Pfau et al., 1998; Price & Zaller, 1993).

Institutional expertise was operationalized as respondents' awareness of, interest in, and knowledge about the presidency, Congress, court system, news media, and public schools. It was assessed with three seven-interval bi-polar scales employed in past research by Susan Fiske, Richard Lau, and Richard Smith (1990) and Vincent Price and John Zaller (1993). While operationalization of awareness and knowledge more often involves the use of objective measures (for a review, see Delli Carpini & Keeter, 1996), more recent work utilizing subjective measures suggests that "self-report" items provide a valid and meaningful indicator (Mondak, 1996).

Reliability ratings of the institutional expertise measure for each institution across the four surveys were presidency, .90, .80, .79, and .83; Congress, .90, .88, .86, and .88; the court system, .80, .89, .85, and .88; the news media, .78, .84, .78, and .88; and the public schools, .92, .92, .91, and .88.

Measures of Media Use

Media use measures have proven controversial, to say the least. Steven Chaffee and Joan Schleuder observe that "exposure to news media has traditionally been the focus of survey research related to public affairs" (1986, p. 78). But, exposure measures alone are deemed inadequate (McLeod & McDonald, 1985), especially in research like this, which endeavors to compare different media (Chaffee & Schleuder, 1986). Chaffee and Schleuder recommend assessing simple media exposure plus attention paid (1986, p. 104). As they explain: "If . . . one anticipates making comparisons between media, . . . then media attention measures are essential. . . . Adding media attention measures to the comparison can reduce the spurious influence of third variables on tests of cognitive effects" (p. 103).

This study operationalized media use as exposure to and attention paid to specific communication media. The investigation employed two ten-point items to assess people's exposure to and attention paid to a given source (Chaffee & Schleuder, 1986; McLeod et al., 1995). The exposure scale ranged from "rarely use" to "frequently use"; the attention scale ranged from "little attention" to "close attention." The exposure item was asked for all communication sources before moving on to the attention item. The first time a medium was mentioned, two examples were offered in order to ensure clarity (e.g., news magazines: *Time* and *Newsweek*). The examples were selected based on their relative popularity within a respective genre in the study area; therefore, they varied some across the four surveys.

Reliability ratings of the media use measures for specific communication sources across the four surveys were newspapers, .75, .67, .81, and .68; news magazines, .83, .55, .84, and .77; television network news, .73, .73, .90, and .77; other national television news (first survey only), .90; local television news, .81, .83, .85, and .70; television news magazines (third and fourth surveys only), .84 and .76; television entertainment talk shows, .94, .77, .86, and .75; political talk radio, .73, .72, .90, and .74; and the Internet (fourth survey only), .87.

Sociodemographics

Sociodemographic factors were used as control variables in our analysis. Relevant respondent sociodemographic variables included gender (males coded high), age, education (operationalized as some high school, high school degree only, some college, four-year college degree only, and advanced study), and political party identification (operationalized as affiliation with Democratic, Republican, or other parties, or as Independent). Dummy variables for Democratic and Republican affiliation were computed from the party identification variable.

Data Analysis Approach

Our attempt to determine the effects of media use on confidence in democratic institutions is riddled with problems of causality. Because our data are cross-sectional, we cannot conclude with absolute certainty that use of print media enhances or undermines confidence levels. After all, individuals' trust in a particular institution may influence how much information he or she seeks about that institution from the print media (or other communication modalities). Also along this line of reasoning, when one examines the relationship between media use and knowledge of an institution, to what extent can one argue temporal precedence? As Susan Fiske and her colleagues put it, "Media exposure conceptually [could] be both a cause and a consequence of expertise" (1990, p. 33). The ability to argue causality from nonlongitudinal survey data is limited when compared to arguing causality based on experimental data (Campbell & Stanley, 1963).

To address this concern, we employed structural equation modeling (SEM) techniques to analyze our data. We ran structural equation models using LISREL, designed to specify "the process underlying the joint distribution of a set of observable variables" (Bielby & Hauser, 1977). SEM assumes that a given set of variables is linearly related (MacCallum, 1995) and tests these relationships against the data collected. The general form of the LISREL model assumes a causal structure among variables, some of which are designated endogenous (dependent) and others exogenous (independent) (Sörbom & Jöreskog, 1981). SEM allows for the estimation for three types of effects: (1) the total effect of a given variable on another, or the part of their total association that is not due to common causes, to correlation among their causes, or to unanalyzed correlation; (2) the indirect effects of a given variable, which are transmitted by variables specified as intervening between the cause and effect of interest in a model; and (3) the direct effect of a variable, or that part of the total effect not transmitted via intervening variables (Alwin & Hauser, 1975, pp. 38–39).

SEM, then, is a way of testing a specified theory about relationships between theoretical constructs (Jöreskog, 1993). In analyzing the relationships between media use, expertise in an institution, and confidence in that same institution, we adopt Karl Jöreskog's (1993) two-step "model generating approach." First, an initial model is specified, based not necessarily on specific hypotheses about single paths between variables but "at least some tentative ideas of what a suitable model should be" (Jöreskog, 1993, p. 313). Second, parameters may be added or subtracted from this original model as long as the changes are meaningful and substantially interpretable.

There is no consensus on what constitutes "good fit" of a given model (Tanaka, 1993). P-values and significance tests based on p-values are conventional ways of making statistical inferences in the social sciences. Significance tests based on p-values are conducted to determine if the null model is "true." Adrian Raftery (1993) argues that the question of whether the null model holds is irrelevant as the researcher knows the answer is "no." "A scientifically more relevant question is, Which model predicts the data better? (That is, under which model are the data more likely to have been observed?)" (Raftery, 1993, p. 164). Because they are prone to give unsatisfactory results in large samples, Raftery (1995) offers a Bayesian Information Criterion (BIC) that takes sample size into account and favors simpler, more parsimonious models than the sequential p-value approach. Thus the evaluation of model fit in this study is based on two statistics: the more traditional chi-square statistic, and the Bayesian Information Criterion.

The next five chapters present the results of our study. Chapter 4 presents the findings of our content analysis, and Chapters 5 through 8 reveal the effects of using particular communication sources on trust in democratic institutions.

Chapter 4

Media Depictions of Institutions

One major source—perhaps *the* major source—of information concerning the condition of the country is, of course, the mass media.
Political scientists Seymour Martin Lipset
and William Schneider (1987, p. 403)

Real news is bad news.
Communication theorist Marshall McLuhan
(in Grossman, 1995, p. 90)

As we noted in Chapter 3, two types of data are required in order to
evaluate the influence of communication media on public confidence: an
analysis of media depictions of institutions, plus survey data on people's
media use patterns and their perceptions of democratic institutions (Miller, Goldenberg, & Erbring, 1979). The first step in this process involves
the systematic content analysis of media depictions.

This chapter reviews past analyses of mass media coverage of democratic institutions and presents the results of two extensive content analyses conducted just before and during the administration of the four
opinion surveys, which we used to assess people's media use and their
confidence in institutions. The methodology of our content analyses was
described in Chapter 3.

PAST RESEARCH ON MEDIA DEPICTIONS

As indicated in Chapters 1 and 2, following the downturn in public
confidence during the late 1960s and early 1970s, scholars began search-

ing for causes. It seemed plausible that one cause of the public's angst over democratic institutions was the mass media's coverage of these institutions. Gary Wamsley and Richard Pride (1972) were among the first to raise this consideration, speculating that *"it is a possibility* that the characteristics of TV news . . . when coupled with new conceptions and evidence on characteristics of audience and effects . . . result in a sum total of effects that is denigrative of political system authority symbols rather than supportive" (1972, p. 449). Michael Robinson went even further, arguing that the mass media—particularly network television news—were responsible for the rising cynicism. His concept of "videomalaise" characterized an insidious process in which the media's negative depictions of institutions instill in viewers a sense of hostility toward institutions, thereby producing deepening cynicism (Robinson, 1975, 1976, 1977).

Since Robinson's early work, researchers have periodically examined the media's depictions of institutions. Most of this research focused on the coverage of one or two traditional news sources, typically network television news and newspapers. These past findings provide a starting point for our search for patterns in mass media depictions of individual institutions.

Television News

In a survey of Oregon residents, Robinson (1974) found that the more time respondents spent viewing the Senate Watergate hearings on television, the greater their chances of reporting negative feelings toward politicians in general and toward the news media in particular. This led him to conclude that the negativity of television news reports produced deepening cynicism toward democratic institutions. In support of this explanation, Robinson employed a combination of laboratory and survey data.

Although his early work did not feature content analysis of television news, Robinson nonetheless assumed strong negativity in the television news reports. "It seems reasonable to assume," he explained, "that these anti-institutional themes reach the audience with one essential message: none of our national policies work, none of our institutions respond, none of our political organizations succeed" (1976, p. 429).

Robinson's point was that news coverage had changed during the 1970s. In response to Vietnam and Watergate, a "new" press had evolved, one with an aggressive and highly cynical attitude. The objective of this "new" journalism is no longer the objective description and explanation of events, which can enhance people's understanding of their world. Rather, the main priority of the "new" press is the uncovering of the failings and foibles of institutions and the people who occupy them. This has the effect, as James Fallows described it, of "portraying public life in America as a race to the bottom" (1996, p. 7). The "new" press truly embodies Marshall McLuhan's lament that "real news is bad news" (Grossman, 1995, p. 90).

Robinson's early work sparked interest in documenting the nature of media news depictions of institutions. Subsequent studies examined the actual content of television news and uncovered a pattern of unabashed negativity, particularly in targeting the presidency and Congress. We discuss these studies in greater detail in Chapter 6.

Suffice it to say, there are two striking voids in the research on television news depictions. First, there are no studies that have examined depictions of democratic institutions offered by other national television news sources (e.g., *CNN Prime News, The NewsHour*), local television news or, for that matter, such nontraditional sources as television news magazines or television entertainment talk shows. However, there is no reason to believe that changes in the culture of journalism depicted by Daniel Hallin (1992), Thomas Patterson (1993), and others have not affected these news sources in much the same way they have the major networks, though, perhaps not quite to the same degree. Second, there are little hard data about media news depictions of democratic institutions other than the presidency and Congress, institutions such as the court system, news media, or the public schools.

Print Media

The limited research to date dealing with print depictions of democratic institutions tends to focus on the presidency and Congress. We review depictions of the presidency in Chapter 4. Regarding Congress, some claim that newspaper depictions are negative in tone, but few who take this position provide independent confirmation (see Davidson, Kovenock, & O'Leary, 1966; Kedrowski, 1988; Patterson & Caldeira, 1990). Samuel Patterson and Gregory Caldeira are typical in their reliance on survey data alone, concluding that "media reportage . . . have a powerful depressing effect on evaluations on Congress" (1990, p. 39).

The fact of the matter is that there are little available data chronicling print media's depictions of Congress. The characterization of Michael Robinson and Kevin Appel nearly 20 years ago of a "paucity of hard research data that . . . describe the content of network news coverage of the House and Senate" (1979, p. 408) is not only still true today, but should be extended to encompass all news media, including newspapers.

Findings from actual content analyses of newspaper coverage of Congress are inconclusive. Charles Tidmarch and John Pitney conducted a content analysis of all references to Congress in ten major newspapers in 1978 and found that hard news coverage was "neutral and balanced," although editorial depictions exhibited a "negative leaning" (1985, p. 480). Robinson (1981) reported a negative slant to newspaper coverage of Congress, but Robinson and Appel (1979) found that network television news was far more hostile in its coverage of Congress than newspapers. Perhaps as a result, studies that we will review in greater detail in Chapter 5 suggest that people's use of traditional print news may enhance confidence in democratic institutions (Becker & Whitney, 1980; Miller & Reese, 1982; O'Keefe, 1980).

Turning to news magazines, content analysis of their coverage of presidential campaigns points to a growing incidence of negative depictions of candidates. Patterson's examination of *Time*'s and *Newsweek*'s "evaluative references" to Democratic and Republican nominees in presidential campaigns from 1960 to 1992 notes a steadily rising proportion of negative versus positive depictions: "Candidates of the 1960s got more favorable coverage than those of the 1970s, who in turn received more positive coverage than those of the 1980's" (1993, p. 20). Negative references exceeded positive ones for the first time in 1980 and, in 1988 and 1992, constituted nearly 60 percent of all evaluative depictions. Patterson, echoing Robinson, argues that journalism norms changed following Vietnam and Watergate, adding that "the antipolitics bias of the press that came out of the closet two decades ago stayed out" (p. 19).

Nontraditional Media

The term "nontraditional media" has been used to refer to any number of communication sources, encompassing such diverse programming as television entertainment talk shows (Meyer, 1993), television tabloids (Weaver, 1994), television political talk shows (Chaffee, Zhao, & Leshner, 1994; McLeod et al., 1996; Newhagen, 1994), and political talk radio (Hollander, 1996). This study operationalizes nontraditional media to include television entertainment talk shows such as *Oprah, Late Night with David Letterman,* and *The Tonight Show,* and television news magazines, such as *60 Minutes, Dateline NBC,* and *20/20.* Political talk radio is treated as a distinct source because it involves a different medium and because of the growing body of research concerning its influence.

There is very little research about nontraditional media depictions of democratic institutions or of their influence on public perceptions of institutions. Research on entertainment talk shows tends to focus on the audience (e.g., Frisby & Weigold, 1994) or talk show guests (Priest & Dominick, 1994). In addition, this research focuses more on daytime than late-night talk shows.

Of the "new" media, political talk radio has generated considerable scrutiny. Political talk radio has grown dramatically during the past decade, with more than 1,000 radio stations featuring a talk format (Herbst, 1995; Jones, 1994).

There is little question about the tone of political talk radio: It is decidedly negative toward most institutions, which are often viewed derisively. Gary Woodward reported that "most [political talk radio programs] . . . feature conservative hosts railing against 'liberal' policies and policy makers" (1997, p. 5). Diane Rehm described talk radio as "a haven for many who are unhappy," adding that "increasingly, . . . talk radio has become a tool with which critics of government lash out, poisoning the dialogue" (1996, p. 140). Jeffrey Katz concluded that "political figures . . . are the main targets of abuse" on talk radio (1991, p. 42).

The few systematic content analyses of political talk radio confirm its negative depictions of most democratic institutions. Murray Levin's analysis of 700 hours of programming from two Boston talk stations in 1977 and 1982 led him to describe talk radio as "a delegitimizing voice" (1987, p. xiii), adding that "talk radio leaves an impression of widespread distress" (p. 21). In another study, Kathleen Hall Jamieson monitored political talk radio during a nine-month period and reported that political talk radio "licenses forms of speech that we have not previously heard in public space, over the air waves" (Fleeson, 1995). In a content analysis of moderate, conservative, and liberal political talk radio programs, Joseph Borrell and Melinda Schwenk concluded that the new genre was not monolithic in its coverage, but acknowledged that "conservative hosts were significantly more likely than liberal hosts to speak out alone without engaging callers or experts" on the subjects including the role of the federal government in taxing and spending, the Congress in general, and education (1997, p. 13).

RESULTS OF THIS INVESTIGATION

With this past research as a backdrop, we now turn to our investigation, which featured two content analyses of media depictions of democratic institutions. The first analysis was conducted between April 3 and 23, 1995, overlapping our first opinion survey; the second between October 21 and November 10, 1996, overlapping the third survey. Both content analyses were comprehensive in scope, featuring the simultaneous examination of the most widely used traditional and nontraditional media.

Data Analysis Approach

To examine potential differences in communication depictions of public confidence in each democratic institution, Multivariate Analysis of Variance (MANOVA) using the Wilk's lambda test, and subsequent one-way Analysis of Variance (ANOVA) on each dependent variable, were computed across communication genre means. In all analyses, the three criterion variables were trust, global attitude, and confidence in the institution, as reflected in the depictions found in the communication source being analyzed.

All significant omnibus effects were followed by subsequent assessment of the pattern of means using Scheffe post-hoc tests. To simplify reporting of these findings, only the results of the omnibus tests are included in the text. Results of the assessment of the pattern of means are summarized in tables. Probability levels were set at .05 for all post-hoc tests.

The number of references to individual institutions varied widely across communication sources. This was especially common when analyses proceeded beyond the presidency and Congress to the institutions of the court system, news media, and public schools.

Whenever a communication source category featured a limited number of references to a particular institution, or n, the risk is considerable that what appears to be a significant finding may, in fact, be nothing more than a statistical anomaly. Hence, all cases involving less than five references were automatically excluded from all statistical analyses. In addition, a harmonic mean was computed in all post-hoc tests. The harmonic mean is designed to adjust the combined n of categories being compared. When the n of each of two categories is similar, the harmonic mean bears a close approximation of the actual combined n of the two categories. However, when the n of two categories differs, the harmonic mean is adjusted downward and more closely reflects the smaller of the two n's. In this way, a harmonic mean protects against statistical anomalies.

In reporting the results of the content analyses, we will initially summarize the findings for individual institutions and then offer an overarching synthesis of media coverage as a whole.

Media Coverage of Individual Institutions

Office of the Presidency. The omnibus MANOVA test indicated significant differences in coverage of the presidency in 1995 ($F(18, 727) = 12.99$, $p < .001$, $R^2 = .23$; significant one-way findings on the dependent measures of trust, $F(6, 260) = 25.69$, $p = .001$, $\eta^2 = .37$; attitude, $F = 32.60$, $p = .001$, $\eta^2 = .43$; and confidence, $F = 33.96$, $p = .001$, $\eta^2 = .44$). Significant differences emerged also in 1996 ($F(18, 1420) = 19.91$, $p < .001$, $R^2 = .19$; significant one-way findings on trust, $F(6, 504) = 56.37$, $p = .001$, $\eta^2 = .40$; attitude, $F = 43.88$, $p = .001$, $\eta^2 = .34$; and confidence, $F = 57.57$, $p = .001$, $\eta^2 = .41$).

Post-hoc results indicated that most communication media were negative in their coverage of the presidency. However, as Table 4.1 reveals, across both data sets political talk radio and, to a somewhat lesser de-

Table 4.1
Media Depictions of the Office of the Presidency

Communication Source	N	Global Attitude		Trustworthiness		Confidence	
1995 Content Analysis							
Newspapers	72	4.06	$(0.39)^f$	4.10	$(0.40)^f$	52.78	$(8.72)^f$
News magazines	14	4.08	$(0.46)^f$	4.00	$(0.21)^f$	49.64	$(6.64)^f$
Network TV news	44	4.47	$(1.12)^h$	4.37	$(1.02)^f$	56.66	$(18.84)^f$
Local TV news	20	4.53	(0.62)	4.71	(0.69)	64.65	(13.27)
Other TV news	41	4.84	(1.00)	4.91	(1.00)	64.29	(15.73)
Entertainment talk shows	26	3.51	$(0.37)^b$	3.78	$(0.29)^b$	44.12	$(5.32)^b$
Political talk radio	50	2.92	$(0.73)^a$	3.16	$(0.62)^a$	33.12	$(10.24)^a$
1996 Content Analysis							
Newspapers	113	3.88	$(0.67)^g$	3.84	(0.74)	49.53	$(10.32)^g$
News magazines	93	3.57	$(0.89)^e$	3.96	$(0.90)^e$	43.91	$(11.45)^e$
Network TV news	68	3.57	$(1.12)^e$	3.43	$(1.01)^d$	43.56	$(16.03)^d$
Local TV news	46	4.29	(1.21)	4.15	(1.23)	55.76	(19.72)
TV news magazines	18	4.14	(0.45)	4.11	(0.32)	51.39	(5.46)
Entertainment talk shows	30	3.21	$(0.81)^d$	3.37	$(0.72)^d$	38.00	$(10.22)^c$
Political talk radio	143	2.48	$(0.76)^a$	2.10	$(1.00)^a$	25.14	$(12.40)^a$

Notes: Entries are means with standard deviations in parentheses. Scheffe post-hoc tests
significant at $p < .05$ for designated items, as follows:

[a] Coverage is negative compared to all other communication sources.
[b] Coverage is negative compared to local TV news, network TV news, other TV news, newspapers, and magazines.
[c] Coverage is negative compared to local TV news, TV news magazines, newspapers, and magazines.
[d] Coverage is negative compared to local TV news, TV news magazines and newspapers.
[e] Coverage is negative compared to local TV news and TV news magazines.
[f] Coverage is negative compared to local TV news and other TV news.
[g] Coverage is negative compared to local TV news.
[h] Coverage is negative compared to other TV news.

gree, television entertainment talk shows were most brutal in their depictions of the presidency. Political talk radio's negative treatment of the
presidency was unsurpassed by any other communication source in both
1995 and 1996. Television entertainment talk shows offered considerable
negative content, producing more negative characterizations of the presidency than local television news, television news magazines, newspapers, or magazines.

Network television news coverage of the presidency was more negative than most other traditional media. It was more negative than local
and other television news coverage in 1995 and more hostile than local
television news, television news magazines, and newspapers in 1996.
Print news coverage was balanced in its depictions of the presidency,

Table 4.2
Media Depictions of Congress

Communication Source	N	Global Attitude		Trustworthiness		Confidence	
1995 Content Analysis							
Newspapers	74	3.87	(0.48)[f]	3.96	(0.43)[f]	49.66	(8.45)[f]
News magazines	13	3.86	(0.39)[f]	4.03	(0.33)[f]	48.85	(6.82)[f]
Network TV news	36	3.54	(1.34)[f]	3.76	(0.92)[f]	45.75	(18.72)[f]
Local TV news	15	4.38	(0.87)	4.49	(0.79)	56.67	(17.29)
Other TV news	43	3.85	(0.77)[f]	3.86	(0.78)[f]	46.81	(12.42)[f]
Entertainment talk shows	26	3.30	(0.33)[a]	3.67	(0.30)[e]	40.08	(6.08)[a]
Political talk radio	22	4.95	(0.95)	4.94	(0.81)	60.52	(14.82)
1996 Content Analysis							
Newspapers	45	3.84	(0.50)	3.98	(0.40)	49.09	(6.72)[h]
News magazines	48	3.60	(0.80)[h]	3.88	(0.61)[h]	43.38	(10.08)[h]
Network TV news	47	3.68	(0.88)[h]	3.60	(0.95)[d]	45.11	(14.05)[g]
Local TV news	15	3.26	(0.95)[e]	3.27	(1.10)[b]	40.33	(13.56)[e]
TV news magazines	8	4.10	(0.80)	4.25	(0.89)	51.88	(10.67)
Entertainment talk shows	10	3.40	(0.81)[g]	4.00	(0.00)	40.50	(11.65)[e]
Political talk radio	10	4.30	(0.55)	4.40	(0.70)	56.00	(9.94)

Notes: Entries are means with standard deviations in parentheses. Scheffe post-hoc tests significant at $p < .05$ for designated items, as follows:

[a] Coverage is negative compared to local TV news, other TV news, political talk radio, newspapers, and magazines.

[b] Coverage is negative compared to TV news magazines, TV entertainment talk shows, political talk radio, newspapers, and magazines.

[c] Coverage is negative compared to local TV news, political talk radio, and magazines.

[d] Coverage is negative compared to TV news magazines, TV entertainment talk shows, and political talk radio.

[e] Coverage is negative compared to TV news magazines, political talk radio, and newspapers.

[f] Coverage is negative compared to local TV news and political talk radio.

[g] Coverage is negative compared to TV news magazines and political talk radio.

[h] Coverage is negative compared to political talk radio.

only negative in comparison with local and other television news in 1995, and local television news and television news magazines in 1996.

The Congress. The omnibus MANOVA test revealed significant differences in media coverage of Congress in 1995 ($F(18, 609) = 7.11, p < .001$, $R^2 = .16$; significant one-way findings on the dependent measures of trust, $F(6, 222) = 9.71, p = .001, \eta^2 = .21$; attitude, $F = 10.64, p = .001$, $\eta^2 = .23$; and confidence, $F = 6.73, p = .001, \eta^2 = .16$); and again in 1996 ($F(18, 490) = 2.93, p < .001, R^2 = .09$; significant one-way findings on trust, $F(6, 176) = 4.09, p = .01, \eta^2 = .12$; attitude, $F = 2.94, p = .01, \eta^2 = .09$; and confidence, $F = 3.43, p = .01, \eta^2 = .10$).

As noted in Table 4.2, with the exception of local television news in

1995, traditional media offered a steady diet of negative coverage of Congress. In 1995, network and other television news, newspapers, and magazines provided negative depictions of Congress compared to the coverage of local television news and political talk radio. However, television entertainment talk show characterizations of Congress were the most hostile. By 1996, local television news was the most negative communication source, surpassing even network television news. Television entertainment talk shows had softened their depictions of Congress some, but remained negative compared to television news magazines and political talk radio. News magazine and, to a lesser degree, newspaper coverage was negative only in comparison with political talk radio. Political talk radio, which provided the most negative coverage of the presidency, offered the most positive coverage of Congress, reflecting its predominant conservative tone and the fact that, in both 1995 and 1996, political talk radio was reacting to a Democratic president and a Republican-controlled Congress.

The Court System. The omnibus MANOVA result was significant for the court system in 1995, $F(9, 90) = 2.20$, $p < .05$, $R^2 = .15$, but none of the one-way ANOVAs achieved statistical significance. The omnibus test was significant in 1996 ($F(18, 476) = 2.79$, $p < .001$, $R^2 = .09$) with significant one-way findings on attitude ($F(6, 174) = 3.94$, $p = .01$, $\eta^2 = .12$) and confidence ($F = 3.04$, $p = .01$, $\eta^2 = .10$) and a marginally significant finding on trust ($F = 2.12$, $p = .06$, $\eta^2 = .07$).

The 1996 content analysis results, depicted in Table 4.3, indicated that political talk radio provided the fewest and most negative depictions of the court system. Network television news coverage and television entertainment talk show characterizations of the courts were negative compared to those of television news magazines and magazines.

The News Media. The omnibus MANOVA test revealed significant differences in communication media coverage of the news media in 1995 ($F(9, 99) = 3.13$, $p < .01$, $R^2 = .18$; significant one-way findings on the dependent measures of trust, $F(3, 44) = 6.13$, $p = .01$, $\eta^2 = .30$; attitude, $F = 4.71$, $p = .01$, $\eta^2 = .25$; and confidence, $F = 6.27$, $p = .01$, $\eta^2 = .30$); and again in 1996 ($F(18, 518) = 3.44$, $p < .001$, $R^2 = .10$; significant one-way results for trust, $F(6, 186) = 7.94$, $p = .001$, $\eta^2 = .20$; attitude, $F = 5.68$, $p = .001$, $\eta^2 = .16$; and confidence, $F = 5.18$, $p = .001$, $\eta^2 = .14$).

Political talk radio provided the most consistently negative depictions of the news media. As Table 4.4 reveals, political talk radio was more hostile toward the news media than television entertainment talk shows and newspapers in 1995 and negative compared to network television news, television news magazines, television entertainment talk shows, and newspapers in 1996.

In addition, other television news coverage of the news media was somewhat negative in 1995, particularly in comparison to newspapers,

Table 4.3
Media Depictions of the Court System

Communication Source	N	Global Attitude		Trustworthiness		Confidence	
1995 Content Analysis							
Newspapers	23	4.01	(0.24)	4.06	(0.26)	50.43	(3.96)
News magazines	1	4.00	(0.00)	4.00	(0.00)	50.00	(0.00)
Network TV news	6	3.97	(0.64)	4.22	(0.62)	52.17	(12.97)
Local TV news	4	4.50	(1.00)	4.58	(1.17)	58.75	(9.33)
Other TV news	8	4.56	(0.63)	4.54	(0.71)	58.62	(10.38)
Entertainment talk shows	6	4.22	(0.89)	4.31	(0.84)	53.33	(11.69)
Political talk radio	0	--	--	--	--	--	--
1996 Content Analysis							
Newspapers	38	3.98	(0.62)	4.16	(0.49)	50.87	(10.71)
News magazines	19	4.16	(0.79)	4.16	(0.90)	51.21	(12.47)
Network TV news	19	3.73	(1.15)[c]	3.53	(1.02)[b]	44.71	(13.75)[d]
Local TV news	65	3.99	(0.56)	3.95	(0.65)	49.92	(9.65)
TV news magazines	18	4.37	(0.52)	4.22	(0.43)	55.83	(7.72)
Entertainment talk shows	18	3.82	(0.58)[c]	3.83	(0.79)	46.94	(8.93)[d]
Political talk radio	4	3.04	(0.28)[a]	3.50	(0.58)[b]	37.50	(6.45)[a]

Notes: Entries are means with standard deviations in parentheses. The results of the one-way ANOVAs for all dependent measures in the 1995 content analysis were insignificant and, therefore, no post-hoc tests were conducted. Scheffe post-hoc tests significant at $p < .05$ for designated items, as follows:

[a] Coverage is negative compared to all other communication media.
[b] Coverage is negative compared to TV news magazines, newspapers, and magazines.
[c] Coverage is negative compared to TV news magazines and magazines.
[d] Coverage is negative compared to TV news magazines.

and surprisingly, local television news coverage was decidedly negative in 1996 compared to most other traditional and nontraditional communication sources.

The Public Schools. The result of the omnibus MANOVA test indicated significant differences in communication media coverage of the public schools in 1995 ($F(9, 132) = 3.46$, $p < .01$, $R^2 = .16$; significant one-way findings on the dependent measures of trust, $F(3, 57) = 5.12$, $p = .01$, $\eta^2 = .21$; attitude, $F = 8.64$, $p = .001$, $\eta^2 = .32$; and confidence, $F = 8.42$, $p = .001$, $\eta^2 = .31$); and again in 1996 ($F(15, 431) = 2.29$, $p < .01$, $R^2 = .07$; significant one-way findings on attitude, $F(5, 159) = 2.38$, $p = .05$, $\eta^2 = .07$; and nearly significant on confidence, $F = 2.01$, $p = .06$, $\eta^2 = .06$). The one-way ANOVA result on trust in the public schools was not significant ($F = 1.52$, $p = .19$, $\eta^2 = .05$).

As shown in Table 4.5, political talk radio and television entertainment talk shows tended to be the most hostile in their references to the public schools. Political talk radio provided a consistent diet of unfavorable

Table 4.4
Media Depictions of the News Media

Communication Source	N	Global Attitude		Trustworthiness		Confidence	
1995 Content Analysis							
Newspapers	10	4.03	(0.49)	3.98	(0.31)	53.50	(12.26)
News magazines	2	3.92	(0.12)	3.83	(0.24)	47.50	(3.54)
Network TV news	2	2.92	(0.00)	4.00	(0.00)	37.50	(3.54)
Local TV news	2	4.00	(0.00)	4.00	(0.00)	50.00	(0.00)
Other TV news	16	2.94	(1.00)[f]	3.01	(0.91)[e]	33.19	(15.88)[f]
Entertainment talk shows	10	3.50	(0.20)	3.68	(0.15)	42.50	(2.64)
Political talk radio	12	3.14	(0.81)[f]	3.32	(0.63)[e]	35.75	(10.75)[f]
1996 Content Analysis							
Newspapers	20	3.79	(0.69)	3.75	(0.72)	47.25	(10.19)
News magazines	18	3.46	(0.96)	3.72	(0.75)	42.63	(14.18)
Network TV news	13	3.44	(2.16)	3.62	(1.89)	45.00	(36.17)
Local TV news	10	2.53	(1.39)[b]	2.30	(1.34)[b]	27.00	(19.47)[a]
TV news magazines	14	3.93	(0.44)	3.93	(0.47)	48.21	(8.43)
Entertainment talk shows	24	3.87	(0.21)	4.00	(0.00)	47.71	(4.42)
Political talk radio	94	3.05	(0.80)[d]	2.95	(1.05)[b]	36.18	(12.69)[c]

Notes: Entries are means with standard deviations in parentheses. Statistical analysis included only entries with an *n* of 5 or more. Scheffe post-hoc tests significant at $p <$ .05 for designated items, as follows:

[a] Coverage is negative compared to network TV news, TV news magazines, TV entertainment talk shows, political talk radio, newspapers, and magazines.

[b] Coverage is negative compared to network TV news, TV news magazines, TV entertainment talk shows, newspapers, and magazines.

[c] Coverage is negative compared to network TV news, TV news magazines, TV entertainment talk shows, and newspapers.

[d] Coverage is negative compared to TV news magazines, TV entertainment talk shows, and newspapers.

[e] Coverage is negative compared to TV entertainment talk shows and newspapers.

[f] Coverage is negative compared to newspapers.

depictions of the public schools compared to the coverage of local media outlets such as television news and newspapers in both years and compared to network television news in 1996. In addition, television entertainment talk shows offered substantially negative characterizations of the public schools, at least as compared to the coverage of local television news in 1995 and to local television news, network television news, and newspapers in 1996.

Synthesis of Findings

The pattern of results suggests that traditional mass media sources, particularly network television news, are negative in their coverage of

Table 4.5
Media Depictions of the Public Schools

Communication Source	N	Global Attitude		Trustworthiness		Confidence	
1995 Content Analysis							
Newspapers	10	3.87	(0.36)	3.95	(0.38)	48.00	(7.15)
News magazines	0	--	--	--	--	--	--
Network TV news	2	3.42	(0.12)	3.75	(0.12)	45.00	(0.00)
Local TV news	24	4.16	(1.00)	4.10	(0.74)	55.37	(15.36)
Other TV news	0	--	--	--	--	--	--
Entertainment talk shows	16	3.71	(0.57)[d]	3.97	(0.52)	47.81	(10.48)[d]
Political talk radio	11	2.83	(0.38)[c]	3.02	(0.32)[c]	33.27	(4.56)[c]
1996 Content Analysis							
Newspapers	84	3.97	(0.53)	4.11	(0.41)	50.05	(8.96)
News magazines	6	3.50	(0.42)	4.00	(0.00)	40.83	(7.36)[e]
Network TV news	17	3.99	(0.92)	4.18	(0.73)	50.29	(12.43)
Local TV news	44	3.86	(1.39)	3.86	(1.37)	48.64	(23.09)
TV news magazines	2	3.58	(0.12)	4.00	(0.00)	42.50	(3.54)
Entertainment talk shows	8	3.04	(0.51)[b]	3.63	(0.52)	38.13	(7.53)[b]
Political talk radio	5	3.23	(0.83)[b]	3.40	(0.89)	37.00	(14.40)[b]

Notes: Entries are means with standard deviations in parentheses. Statistical analysis included only entries with an n of 5 or more. Scheffe post-hoc tests significant at $p <$ .05 for designated items, as follows:

[a] Coverage is negative compared to network TV news, TV news magazines, newspapers, and magazines.

[b] Coverage is negative compared to local TV news, network TV news, and newspapers.

[c] Coverage is negative compared to local TV news, TV entertainment talk shows, and newspapers.

[d] Coverage is negative compared to local TV news.

[e] Coverage is negative compared to network TV news.

national institutions such as the presidency, Congress and, to a lesser degree, the court system. However, its coverage of such institutions as the news media and public schools was more balanced in tone. These results are consistent with past research documenting a pattern of negative network news coverage of the presidency (Center for Media and Public Affairs, 1994; Hallin, 1992; Robinson & Sheehan, 1983; Smoller, 1986, 1990) and Congress (Lichter & Amundson, 1994; Robinson & Appel, 1979). Past research, however, has ignored network news coverage of such institutions as the courts, news media, and public schools. These results suggest that generalizations about the hostility of network news coverage can be extended to the court system, but not to such institutions as the news media or public schools.

Other television news—such as *CNN Prime News* and *The News Hour*—and local television news were less hostile toward democratic institutions; coverage was negative toward Congress and the news media, but positive toward the presidency. Local television news depictions of the presidency and public schools were fairly positive, and its coverage of Congress and the court system was relatively balanced. Local television news depictions of the news media were balanced in 1995, but turned decidedly negative in tone in 1996, perhaps due to the national news media's preoccupation with such sensationalized criminal cases involving Tonya Harding, O. J. Simpson, and the Menendez brothers.

Print media coverage of institutions was more benign, with magazines somewhat more negative than newspapers. Newspapers and magazines were moderately negative in coverage of the presidency and Congress, results that are consistent with previous content analyses findings (Patterson, 1993; Robinson, 1981; Robinson & Appel, 1979; Tidmarch & Pitney, 1985), but were fairly positive in their depictions of the court system, news media, and public schools.

The most surprising finding of the content analyses is the strikingly negative depictions of most institutions on the part of many nontraditional communication sources. Political talk radio was the most aggressively negative communication source in its characterizations of the presidency, court system, and public schools, and one of the most negative media in its depictions of the news media. By contrast, it was more positive than any other communication source in its coverage of Congress.

The results for political talk radio carry two implications. First, they confirm recent findings of Levin (1987), Jamieson (in Fleeson, 1995), and Rehm (1996) that document a pattern of hostility on the part of political talk radio toward democratic institutions. Second, the results help clarify the inconsistency in past findings about the influence of talk radio on confidence. Political talk radio's tone and, thus its potential influence, varies across specific institutions. It was very positive in its depictions of Congress, but highly negative toward all other institutions.

This pattern suggests that judgments about media influence on public perceptions of confidence must be confined to specific communication sources, concerning individual institutions and at particular points in time. The results indicate that media vary in their tone of coverage about specific institutions. Further, the coverage from specific communication modalities changes as the circumstances change. Prior to the Republican sweep of both houses of Congress in 1994, the Times Mirror Center for the People and the Press revealed that political talk radio was especially hostile toward Congress. One to two years later, our results indicate that political talk radio was more positive than all other sources in its depiction of Congress.

Besides political talk radio, television entertainment talk shows were consistently hostile toward most institutions. The media genre of television entertainment talk shows was one of the more negative in characterizations of the presidency, Congress, the court system, and public schools. Not surprisingly, perhaps, it was the most positive in its references to the news media. This genre has been ignored in past research (Priest & Dominick, 1994). However, results of our content analyses suggest that television entertainment talk shows provide a steady stream of negative references to most democratic institutions and, thus, manifest the potential to influence perceptions of viewers about institutions.

In contrast to their reputation for aggressive investigative reporting, television news magazines provided the most consistently positive coverage of all democratic institutions. One plausible explanation is found in the focus of coverage of television news magazine stories. Fallows's (1996) examination of five years' worth of program logs for *60 Minutes*—the first, and still the most popular, television news magazine show—revealed a concentration of stories on the entertainment industry and celebrities, while "barely one-fifth of the stories concerned economics, the real workings of politics, or any other issue of long-term national significance" (p. 57).

CONCLUSION

Past content analyses of mass media coverage of democratic institutions have focused on depictions from one or two traditional news sources—typically network television news, the print media, and most recently, political talk radio—of a limited number of institutions, most often the presidency and Congress. This past research documents a pattern of increasing hostility in network news coverage of the presidency and Congress. In addition, recent research documents a persistent pattern of negativity on the part of political talk radio toward democratic institutions. No studies have scrutinized the coverage of other communication media (e.g., traditional media such as "other" and local television news and nontraditional media such as television news magazines and television entertainment talk shows), or any media coverage of institutions such as the court system, news media, or public schools.

Results of two content analyses conducted as part of this investigation reveal that, although traditional media are often negative in their depictions of institutions, nontraditional sources—political talk radio and, to a lesser extent, television entertainment talk shows—provide the most hostile depictions of democratic institutions.

Systematic assessment of the communication media's coverage of institutions is a prerequisite to assessing the influence of the media on public perceptions of confidence, as Arthur Miller, Edie Goldenberg, and Lutz Erbring (1979) have emphasized. Once the pattern of media coverage is known, we can examine people's media use habits and their perceptions of institutions, confident in the view that, if a particular communication source depicts an institution negatively, and if people who utilize that source for information about public affairs view the respective institution in much the same way as the source depicts it, then the source may be partly responsible for those perceptions. As Lipset and Schneider remind us, "One major source—perhaps *the* major source—of information concerning the condition of the country is . . . the mass media" (1987, p. 403).

## Chapter 5

The Print Media's Contribution

The man who never looks into a newspaper is better informed than
he who reads them, inasmuch as he who knows nothing is nearer to
the truth than he whose mind is filled with falsehoods and errors.
　　　Founding Father Thomas Jefferson (Letter to John Novell, 1807)

The press is no substitute for institutions. It is like the beam of a
searchlight that moves restlessly about, bringing one episode and
then another out of darkness into vision.
　　　　Political philosopher Walter Lippmann (1922, p. 229)

Discussion of the pivotal role of newspapers in democratic societies can
be traced back to Alexis de Tocqueville (1848/1969), who believed that
newspapers not only guaranteed liberty, but also maintained civilization.
Newspapers, he wrote, were capable of bringing people together by giving "publicity to the feeling or idea that had occurred to them all simultaneously but separately" (p. 518).

The pedestal upon which newspapers rested was a sturdy one, at least
until Walter Lippmann, in his classic book *Public Opinion* (1922), questioned whether the press could indeed disseminate truth and enlighten
the public. Similar questions remain to this day, but today, attention
tends to focus more on television than print news.

The attention that television has garnered is not surprising given the
speed with which the medium has become the foremost source of political information for most Americans. Burns Roper (Roper Organization,
1981), in documenting trends in television use over two decades, found

that beginning in 1963, more Americans reported getting most of their news from television (55 percent) than from newspapers (53 percent), radio (29 percent), magazines (6 percent), or interpersonal sources (4 percent). Today, the figures have become even more extreme. Over two-thirds (69 percent) of American adults report television as their primary source of political information. Its lead over other channels of information has increased substantially. Today, newspapers are a distant second (37 percent), and radio (14 percent), magazines (5 percent), and interpersonal sources (7 percent) lag even further behind as primary sources of news and information (Roper Starch Worldwide, 1997).

The overwhelming presence of television in the contemporary media landscape makes it a prime target for researchers investigating a variety of social problems. Its omnipotence stems in part from its power to act as the "common storyteller of our age" (Gerbner et al., 1994, p. 18), disseminating images and messages to a broad audience. Television's visual and verbal streams can play a crucial role in shaping the perceptions of reality—including political reality—for millions of people in all walks of life (Graber, 1993, p. 2). Newspapers, on the other hand, are perceived as an information channel, better at relating abstract ideas and factual details (Robinson & Davis, 1990). Perhaps for this reason, research in political communication comparing newspapers and television has credited the former with doing a better job fulfilling democratic ideals, including that of providing for an informed citizenry (Guo & Moy, 1998).

When we examine mass media effects on public confidence, the picture painted is no different. By the end of Chapter 6, we will learn exactly how the print media and television news influence confidence levels. In this chapter, we review the limited research on the print media as it relates to confidence in democratic institutions and present our findings on its contribution to confidence levels.

THE CONTENT OF NEWSPAPERS AND NEWS MAGAZINES

Newspapers

As we noted in Chapter 4, the research linking newspapers with confidence in democratic institutions is limited, and one cannot explore this area without noting the seminal work of Arthur Miller, Edie Goldenberg, and Lutz Erbring (1979), which involved a content analysis of 94 newspapers published in 1974. Each front-page article was analyzed for media criticism toward a given institution. Miller and colleagues found that among those articles that implicated a political figure or institution, nearly two-thirds (63 percent) were neutral, and 31 percent contained adverse criticism of some sort. Their content analyses also revealed that over half of all articles referring to confidence in government contained critical references.

Of note is their finding that newspaper articles quite often directed criticism toward the president (Gerald Ford at the time), but that "criticism of the *presidency* was virtually nonexistent" (Miller, Goldenberg & Erbring, 1979, p. 72; italics added). Although Congress as an institution did come under attack, the researchers noted that many of these criticisms were comments that President Ford had made. Their analyses of the NES data showed that media criticism was a strong predictor of cynicism.

Despite Miller et al.'s findings that newspapers did not print criticisms of the presidency during Ford's administration, Ralph Dowling's (1989) analysis of the print media revealed that they portrayed the presidency as a weak institution during Jimmy Carter's involvement in the Iran hostage crisis. These particular findings, however, were based on editorials and letters to the editor, not front-page articles as analyzed by Miller and colleagues. Dowling concluded that a "weak-Carter-persona" portrayed in the print media contributed to Ronald Reagan's landslide victory in the 1980 presidential election, which would subsequently mark "a renewal of patriotism" (p. 145). Dowling's comment may have been made retrospectively, but it echoes print media's coverage of transition periods in the White House.

Karen Johnson (1986) examined the print media coverage of three presidential transitions (Johnson-Nixon, Ford-Carter, and Carter-Reagan) and found that outgoing presidents are depicted very negatively during this period. For example, the *New York Times* wrote:

While Mr. Johnson's absence may make some hearts grow fonder, neither sentimental memory nor benevolent history is going to restore him or his years . . . he led the nation into the most corrosive internal disunity of modern times. (Wicker, 1969, p. E23)

However, another more prominently placed article appearing in the *New York Times* that same day placed the outgoing president in a favorable light relative to Richard Nixon. Referring to Lyndon Johnson's last State of the Union address, Robert Semple, Jr. (1969) wrote:

Mr. Johnson is surer about what he wants Richard Nixon to do for the country than Mr. Nixon is about doing it. The outgoing President departs with a sense of priorities and a program firmly in mind. Mr. Nixon may have a sense of priorities, but so far he has no visible program. Nor does he have many of his own people in place in Washington. With only a day left before he assumes full power, Mr. Nixon has filled only a quarter of the 300 or so top jobs in his Administration—the rest are holdovers. (p. E1)

Similarly, a month after Carter defeated Ford in 1976, the *New York Times* noted that "Mr. Ford, who used to boast of his accessibility and 'open Presidency,' seems to have vanished effectively from public view since the election. . . . On the few occasions when he has made a public appearance, he has looked hollow-eyed and grim" (Shabecoff, 1976, p. B8).

During the Carter-Reagan transition, coverage of Carter was not particularly glowing. Edward Walsh (1981), in recapitulating the Carter administration, described it as a "flawed presidency of good intentions," one in which Carter's "inexperience and uncertainty showed themselves early and often during his tenure as his administration lurched from one crisis to the next" (p. C1). The *Washington Post* printed a story that did nothing to help either Carter or Reagan. "At the center of the Carter legacy is an institution in trouble. A supreme office was trivialized to the point where it became thinkable for an actor to be elected president" (Kraft, 1981, p. C7).

Does Congress fare any better in print media depictions? It depends, according to Charles Tidmarch and John Pitney (1985). Like Dowling, they content-analyzed ten newspapers during the summer of 1978. Hard news about Congress, they concluded, "is rarely classifiable as explicitly negative" (p. 480). However, hostility toward Congress on the part of editorialists was evident, with the *Los Angeles Times* printing ten negative editorials per single positive editorial, and the *Denver Post* being the most balanced, with 1.1 negative editorials for each positive one.

In addition to these past studies, anecdotal evidence reveals that democratic institutions have been portrayed both favorably and not so favorably by our local newspapers. For instance, a front-page story in April 1995 cast President Bill Clinton in very positive light as he hailed American troops in Port-au-Prince, Haiti, for successfully keeping the peace (O'Connor, 1995). Another article lauded Clinton for advocating stronger child-support laws (Benac, 1995). Yet stories of campaign financing allegations were not uncommon, as articles implicated Clinton, his 1996 presidential opponent Bob Dole, and Congress:

Spend more, win more. . . . The better fundraisers managed to build moats around once-vulnerable campaign castles, while the few who lagged in dollars ultimately fell to better financed challengers. (Solomon, 1996, p. 1A)

Nor did the criminal court system or the news media escape unscathed. In the story of Richard Jewell, the Olympic Park guard who was accused of a pipe bombing during the 1996 Summer Games in Atlanta, Georgia, the hero-turned-suspect lashed out at the FBI and the media. Jewell was quoted as saying, "I felt like a hunted animal, followed constantly, waiting to be killed" (Meyer, 1996, p. 2A).

During the O. J. Simpson trial, the *Wisconsin State Journal* questioned the degree to which the trial had degenerated into a circus. Editors wondered who the true defendant was in the trial. Was it defense lawyer Johnnie Cochran, who was accused of devoting his life to appearing on *Geraldo*, or was it prosecutor Marcia Clark for giving her mother-in-law photos of herself topless, only to have them appear later in tabloids?

This trial should be serious business. . . . It's a shame that it has degenerated into low drama. It doesn't speak well for the participants, and unfortunately, it doesn't say much about the rest of us either. (*Wisconsin State Journal*, 1995, p. 7A)

Finally, local newspaper coverage of the public school system warrants attention. As Table 4.5 indicated, the number of articles about public schools was considerably higher in 1996 than in 1995. This marked increase in coverage stems from the fact that beginning in the summer of 1995, the *Wisconsin State Journal* and other local media took part in a civic journalism project involving schools in the area. The "Schools of Hope" project was launched August 27, 1995, with the goal of addressing racial inequities, balancing school budgets, and ensuring academic success for all students (Denton, 1995). Over the next year and a half, the local media made attempts to collaborate with educators, parents, students, and various other interested parties. Students were polled to see how they felt about a potential pairing of two schools (*Wisconsin State Journal*, 1995). Special forums on school-related issues were held, with times and locations published in the newspapers. Coverage of the public school system by newspapers overall was not positive or negative, as our content analyses indicated.

News Magazines

Weekly news magazines such as *Time, U.S. News & World Report,* and *Newsweek* share newspapers' responsibility for informing their readers of current political and social events. Because they offer readers an opportunity for coverage that is typically more in-depth than that of newspapers, these weekly news magazines allow readers to better understand the nuances of the political events and social problems that face the American public.

Cross-medium comparisons often are made between newspapers and television, and the former is often considered superior in its ability to convey political information to its audience. This argument is based on, among other things, the belief that more information is better (see Guo & Moy, 1998 for a review). If we extend this comparison to include news magazines—with their lengthy expositions and color photographs—can we conclude that readers are learning more from news magazines than either newspapers or television? Perhaps, but one must question the quality of the content that is being conveyed by news magazines and not simply the quantity. After all, news magazines are not unbiased in their coverage of democratic institutions, particularly the presidency.

As we noted in Chapter 4, the ratio of favorable to unfavorable references to major-party nominees in *Time* and *Newsweek* was approximately three-to-one in 1960. By 1992, the ratio had reversed itself to stand at two-to-three (Patterson, 1993). Articles in *Time* also tended to report more on the personal inadequacies of presidents from 1945 onwards (Hart, Smith-Howell, & Llewellyn, 1990). These findings would suggest that news magazine coverage of the presidency has become increasingly negative over the past half century.

However, other researchers would refute this sweeping generalization. John Merrill (1965), in a content analysis of *Time* articles, found distinct differences in coverage of the administrations of Presidents Harry S. Truman, Dwight D. Eisenhower, and John F. Kennedy. His analyses revealed that virtually all biases concerning Truman (in 1951) were negative. Conversely, 81 of 82 biases found in coverage of Eisenhower (1955) were positive, and nearly 70 percent of biased references concerning Kennedy were positive.

The anti-Truman and pro-Eisenhower stance that appeared to be taken by *Time* led other researchers to revisit the presidential stereotypes conveyed by the news magazine (Fedler, Meeske, & Hall, 1979). Fred Fedler and his colleagues found *Time* coverage was ambivalent toward Johnson but strongly in favor of Nixon before Watergate. Ford received moderately favorable coverage, and Carter received relatively critical coverage (1979, p. 359).

Our investigation of news magazine coverage of democratic institutions revealed some negative coverage of the presidency. In its 1996 post-election issue, *Time's* cover story tackled the Clinton fund-raising scandal. The title on the cover page read "The Money Trail," while the title in the table of contents read "The Stink of Money" (*Time*, 1996).

But coverage extended to other democratic institutions. In a special issue on balancing the budget, *Time's* cover image was of a meat cleaver underneath the headline "The Budget Revolution." The text on the cover read:

This time it's serious. The chopping has begun. For the first time in decades, Congress is committed to balancing the budget. It will mean slashing as much as $1.4 trillion and cutting programs that affect virtually every American citizen. But surprise of surprises: people want it that way. The tough choices are on the table, and it's about time. (*Time*, 1995)

Time's coverage of the news media may have very likely undermined confidence in newspapers when Ann Blackman and colleagues wrote how certain newspapers, such as the *San Francisco Examiner*, run foreign news without any overseas correspondents on staff (Blackman, Bonfante et al., 1996). They cite former *Atlanta Journal-Constitution* editor Bill Kovach:

Newspapers are trying to save money in the newsrooms, but they are undercutting the quality of their news reports. It's taking the life right out of them. (p. 68).

But the print media are not the only ones suffering, according to another *Time* article. In fact, budget reductions at the TV networks have reduced the number of actual stories.

What has exploded is not news, but *talk* about the news: commentary, not information. Which makes the news explosion both more democratic and more suspect. Everyone from Kathie Lee to call-in viewers on Larry King Live has a viewpoint, and every viewpoint gets a hearing. . . . MSNBC fills its airtime with a corps of interchangeable "contributors" who offer seat-of-the-pants opinions on whatever the big story of the day happens to be. It's cocktail party chat passing for journalism. (Blackman, Cohen et al., 1996, p. 62)

Where the criminal court system is concerned, news magazines flooded their pages with coverage of the O. J. Simpson trial. At one end of the spectrum was a two-page spread of Simpson trivia, including the number of times each lawyer spoke during the trial (ranging from 12,000 times for Robert Shapiro to over three times that much for Marcia Clark) and the asking price of Simpson's first pro football helmet, estimated at $25,000 (Seter, Ito, & Bennefield, 1995). At the other extreme was a 17-page, behind-the-scenes look at the trial of the century, showing pictures from the defense team before the trial began to Simpson's family celebrating his acquittal (Chua-Eoan & Gleick, 1995).

As we noted in Table 4.5, magazine coverage of schools was scarce. In 1996, *U.S. News & World Report* ran a cover story on the standards of the American public school system. The article included statistics demonstrating, for instance, that the U.S. math curriculum is less demanding than in other countries and that students in the United States spend an average of 178 days in school each year compared with 240 for students in Japan (Toch et al., 1996, p. 56).

A Caveat

Trends in print media coverage of democratic institutions are merely that—trends. If the trend in coverage moves toward greater negativity, we cannot conclude that *all* coverage is negative. When the public learned of Watergate, newspapers and news magazines were quick to criticize Congress for not reacting quickly enough (Rozell, 1994), but later the *New York Times* praised Congress for the role it played, concluding that "the country can rightly feel that a thorough, conscientious and non-partisan job has been done" (*New York Times*, 1974). Similarly, press coverage of Congress was negative in late 1990 as legislators debated whether to continue with sanctions against Iraq or to grant President George Bush the authority to wage war. Yet, once Congress had voted, it was portrayed in a considerably different light:

One by one, congressmen and senators took the floor and reached for the legacy of history, for Kennedy and Roosevelt and Churchill. They spoke, too, of their children, and the children of their constituents, and of past wars and the lessons they taught. Throughout the debate was the wrenching, sobering consciousness of their own responsibility. (Toner, 1991, p. 12)

Although this chapter deals with the influence of print media on confidence in democratic institutions, we must note that newspaper and news magazine coverage of a single event may differ markedly. This point is easily illustrated by the 1998 sex scandal involving President Clinton and former White House intern Monica Lewinsky. The *New York Times* ran a front-page story with the headline "Subpoenas Sent as Clinton Denies Reports of an Affair with Aide at White House" (Clines & Gerth, 1998). That same day, the *Times* printed excerpts from statements issued by the White House as well as excerpts of interviews that Clinton had held with Jim Lehrer for *The News Hour with Jim Lehrer*, and Robert Siegel and Mara Liasson for National Public Radio's *All Things Considered*. In the following week, the *Times* published several articles that sought to answer a number of questions: Who was Monica Lewinsky? (Henneberger, 1998); How was the First Lady reacting to Lewinsky's allegations? (Clines, 1998); What was Congress' reaction to the sex scandal? (Alvarez, 1998); Has the role of the Internet changed after cyberspace columnist Matt Drudge broke the story? (Schiesel, 1998).

Time magazine published a special report the week after the scandal broke. Like the *New York Times*, it offered detailed exposition on various characters in the "sordid tale that imperils the president" (*Time*, 1998). The 30-plus pages of articles, commentary, photos, and poll results in the February 2 issue were followed by another 30-plus pages of coverage in the February 9 issue. The cover of *Time*'s February 16 issue was the third consecutive cover devoted to the sex scandal, but coverage had dropped to about two-thirds of the coverage from the previous two weeks.

Like *Time*, *U.S. News & World Report* made the scandal its cover story in both its February 2 and February 9 issues. In contrast to *Time*, *U.S.*

News & World Report devoted considerably fewer column inches to the story. After two weeks, in its February 16 issue, *U.S. News & World Report* had moved the scandal off its cover, opting instead for coverage of IBM. Barring an item in "Washington Whispers" and John Leo's column, which addressed sexual harassment that week, only one article involving the Lewinsky scandal appeared in the February 16 issue.

Thus, generalizations of media coverage must be made with caution. We must note here that differences in news magazine coverage of democratic institutions (e.g., the coverage in *Time* vs. *U.S. News & World Report*) do not pose a problem as our sample design for the content analyses was weighted to account for differences in the publications' circulation in the area. In other words, our content analyses were designed to reflect the media content consumed by residents in the area.

Content and Public Confidence

While content analyses of print media coverage of democratic institutions (particularly the presidency and Congress) are popular, few scholars after Miller et al. (1979) have empirically examined the link between such coverage and confidence in these institutions. In two studies, Lee Becker discovered that people who relied on newspapers for news tended to evaluate local government more favorably than those who relied on television for news (Becker, Sobowale, & Casey, 1979; Becker & Whitney, 1980). Evaluations of national government were assessed in a study comparing those who followed the Watergate hearings in the newspaper and those who relied on television. Jack McLeod and colleagues found that young adults who followed the hearings in the print media thought Watergate was a political anomaly and did not blame the political system for the events that had transpired (McLeod, Brown, Becker, & Ziemke, 1977).

Thomas Patterson (1993), who found increasingly negative references to presidential candidates in news magazines from 1960 to 1992, also found that public opinion toward these candidates followed a trend that mirrored magazine coverage. *Time*'s coverage of George Bush's personal qualities during the 1992 presidential campaign was correlated with his standings in Gallup public opinion surveys (Johnson & Shields, 1995).

FINDINGS FROM OUR STUDY

Who's Reading?

It is not surprising that use of print media is concentrated among certain segments of society, with education playing a key role. As early as the 1940s, readership studies have revealed that newspaper reading

Table 5.1
Predicting Readership of Newspapers and News Magazines

	Newspapers		News Magazines	
	β	s.e. (β)	β	s.e. (β)
Sex (Male)	.074	(.056)	.013	(.056)
Age	.008	(.002)**	-.005	(.002)**
Education	.040	(.018)*	.095	(.018)**
Income	.078	(.021)**	.080	(.021)**
Democrat	-.012	(.063)	-.005	(.063)
Republican	-.043	(.074)	-.060	(.074)

Note: Entries are coefficients from ordinary least squares regression with standard errors in parentheses.

* p < .05
** p < .01

tends to increase with age, education, and economic status, though readership tends to drop off among those above 50 years of age (Schramm & White, 1949; Stone, 1987; see also Schönbach et al., 1999).

Our data show that these same demographic variables predict newspaper reading among our respondents, as shown in the first two columns of Table 5.1. Although the average level of news magazine readership among our respondents is lower than that of newspaper reading (3.94 out of 10, compared with 6.72; use of the two is correlated at .32), news magazines attract a slightly different type of reader: the more educated and affluent, but younger, individual.

The Power of Print

For each institution examined in this investigation, we present the paths of influence for each communication modality. To borrow an analogy from Norman Nie, Jane Junn, and Kenneth Stehlik-Barry, path diagrams can be thought of as "volumes of water moving through interconnected streams" (1996, p. 54). For ease of presentation, we show only the direct effects between the following variables: demographics and media use; media use and expertise in a given institution; media use and confidence in that institution; and expertise and confidence in an institution. Specific coefficients for each path are omitted from these diagrams; they may be found, however, in the appendices to Chapter 5. Paths between exogenous variables (demographics and political party identification) and endogenous variables (media use, expertise in a given

Figure 5.1
Direct Effect of Newspaper Reading on Evaluation

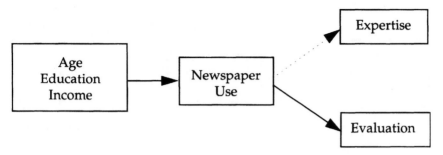

Note: Solid line from newspaper use to evaluation denotes the direct effect. A direct effect
of newspaper reading on expertise may or may not exist in models where there is a
direct effect on evaluation of a given institution.

institution, and evaluations of that institution) are denoted by gammas
(γ), while paths between pairs of endogenous variables are denoted by
betas (β). All paths are positive unless otherwise noted.

It is conceivable that a demographic variable (e.g., one's age or education) may influence one's perceptions of the office of the presidency
both directly as well as indirectly through media use and expertise. Direct, indirect, and total effects are noted in the appendices to this chapter.

Describing the influence of newspaper reading on public confidence
would entail presenting 15 models (three criterion variables—global attitude, trust, and confidence—for each of five democratic institutions).
Rather than detailing each of the 15 models, we note three distinct models of influence in Figures 5.1 to 5.3.

Figure 5.1 depicts a model in which media use influences evaluations
directly. In other words, exposure and attention to newspapers will have
a direct impact on respondents' global attitude, confidence, or trust in a
given institution. The dotted line in Figure 5.1, from newspaper reading
to expertise in a particular institution, may or may not exist, although
there may be a direct media effect on confidence. Put another way, media
use may enhance or undermine confidence in an institution but not necessarily influence awareness, interest, or knowledge of that institution.
This is in stark contrast to Figure 5.2, which depicts a model of influence
such that media use influences evaluations *only* through expertise; media
use impacts confidence only because it affects expertise, and expertise
affects confidence. Finally, Figure 5.3 depicts a model in which media
use influences evaluations both directly and indirectly through expertise.

Although specific coefficients are not presented here but rather in Appendix Tables 5.1 through 5.5, our data revealed that *in all cases, newspaper reading enhanced evaluations of the five democratic institutions*. As

Figure 5.2
Indirect Effect of Newspaper Reading on Evaluation

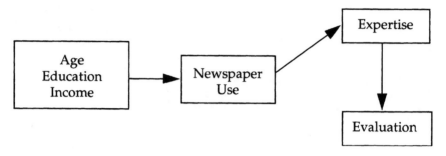

noted in Table 5.2, which summarizes the paths of influence for each criterion variable, the effects of newspaper reading on respondents' global attitude toward the office of the presidency, Congress, the court system, the news media, and the public schools were direct and indirect. That is, reading newspapers enhanced confidence levels directly and increased respondents' expertise (awareness, knowledge, and interest) in these institutions, which in turn enhanced evaluations. This model held for two-thirds of the criterion variables—all three evaluations of the news media and public school system; global attitude toward the presidency, Congress, and the court system; and trust in the courts.

There were a number of instances in which newspaper reading had only indirect effects on evaluations of institutions—specifically, confidence and trustworthiness of the presidency and Congress. In other words, it was only by increasing knowledge and awareness of these institutions that newspaper reading affected these evaluations.

Finally, the sole case in which reading newspapers exerted only a direct effect was with the 0–100 confidence rating of the court system. Respondents' knowledge or interest in the criminal court system had no bearing on the rating they gave of the institution.

Turning to the influence of reading news magazines on evaluations of institutions, 14 of the 15 effects were indirect, as shown in Table 5.3. Only for evaluations of the public school system did reading news magazines exert both a direct and an indirect effect. Like newspaper reading, reading news magazines such as *Time, Newsweek,* and *U.S. News & World Report* ultimately enhanced confidence levels in the various democratic institutions.

The fact that newspaper reading does not exert the same pattern of influences on all 15 evaluations needs to be highlighted for a number of reasons. First, the lack of consistent effects suggests that these three measures are not tapping the same construct. As we noted in Chapter 1, the concept of confidence is not unidimensional. These measures cer-

Figure 5.3
Direct and Indirect Effects of Newspaper Reading on Evaluation

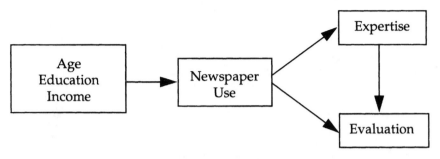

tainly are related, but the fact that each has different demographic predictors attests to their construct validity. For instance, in Appendix Table 5.1, one can see that global attitudes toward the office of the presidency are predicted positively by being female, older, and a Democrat, and negatively by being Republican. More simply, females, older respondents and Democrats tended to hold favorable attitudes toward the presidency, while Republicans were likely to express less favorable attitudes. While political partisanship still predicts one's evaluation of the presidency on the 0–100 confidence rating, gender, income, and age no longer have a direct impact. Rather, the only demographic predictor of the thermometer rating is education ($\gamma = .08$). In the case of trustworthiness as the criterion variable, age is the only predictor other than political partisanship. The differences in total effects of all variables may be gleaned from the appendices, but suffice it to say, such differences illustrate empirically that confidence is a multidimensional concept. Thus, differences across studies of political trust, political legitimacy, or cynicism may not be surprising.

Second, newspaper effects differed across measures and institutions, while the effects of news magazines were virtually constant, working indirectly through expertise. Could these differences stem from variations in the content of newspapers versus national news magazines? Because they do not face the space and time constraints imposed on broadcast media, newspapers and news magazines are capable of contextualizing events, providing background information, and covering issues in depth. Newspapers such as the *New York Times* have printed entire State of the Union addresses and excerpts from Senate hearings and, relative to television's "episodic" news, can provide more thematic coverage (Iyengar, 1991). But the fact that news magazines are published weekly allows them to provide even greater richness and texture to a story or issue.

Our findings indicate that reading news magazines—and newspapers

Table 5.2
Effects of Reading Newspapers on Evaluations of Democratic Institutions:
Summary Table

	Presidency	Congress	Court System	News Media	Public Schools
Global Attitude	Direct and indirect effects	Direct and indirect effects	Direct and indirect effects	Direct and indirect effects	Direct and indirect effects
Trustworthiness	Indirect effect only	Indirect effect only	Direct and indirect effects	Direct and indirect effects	Direct and indirect effects
Confidence	Indirect effect only	Indirect effect only	Direct effect only	Direct and indirect effects	Direct and indirect effects

Note: Effects are noted based on probability levels set at p = .05.

to a lesser degree—influenced evaluations of various democratic institutions, highlighting the role of cognitive factors such as knowledge,
interest, and awareness. This "expertise" serves as a link between people's use of the print media and their evaluations of democratic institutions. In 29 of the 30 models, reading a newspaper or news magazine
raised levels of awareness, interest, and knowledge of a given institution,
which in turn enhanced evaluations of institutions.

The positive influence of print media is apparent in our data. As
shown in Appendix Tables 5.1 to 5.5, reading newspapers led to more
positive expressions of global attitudes, "warmer" confidence ratings,
and reports of greater trustworthiness in each of the five democratic
institutions. The positive effects of newspaper reading worked both directly, and indirectly through expertise (see "Newspaper Use" column
in each appendix table, and as summarized in Table 5.2). Similarly, reading weekly news magazines enhanced evaluations of democratic institutions, as shown in Appendix Tables 5.6 to 5.10. However, in nearly all
the models we tested, news magazine reading worked only through expertise.

These positive effects are found despite the slightly negative depictions
that our content analyses revealed in Chapter 4. The negativity reflected
in our content analyses is somewhat consistent with earlier research
showing that the print media may indeed be negative in their depictions
of certain institutions (e.g., Patterson, 1993). Moreover, with the exception of Congress, coverage of all institutions tended to be greater in 1996
than in 1995, potentially due to the 1996 elections.

Why would slightly negative depictions of democratic institutions by
newspapers and news magazines *enhance* evaluations of these institu-

Table 5.3
Effects of Reading News Magazines on Evaluations of Democratic
Institutions: Summary Table

	Presidency	Congress	Court System	News Media	Public Schools
Global Attitude	Indirect effect only	Indirect effect only	Indirect effect only	Indirect effect only	Direct and indirect effects
Trustworthiness	Indirect effect only	Indirect effect only	Indirect effect only	Indirect effect only	Direct and indirect effects
Confidence	Indirect effect only	Indirect effect only	Indirect effect only	Indirect effect only	Direct and indirect effects

Note: Effects are noted based on probability levels set at $p = .05$.

tions? One explanation lies in the general patterns of media use among individuals. As we noted earlier in this chapter, newspapers are no longer the primary source of political information for Americans. They were displaced decades ago by television news (Roper, 1981), and today's media landscape is even more fractured as new technologies allow audience members to listen to nationally syndicated political talk radio shows and turn to cyberspace for constantly updated news. Given these circumstances, when analyzing the effects of each communication modality, we must control for the use of other media. In this case, reading newspapers was residualized for use of all other media except news magazines, and vice versa. After all, media use patterns have been shown to fall along a unidimensional scale, one extreme including only those who watch television and the other extreme including those who read newspapers and news magazines (Mutz, 1994). Indeed, a zero-order correlation of .32 between reading newspapers and reading news magazines offered an empirical basis for controlling for use of other media.

Given these analyses, we can interpret the effects of reading newspapers and news magazines as follows: After taking into account use of all other media, reading newspapers and news magazines enhances evaluations of democratic institutions. Our findings for local and network television news, which are presented in Chapter 6, are markedly different.

Appendix Table 5.1
Effects of Demographics, Party Identification, Newspaper Use, and Institutional Expertise on Evaluations of the Office of the Presidency

	Sex (M)	Age	Education	Income	Democrat	Republican	Newspapers	Expertise	R²
Newspaper Use	--	(γ).13**	(γ).07*	(γ).11**	--	--	(β).13**		.04
	--	--	--	--	--	--	--		
	--	.13**	.07*	.11**	--	--	.13**		
Expertise	(γ).08**	(γ).25**	(γ).25**	--	(γ).12**	(γ).09**	(β).13**	(β).24**	.18
	--	.02**	.01*	.01**	--	--	.03**	--	
	.08**	.26**	.26**	.01**	.12**	.09**	.13**	.24**	
Global Attitude	(γ)-.06**	(γ).09**	(γ).05#	--	(γ).09**	(γ)-.17**	(β).07**	(β).24**	.16
	.02**	.07**	.07**	.01**	.03**	.02**	.03**	--	
	-.05#	.17**	.12**	.01**	.11**	-.15**	.10**	.24**	
Trust-worthiness	(γ)-.05#	(γ).12**	--	--	(γ).07*	(γ)-.17**	--	(β).19**	.11
	.02**	.05**	.05**	.00**	.02**	.02**	.02**	--	
	-.03	.17**	.05**	.00**	.09**	-.15**	.02**	.19**	
Confidence	--	--	(γ).08**	--	(γ).12**	(γ)-.11**	--	(β).14**	.08
	.01**	.04**	.04**	.00**	.02**	.01**	.02**	--	
	.01**	.04**	.12**	.00**	.14**	-.10**	.02**	.14**	

Notes: This appendix table condenses three models, each of which includes sociodemographics, party identification, media use, institutional expertise, and *one* of three criterion variables (shown in the last three rows: global attitude, trustworthiness, or confidence). Entries in each cell are standardized direct, indirect, and total effects, respectively. Direct effects and indirect effects may not add up to total effects due to rounding. The χ^2 statistic for the global attitude model is 2.65 (5, N = 1278, p = .75), 2.40 (7, N = 1278, p = .93) for trustworthiness, and 6.65 (8, N = 1278, p = .58) for confidence.

# p < .10
* p < .05
** p < .01

Appendix Table 5.2
Effects of Demographics, Party Identification, Newspaper Use, and Institutional Expertise on Evaluations of Congress

	Sex (M)	Age	Education	Income	Democrat	Republican	Newspapers	Expertise	R²
Newspaper Use	–	(γ).13**	(γ).07*	(γ).11**	–	–			.04
	–	–	–	–	–	–			
	–	.13**	.07*	.11**	–	–			
Expertise	(γ).13**	(γ).21**	(γ).26**	–	(γ).07*	(γ).09**	(β).15**		.18
	–	.02**	.01*	.02**	–	–	–		
	.13**	.23**	.26**	.02**	.07*	.09**	.15**		
Global Attitude	(γ)-.06*	(γ)-.10**	(γ)-.06*	–	–	(γ).09**	(β).06*	(β).30**	.10
	.04**	.08**	.08**	.01*	.02*	.03**	.04**	–	
	-.02	-.02	.03	.01**	.02*	.11**	.11**	.30**	
Trust-worthiness	–	–	(γ)-.06*	–	–	(γ).07*	–	(β).18**	.04
	.02**	.04**	.05**	.00**	.01*	.02**	.03**	–	
	.02**	.04**	-.01	.00**	.01*	.08*	.03**	.18**	
Confidence	(γ)-.08**	(γ)-.07*	–	–	–	(γ).12**	–	(β).17**	.05
	.02*	.04**	.05**	.01*	.01*	.01**	.03**	–	
	-.05#	-.03	.05**	.01*	.01*	.14**	.03**	.17**	

Notes: This appendix table condenses three models, each of which includes sociodemographics, party identification, media use, institutional expertise, and *one* of three criterion variables (shown in the last three rows: global attitude, trustworthiness, or confidence). Entries in each cell are standardized direct, indirect, and total effects, respectively. Direct effects and indirect effects may not add up to total effects due to rounding. The χ² statistic for the global attitude model is 4.61 (6, N = 1278, p = .59), 8.86 (9, N = 1278, p = .45) for trustworthiness, and 5.50 (7, N = 1278, p = .60) for confidence.

\# p < .10
* p < .05
** p < .01

101

Appendix Table 5.3

Effects of Demographics, Party Identification, Newspaper Use, and Institutional Expertise on Evaluations of the Court System

	Sex (M)	Age	Education	Income	Democrat	Republican	Newspapers	Expertise	R²
Newspaper Use	--	(γ).13**	(γ).07*	(γ).11**	--	--			.04
	--	--	--	--	--	--			
	--	.13**	.07*	.11**	--	--			
Expertise	--	--	(γ).09**	(γ).07*	--	--	(β).18**		.05
	--	.02**	.01*	.02**	--	--	--		
	--	.02**	.10**	.09**	--	--	.18**		
Global Attitude	--	--	(γ).08**	(γ).09**	(γ).08**	--	(β).09**	(β).12**	.06
	--	.01**	.02**	.02**	--	--	.02**	--	
	--	.01**	.10**	.11**	.08**	--	.11**	.12**	
Trust-worthiness	--	(γ).05#	(γ).11**	(γ).10**	--	--	(β).07*	(β).07*	.05
	--	.01*	.01*	.01**	--	--	.01*	--	
	--	.06*	.12**	.11**	--	--	.08*	.07*	
Confidence	--	--	(γ).13**	(γ).08**	(γ).07**	--	(β).09**	--	.05
	--	.01**	.01#	.01**	--	--	--	--	
	--	.01**	.14**	.09**	.07**	--	.09**	--	

Notes: This appendix table condenses three models, each of which includes sociodemographics, party identification, media use, institutional expertise, and *one* of three criterion variables (shown in the last three rows: global attitude, trustworthiness, or confidence). Entries in each cell are standardized direct, indirect, and total effects, respectively. Direct effects and indirect effects may not add up to total effects due to rounding. The χ² statistic for the global attitude model is 7.20 (10, N = 1278, p = .71), 11.96 (10, N = 1278, p = .29) for trustworthiness, and 10.31 (11, N = 1278, p = .5) for confidence.

\# p < .10
* p < .05
** p < .01

Appendix Table 5.4
Effects of Demographics, Party Identification, Newspaper Use, and Institutional Expertise on Evaluations of the News Media

	Sex (M)	Age	Education	Income	Democrat	Republican	Newspapers	Expertise	R²
Newspaper Use	–	(γ) .13**	(γ) .07*	(γ) .11**	–	–			.04
	–	–	–	–	–	–			
	–	.13**	.07*	.11**	–	–			
Expertise	–	(γ) .13**	(γ) .12**	–	–	–	(β) .24**		.10
	–	.03**	.02**	.03**	–	–	–		
	–	.16**	.13**	.03**	–	–	.24**		
Global Attitude	(γ) -.06*	–	(γ) -.13**	–	(γ) .06*	(γ) -.07*	(β) .08**	(β) .33**	.15
	–	.06**	.05**	.02**	–	–	.08**	–	
	-.06*	.06**	-.08**	.02**	.06*	-.07*	.16**	.33**	
Trust-worthiness	(γ) -.05#	(γ) .08**	(γ) -.10**	–	(γ) .10**	–	(β) .07**	(β) .23**	.09
	–	.04**	.03**	.01**	–	–	.05**	–	
	-.05#	.13**	-.07*	.01**	.10**	–	.13**	.23**	
Confidence	–	–	(γ) -.09**	–	(γ) .09**	–	(β) .05#	(β) .22**	.10
	–	.04**	.03**	.01**	–	–	.05**	–	
	–	.04**	-.06*	.01**	.09**	–	.10**	.22**	

Notes: This appendix table condenses three models, each of which includes sociodemographics, party identification, media use, institutional expertise, and *one* of three criterion variables (shown in the last three rows: global attitude, trustworthiness, or confidence). Entries in each cell are standardized direct, indirect, and total effects, respectively. Direct effects and indirect effects may not add up to total effects due to rounding. The χ² statistic for the global attitude model is 9.01 (9, N = 1278, p = .44), 7.90 (9, N = 1278, p = .54) for trustworthiness, and 10.58 (11, N = 1278, p = .48) for confidence.

\# p < .10
* p < .05
** p < .01

Appendix Table 5.5
Effects of Demographics, Party Identification, Newspaper Use, and Institutional Expertise on Evaluations of the Public School System

	Sex (M)	Age	Education	Income	Democrat	Republican	Newspapers	Expertise	R²
Newspaper Use	–	(γ).13**	(γ).07*	(γ).11**	–	–			.04
	–	–	–	–	–	–			
		.13**	.07*	.11**	–	–			
Expertise	(γ)-.09**	(γ).05#	(γ).14**	(γ).10**	–	–	(β).08**		.06
	–	.01*	.01#	.01*	–	–	–		
	-.09**	.06*	.14**	.10*	–	–	.08**		
Global Attitude	(γ)-.07**	–	–	–	(γ).06*	(γ)-.09**	(β).09**	(β).27**	.11
	-.02**	.03**	.04**	.04**	–	–	.02**	–	
	-.10**	.03**	.04**	.04**	.06*	-.09**	.11**	.27**	
Trust-worthiness	–	–	–	–	(γ).09**	–	(β).07*	(β).22**	.07
	-.02**	.02**	.04**	.03**	–	–	.02**	–	
	-.02**	.02**	.04**	.03**	.09**	–	.09**	.22**	
Confidence	–	–	–	–	(γ).10**	–	(β).06*	(β).22**	.07
	-.02**	.02**	.04**	.03**	–	–	.02**	–	
	-.02**	.02**	.04**	.03**	.10**	–	.08**	.22**	

Notes: This appendix table condenses three models, each of which includes sociodemographics, party identification, media use, institutional expertise, and *one* of three criterion variables (shown in the last three rows: global attitude, trustworthiness, or confidence). Entries in each cell are standardized direct, indirect, and total effects, respectively. Direct effects and indirect effects may not add up to total effects due to rounding. The χ² statistic for the global attitude model is 3.63 (8, N = 1278, p = .89), 9.25 (10, N = 1278, p = .51) for trustworthiness, and 8.18 (10, N = 1278, p = .61) for confidence.

\# p < .10
* p < .05
** p < .01

104

Appendix Table 5.6
Effects of Demographics, Party Identification, News Magazine Use, and Institutional Expertise on Evaluations of the Office of the Presidency

	Sex (M)	Age	Education	Income	Democrat	Republican	News Magazines	Expertise	R^2
News Magazine Use	--	(γ) -.07**	(γ).15**	(γ).11**	--	--			.04
	--	--	--	--	--	--			
	--	-.07**	.15**	.11**	--	--			
Expertise	(γ).09**	(γ).27**	(γ).24**	--	(γ).12**	(γ).09**	(β).10**		.18
	--	-.01*	.02**	.01**	--	--	--		
	.09**	.27**	.26**	.01**	.12**	.09**	.10**		
Global Attitude	(γ)-.07*	(γ).10**	(γ).05*	--	(γ).09**	(γ)-.17**	--	(β).25**	.15
	.02**	.07**	.07**	.00**	.03**	.02**	.03**	--	
	-.04	.17**	.12**	.00**	.12**	-.15**	.03**	.25**	
Trust-worthiness	--	(γ).13**	--	--	(γ).08**	(γ)-.17**	--	(β).18**	.11
	.02**	.05**	.05**	.00**	.02**	.02**	.02**	--	
	.02**	.18**	.05**	.00**	.10**	-.15**	.02**	.18**	
Confidence	--	--	(γ).08**	--	(γ).12**	(γ)-.11**	--	(β).14**	.08
	.01**	.04**	.04**	.00*	.02**	.01**	.02**	--	
	.01**	.04**	.12**	.00*	.14**	-.10**	.02**	.14**	

Notes: This appendix table condenses three models, each of which includes sociodemographics, party identification, media use, institutional expertise, and *one* of three criterion variables (shown in the last three rows: global attitude, trustworthiness, or confidence). Entries in each cell are standardized direct, indirect, and total effects, respectively. Direct effects and indirect effects may not add up to total effects due to rounding. The χ^2 statistic for the global attitude model is 2.19 (6, N = 1278, p = .90.6), 5.22 (8, N = 1278, p = .73) for trustworthiness, and 5.05 (8, N = 1278, p = .75) for confidence.

\# p < .10
* p < .05
** p < .01

105

Effects of Demographics, Party Identification, News Magazine Use, and Institutional Expertise on Evaluations of Congress

	Sex (M)	Age	Education	Income	Democrat	Republican	News Magazines	Expertise	R^2
News Magazine Use	--	(γ) -.07**	(γ) .15**	(γ) .11**	--	--			.04
	--	-	-	-	--	--			
	--	-.07**	.15**	.11**	--	--			
Expertise	(γ) .14**	(γ) .24**	(γ) .25**	-	(γ) .07*	(γ) .09**	(β) .12**		.17
	-	-.01*	.02**	.01**	-	-	-		
	.14**	.23**	.27**	.01**	.07*	.09**	.12**		
Global Attitude	(γ) -.07*	(γ) -.07**	(γ) -.07*	(γ) .05#	-	(γ) .09**	.04**	(β) .31**	.10
	.04**	.07**	.08**	.00**	.02*	.03**	.04**	-	
	-.02	-.02	.03	.00#	.02*	.11**		.31**	
Trust-worthiness	-	-	(γ) -.06*	-	-	(γ) .07*	-	(β) .18**	.04
	.03**	.04**	.05**	.00**	.01*	.01**	.02**	-	
	.03**	.04**	-.01	.00**	.01*	.08**	.02**	.18**	
Confidence	(γ) -.07**	(γ) -.07*	-	-	-	(γ) .12**	-	(β) .17**	.05
	.02**	.04**	.05**	.00**	.01*	.01**	.02**	-	
	-.05#	-.03	.05**	.00**	.01*	.14**	.02**	.17**	

Notes: This appendix table condenses three models, each of which includes sociodemographics, party identification, media use, institutional expertise, and *one* of three criterion variables (shown in the last three rows: global attitude, trustworthiness, or confidence). Entries in each cell are standardized direct, indirect, and total effects, respectively. Direct effects and indirect effects may not add up to total effects due to rounding. The χ^2 statistic for the global attitude model is 1.06 (6, N = 1278, p = .98), 6.07 (9, N = 1278, p = .73) for trustworthiness, and 6.65 (8, N = 1278, p = .57) for confidence.

\# p < .10

* p < .05

** p < .01

Appendix Table 5.8
Effects of Demographics, Party Identification, News Magazine Use, and Institutional Expertise on Evaluations of the Court System

	Sex (M)	Age	Education	Income	Democrat	Republican	News Magazines	Expertise	R²
News Magazine Use	--	(γ) -.07**	(γ) .15**	(γ) .11**	--	--			.04
	--	--	--	--	--	--			
	--	-.07**	.15**	.11**	--	--			
Expertise	--	(γ) .08**	(γ) .08**	(γ) .07*	--	--	(β) .13**		.04
	--	-.01*	.02**	.01**	--	--	--		
	--	.07*	.10**	.08**	--	--	.13**		
Global Attitude	--	--	(γ) .09**	(γ) .10**	(γ) .08**	--	--	(β) .13**	.06
	--	.01*	.01**	.01*	--	--	.02**	--	
	--	.01*	.10**	.11**	.08**	--	.02**	.13**	
Trust-worthiness	--	(γ) .06*	(γ) .11**	(γ) .10**	--	--	--	(β) .07**	.04
	--	.01#	.01*	.01#	--	--	.01*	--	
	--	.06*	.12**	.11**	--	--	.01*	.07**	
Confidence	--	--	(γ) .13**	(γ) .08**	(γ) .07*	--	--	(β) .06*	.04
	--	.00	.01#	.00#	--	--	.01#	--	
	--	.00	.14**	.09**	.07*	--	.01#	.06*	

Notes: This appendix table condenses three models, each of which includes sociodemographics, party identification, media use, institutional expertise, and *one* of three criterion variables (shown in the last three rows: global attitude, trustworthiness, or confidence). Entries in each cell are standardized direct, indirect, and total effects, respectively. Direct effects and indirect effects may not add up to total effects due to rounding. The χ^2 statistic for the global attitude model is 4.20 (10, N = 1278, p = .94), 7.69 (10, N = 1278, p = .66) for trustworthiness, and 4.12 (10, N = 1278, p = .94) for confidence.

# p < .10
* p < .05
** p < .01

Appendix Table 5.9
Effects of Demographics, Party Identification, News Magazine Use, and Institutional Expertise on Evaluations of the News Media

	Sex (M)	Age	Education	Income	Democrat	Republican	News Magazines	Expertise	R^2
News Magazine Use	—	(γ) -.07**	(γ) .15**	(γ) .11**	—	—			.04
	—	—	—	—	—	—			
	—	-.07**	.15**	.11**	—	—			
Expertise	—	(γ) .17**	(γ) .11**	—	—	—	(β) .13**		.06
	—	-.01*	.02**	.01**	—	—	—		
	—	.16**	.13**	.01**	—	—	.13**		
Global Attitude	(γ) -.05*	(γ) .05#	(γ) -.12**	—	(γ) .06*	(γ) -.07*	—	(β) .34**	.14
	—	.05**	.05**	.00**	—	—	.04**	—	
	-.05*	.10**	-.08**	.00**	.06*	-.07*	.04**	.34**	
Trust-worthiness	—	(γ) .10**	(γ) -.10**	—	(γ) .10**	—	—	(β) .24**	.09
	—	.04**	.03**	.00**	—	—	.03**	—	
	—	.13*8	-.07*	.00**	.10**	—	.03**	.24**	
Confidence	—	—	(γ) -.09**	—	(γ) .09**	—	—	(β) .24**	.07
	—	.04**	.03**	.00**	—	—	.03**	—	
	—	.04**	-.06*	.00**	.09**	—	.03**	.24**	

Notes: This appendix table condenses three models, each of which includes sociodemographics, party identification, media use, institutional expertise, and *one* of three criterion variables (shown in the last three rows: global attitude, trustworthiness, or confidence). Entries in each cell are standardized direct, indirect, and total effects, respectively. Direct effects and indirect effects may not add up to total effects due to rounding. The χ^2 statistic for the global attitude model is 4.33 (9, N = 1278, p = .89), 7.05 (11, N = 1278, p = .79) for trustworthiness, and 7.41 (12, N = 1278, p = .83) for confidence.

\# p < .10

* p < .05

** p < .01

Appendix Table 5.10

Effects of Demographics, Party Identification, News Magazine Use, and Institutional Expertise on Evaluations of the Public School System

	Sex (M)	Age	Education	Income	Democrat	Republican	News Magazines	Expertise	R²
News Magazine Use	--	(γ) -.07**	(γ) .15**	(γ) .11**	--	--			.04
	--	--	--	--	--	--			
	--	-.07**	.15**	.11**	--	--			
Expertise	(γ) -.09**	(γ) .07*	(γ) .13**	(γ) .10**	--	--	(β) .07*		.06
	--	-.01#	.01*	.01*	--	--	--		
	-.09**	.06*	.14**	.10**	--	--	.07*		
Global Attitude	(γ) -.07**	--	--	--	(γ) .06*	(γ) -.09**	(β) .04#	(β) .28**	.11
	-.02**	.01#	.05**	.03**	--	--	.02*	--	
	-.09**	.01#	.05**	.03**	.06*	-.09**	.06*	.28**	
Trust-worthiness	--	--	--	--	(γ) .06*	(γ) -.06#	(β) .07*	(β) .22**	.07
	-.02**	.02**	.04**	.03**	--	--	.02**	--	
	-.02**	.02**	.04**	.03**	.06*	-.06#	.09**	.22**	
Confidence	--	--	--	--	(γ) .10**	--	(β) .06*	(β) .22**	.07
	-.02**	.02**	.04**	.03**	--	--	.02**	--	
	-.02**	.02**	.04**	.03**	.10**	--	.08**	.22**	

Notes: This appendix table condenses three models, each of which includes sociodemographics, party identification, media use, institutional expertise, and *one* of three criterion variables (shown in the last three rows: global attitude, trustworthiness, or confidence). Entries in each cell are standardized direct, indirect, and total effects, respectively. Direct effects and indirect effects may not add up to total effects due to rounding. The χ² statistic for the global attitude model is 2.89 (8, N = 1278, p = .94), 5.92 (9, N = 1278, p = .75) for trustworthiness, and 8.18 (10, N = 1278, p = .61) for confidence.

# p < .10

* p < .05

** p < .01

## Chapter 6

The Effects of Traditional Television News

Is Americans' involvement with television a dangerous one?
Communications scholar Jib Fowles (1992, p. 32)

The appearance of television on the American media landscape brought to a crescendo the cry that media are to blame for society's problems. In the political arena, the rapid adoption of television coincided with a steady decline in voter turnout (see Rosenstone & Hansen, 1993 for a review). According to data from the Center for Political Studies, nearly three-quarters of the most politically apathetic citizens reported television to be the medium they used most often; for the most politically involved respondents, that figure was under 60 percent (Bennett, 1986). Supporting data come from Stephen Shaffer (1981) who found that between 1960 and 1976, voter turnout declined only 1.5 percent for those most reliant on newspapers, compared to over 10 percent for those least reliant on newspapers.

Television has been charged also with ills outside the voting booth. Robert Putnam (1995) asserts that television is the only medium to contribute to America's decline in social capital by privatizing citizens' leisure time. Putnam observes that the time citizens used to spend with their neighbors, bowling leagues, and civic associations is now spent in front of the television set. In contrast, newspaper reading is positively related to such civic engagement.

In addition, conventional wisdom maintains that newspapers are superior to television in imparting political information (e.g., Robinson & Levy, 1986, 1996). For some, this is not surprising given how television news often performs the same function as a headline service, as noted by Walter Cronkite (Comstock, 1980). But it is not just time constraints that limit the usefulness of television news as a learning tool. Scholars have suggested that television news tends to hamper learning as it places greater emphasis on personalities and pictures (e.g., Hallin, 1986). This position, however, does not appear to dampen Doris Graber's (1996) optimism over the role of visuals. While she does not deny the potential of television news stories to distort pictures (literally), Graber suggests that audiovisual information is helpful to society at large. Individuals learn to process visual cues a lot earlier than they do verbal cues, and thus, audiovisual cues can reach a much broader audience, starting at a much younger age.

Despite the ongoing debate over these specific arguments, one concern remains: that relative to newspapers, television may play a detrimental role in our political system, serving to undermine democratic processes. Where confidence in democratic institutions is concerned, the argument is no different. Newspaper reading is believed to increase citizens' trust in government, while television viewing purportedly erodes it. In this chapter, we discuss in greater detail how "traditional" television news programs (network news and local news) are related to confidence in institutions.

TELEVISION NEWS

It is easy to talk about television news as a single entity, but the term obscures general differences between local and network news. For instance, network news airs for a half-hour in the early evening, and tends to focus on events in our nation's capital and major cities. It often is supplemented with stories concerning other nations and international cities. Moreover, the stories broadcast by each of the three network news programs tend to cover the same content (Ansolabehere, Behr, & Iyengar, 1993).

Local television news, on the other hand, is generally broadcast in the early evening *and* after prime-time programming. Anyone who watches local news knows it is more than just the recapping of national and international events; each broadcast comes complete with weather and sports. Stephen Hess's (1996) informal analysis of local broadcasts from 35 cities indicated that on average, news accounted for approximately two-thirds of the newscast, with national and world news taking up 15 percent. This figure changes with the size of the market: the top 25 markets average 73 percent news; the smaller markets, 60 percent. While network news may be uniform in content, Hess concluded that local news broadcasts *appear* the same across different cities—from the nearly standard anchor desk to the rapport between the anchor team to the lack of facial hair on male anchors. A more notable difference between network and local news concerns how the former tends to deal with events or issues associated with specific places; in contrast, local news broadcasts are marked by "the absence of place, a sense that this news is special to this locale" (Hess, 1996, p. 120). That is, local news stories tend not to feel connected to the *place* they are supposed to represent.

Of particular relevance to our study is the fact that coverage of democratic institutions tends to differ between the two communication modalities. Not surprisingly, there tends to be less coverage of democratic institutions in local news broadcasts than in national news broadcasts. In her content analysis of local broadcasts in Philadelphia, Phyllis Kaniss (1991) found that the coverage of isolated incidents such as crimes, accidents, or fires was equally, if not more, prominent than coverage of government and policy. She attributed the proclivity for such coverage to the fact that crimes and fires are better than policy stories at providing sound bites and visuals. When stories about government do appear, they tend to be covered from a "sexy" or "humanistic" perspective (p. 120). This type of coverage potentially limits the amount of political information conveyed and certainly places constraints on the *quality* of political information conveyed.

Is network news and local news coverage of democratic institutions equally negative? We began discussion of this issue in Chapter 4, noting Michael Robinson's (1974) seminal work in the area. We now present in greater detail a review of past research on television news content.

TELEVISION NEWS NEGATIVITY

Content analyses of network television news coverage of the presidency document increasing negativity. In a study of network television news coverage during the 1980 election campaign in which the major players were incumbent Democratic President Jimmy Carter, Republican challenger Ronald Reagan, and intra-party challenger Edward Kennedy— Michael Robinson and Margaret Sheehan (1983) found that negative news stories outnumbered positive ones by a two-to-one margin. In a follow-up study of network news coverage during the 1984 campaign, Robinson reported that the margin of negative versus positive coverage of incumbent President Reagan was five-to-one (Patterson, 1991, p. 157). If anything, the margin has grown since then.

Two longitudinal studies of network television news coverage of the presidency also point to increasing negativity. Daniel Hallin (1992) studied network television news campaign coverage from 1968 to 1988 and found a pronounced trend of rising negativism. As late as 1968, there was an approximate balance in positive and negative stories, but from 1980 through 1988 "negative stories *clearly* predominated" (1992, pp. 14–

15, emphasis added). Hallin placed most of the blame for the growing negativism on two emerging trends in network television journalism: the displacement of journalist's words with those of the newsmakers, coupled with the shrinking sound bite.

In another study from roughly the same period, Fred Smoller (1986, 1990) analyzed 5,292 CBS news stories from 1969 through 1985. During the Nixon, Ford, and Carter presidencies, and Reagan's first term, he found most coverage was neutral but that "60 percent of [the] directional coverage was negative" (1986, p. 40). Smoller documented an increasingly negative tone in overall CBS news coverage of the presidency, also noting the negativity peaked during each officeholder's fourth year in office.

In a more recent content analysis, the Center for Media and Public Affairs (1994) examined network television news coverage of President Bill Clinton. It found that 62 percent of all evaluations of Clinton during his first 18 months in office by network news "sources" or "reporters" were negative. All together, the network newscasts offered up 2,400 negative comments on Clinton, averaging five per newscast. The study concluded: "It is not public opinion which is influencing news coverage, but the news that is driving opinion" (1994, p. 7). This study also featured an analysis of public opinion poll results to provide the kind of interconnected data that we maintain is essential in assessing the influence of mass media on confidence.

Congress fares no better in network coverage. Michael Robinson and Kevin Appel (1979) studied coverage of Congress during a one-month period in 1976 and found that although most stories were neutral in tone, all stories that contained a slant were negative. They concluded that network television news surpasses print news in its negative content and tone toward Congress (1979, p. 415). This pattern appears to have escalated since the 1970s. S. Robert Lichter and Daniel Amundson indicate that television network news coverage of Congress has grown increasingly "jaundiced" during the past two decades (1994, p. 140).

Research shows, however, that Congress fares somewhat better in *local* news coverage. Michael Robinson (1981) attributes this difference to the relative size of the two types of media. In other words, national news media have greater access to a larger pool of newsmakers, while local news media, by definition, are rooted in their localities and need repeated access to the same people. He likens the national news media to consultants, and local news media to foremen: "Consultants do their work and get out, while foremen have to stay put. For the most part, consultants are tougher than foremen; like the national press, consultants are expected to be tough" (Robinson, 1981, p. 86). Size notwithstanding, Robinson (1981) explains that the difference in negativity between local and network news comes down to *what* the various media cover. His content analysis revealed that 83 percent of stories that were negative toward Congress were about the institution and not individual members. Covering the institution as a whole, as the national networks usually do, makes it an easier target.

We noted earlier that there has been little research that has systematically examined television news depictions of other democratic institutions. But this may quickly change as cameras are allowed to enter the courtroom. Televised coverage of trials may have severe repercussions on public confidence in the court system.

The trial that best illustrates this potential danger is, obviously, the O. J. Simpson trial. For over a year, Americans were riveted to their television sets, tuned into a trial that involved sex and murder intertwined with strains of racial conflict. Presiding Judge Lance Ito had allowed cameras into his courtroom, hoping to educate viewers, but his plan backfired. Rather than learning about the criminal justice systems, viewers were entertained by the overkill of media coverage that turned a "murder trial into political theater" (Thaler, 1997, p. 287).

Andrew Tyndall (1998), publisher of the *Tyndall Report*, a weekly analysis of network broadcast news, concluded that the media treated the trial much as they treated a "continuing story" such as the war in Bosnia. Network news gave the trial over 27 hours of coverage over 40 weeks, making the criminal trial the second most prominent story in the period from 1987 to 1997. Coverage of the trial superseded that of the war in Yugoslavia, the events in Tiananmen Square, and the collapse of the Soviet Union. The only story that commanded greater network coverage was the crisis in the Persian Gulf.

The O. J. Simpson trial very well may have set a precedent for subsequent high-profile trials. When Timothy McVeigh was put on trial for the bombing of the Federal Building in Oklahoma City, legal analysts questioned the impact of lawyers who rely increasingly on drama and entertainment. Legal analyst Andrew Cohen (1998) surmised that lawyers will become increasingly theatrical, making greater use of videotapes, audiotapes, and overhead presentations. These dramatic moments make for better news coverage from the perspective of an audience whose attention span has diminished, but concerns remain over televised coverage of court proceedings. Partly as a result of these concerns, courtroom cameras were not permitted in the McVeigh trial. Judge Judith Kaye (1998), chief judge of the state of New York and chief judge of the Court of Appeals of the state of New York, writes:

By tradition and by explicit prohibition, judges do not comment on pending matters. Sitting judges can't hold press conferences about their decisions.... A decision should stand as the last word. But this means that when judges are sound bitten, they can't bite back.... The cumulative effect of this coverage is

Table 6.1
Predicting Viewership of Network and Local Television News

	Network News		Local News	
	β	s.e. (β)	β	s.e. (β)
Sex (Male)	-.031	(.056)	-.073	(.056)
Age	.006	(.002)**	.006	(.002)**
Education	.012	(.018)	-.057	(.018)**
Income	-.063	(.021)**	.036	(.021)
Democrat	.024	(.063)	.089	(.063)*
Republican	-.160	(.074)*	-.004	(.074)

Note: Entries are coefficients from ordinary least squares regression with standard errors in parentheses.
* p < .05
** p < .01

less informed and more cynical citizens, who are less likely to trust and respect their system of justice and more likely to write off the judiciary as yet another public institution that is hopelessly out of touch. (p. 77)

MIXED INFLUENCE OF TELEVISION NEWS

Who's Watching?

Americans have become increasingly reliant on television as their primary source of political information (Roper Organization, 1981; Roper Starch Worldwide, 1997), and the penetration rate of television sets into American households is nearly 100 percent (DeFleur & Dennis, 1998). These data would suggest that *everyone* is watching television and getting their political information from television. This is certainly not the case.

Our data indicate that television news viewing is not equally distributed among individuals. According to the ordinary least squares regression analyses shown in Table 6.1, one's gender did not affect the degree to which one watched either network or local news, but older people were significantly more likely to watch the news than younger people. Viewership also was related to indicators of socioeconomic status: lower income respondents were more likely to watch network news, and respondents with lower education levels were more likely to watch local news. Finally, Democrats revealed a greater proclivity for watching local news, while Republicans were less likely to watch network news.

Effects of Television News

Previous studies comparing the effects of newspaper and television coverage on the confidence levels of audience members have tended to favor newspapers (e.g., Becker & Whitney, 1980; Miller & Reese, 1982). In other words, reliance on television news tends to erode confidence levels whereas newspaper use tends to have the opposite effect.

According to our content analyses, network news coverage of democratic institutions was indeed negative, but this generalization is limited to certain time periods and certain institutions. On the one hand, network coverage of the presidency, Congress, and to a lesser degree, the court system was found to be generally more negative than coverage by the other media. On the other hand, we found that the depictions of the news media and the school system by network news did not differ significantly from other media's depictions.

Our content analyses also suggest that "television news" may be too broad a term to use in studies of mass media and trust in institutions. After all, our content analyses show that the tone of local news coverage of institutions was not always consonant with that of network news. In 1995, local news (and other TV news) coverage of the office of the presidency was most positive (as shown earlier in Table 4.1), and while network news coverage was still favorable, it was significantly less so than local news. Local news coverage maintained its tone and tenor through 1996, but network news coverage had become more negative toward the presidency. Network news coverage of Congress remained consistently negative throughout the period under study. In contrast, the relatively positive tone of congressional coverage by local news took a nosedive between 1995 and 1996. Finally, while both network and local news aired stories that portrayed the news media in a negative light, local news was significantly harsher in its coverage.

Despite these differences, similarities emerged between the two modalities. Both network news and local news covered the court system in a similar light, just as coverage of local schools did not differ significantly between the two. Nevertheless, our content analyses reveal that more differences than similarities exist between the two. Thus any conclusions drawn about the content of "television news" need to be qualified. Do the *effects* of viewing network and local television need to be similarly qualified? Our structural equation models indicate a categorical "yes."

Effects of Network News Viewing

Office of the Presidency. As we noted in Chapter 4 and earlier in this chapter, the body of research overwhelmingly points to the detrimental effects of television news on citizens' confidence. Our data show that while watching network news exerted a direct negative impact on viewers' global attitude toward the office of the presidency (see Figure 6.1 and Appendix Table 6.1), viewing network news also enhanced one's level of interest, awareness, and knowledge of the presidency, which in

Figure 6.1
Effects of Watching Network TV News on Evaluations of the Presidency

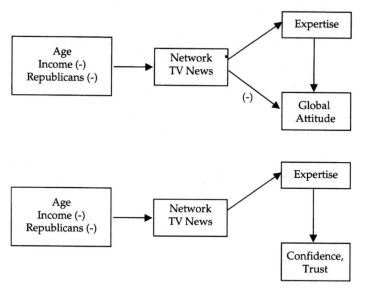

Note: Total effects of network news viewing on global attitude were not statistically significant.

turn enhanced evaluations of the presidency. In other words, after taking into account the degree to which one used other communication modalities and one's level of expertise in the presidency, watching network news did not have a significant total effect on one's global attitude toward the presidency. Where the other two criterion variables—confidence and trustworthiness—were concerned, watching network news had no direct effect. Rather, it enhanced confidence levels and feelings of trustworthiness indirectly through increasing expertise. Research not controlling for these effects simultaneously would come to a different conclusion.

Therefore, our data do not indicate that watching network news is a detriment to evaluations of the office of the presidency. We must reiterate, however, that our analyses have taken into account the use of other media. Watching network television news *alone* may erode confidence, and our content analyses did show more negative portrayals of the presidency by network news in 1996 (compared to 1995), but we find that *after controlling for use of other media, network news viewing enhances evaluations of the presidency.*

Congress. Consistently negative in tone in its coverage of Congress, network news had a negative impact on how viewers felt about this institution. After taking into account use of all other media, network

Figure 6.2
Effects of Watching Network TV News on Evaluations of Congress and the Court System

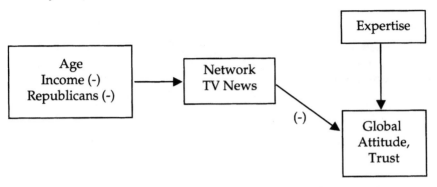

news viewing had a significant negative impact on individuals' global attitude toward and trust in Congress (both coefficients at (β = −.08). Moreover, there were no "buffering" positive effects of network news viewing on expertise. One's expertise in Congress did have a positive effect on all evaluations, but expertise was *not* influenced by watching network news. Figure 6.2 thus illustrates these two distinct and direct influences on evaluations of Congress—one for network news, and one for expertise in Congress. Network news viewing had no bearing on the 0–100 confidence rating of Congress.

The Court System. As reflected also in Figure 6.2, the relationships that emerged for Congress among network news viewing, institutional expertise, and evaluations of the institution were nearly identical for the court system. Watching network news had a direct, negative impact on one's global attitude (β = −.06) and trust in the court system (β = −.07). Again, exposure and attention to network news did not affect how aware, interested, or knowledgeable one was about the court system, but expertise did enhance all evaluations. The only difference in direct effects between Congress and the court system involved the magnitude of the effects. Expertise in each institution had a positive impact on evaluations of the institution, but the coefficients for the court system were significantly lower than the corresponding ones for Congress.

The News Media. As Figure 6.3 shows, only one effect emerged for network news viewing on perceptions of the news media: news viewing increased expertise in the news media, which in turn resulted in more positive evaluations of this institution. Thus the effects of network news viewing were positive and indirect (β = .02 and .03, shown in Appendix Table 6.4).

The Public Schools. Conspicuously absent from Appendix Table 6.5 are

Figure 6.3
Effects of Watching Network TV News on Evaluations of the News Media

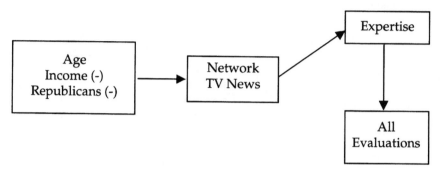

effects of network news viewing on perceptions of the public school system. Expertise, however, did exert a consistently strong positive impact on all evaluations: the greater one's interest, awareness, and knowledge of the school system, the more favorable their evaluations of this institution. While expertise did influence evaluations of public schools, network news viewing did not increase expertise.

The Effects of Local News Viewing

The Office of the Presidency. As we noted earlier, local news coverage of the presidency differed significantly from network news coverage. In general, local news coverage was more positive. Indeed, the tone of such coverage translated into more positive evaluations of the presidency. As shown in Figure 6.4, effects were direct, not working through expertise. Put another way, watching local news did not affect levels of expertise in the presidency. Expertise levels did, however, have a positive impact on all evaluations.

The News Media. According to our content analyses, local television news was the communication source that generated the least amount of content related to the news media. Yet what coverage did exist was the harshest of all the modalities we studied. Despite this tone of coverage, watching news from the local network affiliates *enhanced* all evaluations of the news media. This positive effect worked two ways: directly, and indirectly (with marginal significance) through expertise related to the news media. Only the direct and statistically significant path is shown in Figure 6.4.

The Public Schools. The effects of watching local news on perceptions of the public school system were similar to those of local news viewing on the office of the presidency: direct only (see Figure 6.4). In other

Figure 6.4
Effects of Watching Local Television News on Evaluations of the Presidency, the News Media, and the Public Schools

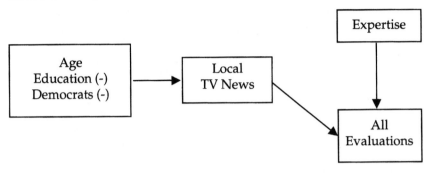

words, watching local television news had a direct positive effect on respondents' evaluations of the public schools. Appendix Table 6.10 indicates a marginally significant effect of viewing as expertise, not shown in Figure 6.4.

The Congress and Court System. Our content analyses indicate that local news coverage related to Congress took a turn for the worse from 1995 to 1996. The negativity in coverage, however, did not translate into any effect on evaluations of Congress. Expertise in Congress did enhance confidence, trust, and global attitude, but local news viewing did not influence expertise. The same pattern of effects emerged in the case of local news viewing and evaluations of the court system. This latter set of findings is more consistent with the relatively balanced coverage found in our content analyses (noted earlier in Table 4.3).

CONCLUSION

In response to Jib Fowles's (1992) query about whether Americans' involvement with television was a dangerous one, many would respond in the affirmative. Previous research has linked television to a gamut of political and social ills, at least relative to newspapers. The comparison of print versus broadcast news is no different where confidence in institutions is concerned.

Our data indicate that reading newspapers and news magazines led to more favorable evaluations of various democratic institutions. These effects were direct and indirect, working through what we term "institutional expertise." More notably, this pattern of results emerged after we controlled for people's use of other media—including television news, entertainment programming, and political talk radio. But most notably, *the effects of exposure and attention to print media on confidence in these institutions were consistently positive.*

Table 6.2

Effects of Watching Network TV News on Evaluations of Democratic
Institutions: Summary Table

	Presidency	Congress	Court System	News Media	Public Schools
Global Attitude	Direct and indirect effects	Direct effect only (negative)	Direct effect only (negative)	Indirect effect only	None
Trustworthiness	Indirect effect only	Direct effect only (negative)	Direct effect only (negative)	Indirect effect only	None
Confidence	Indirect effect only	None	None	Indirect effect only	None

Note: Effects are noted based on probability levels set at $p = .05$.

Table 6.3

Effects of Watching Local Television News on Evaluations of Democratic
Institutions: Summary Table

	Presidency	Congress	Court System	News Media	Public Schools
Global Attitude	Direct effect only	None	None	Direct effect only	Direct effect only
Trustworthiness	Direct effect only	None	None	Direct effect only	Direct effect only
Confidence	Direct effect only	None	None	Direct effect only	Direct effect only

Note: Effects are noted based on probability levels set at $p = .05$.

In contrast, watching television news had mixed effects on confidence.
As noted in Table 6.2, watching network news had a direct effect on
perceptions of three of the five democratic institutions under review—
the office of the presidency, Congress, and the court system—and all
such direct effects were *negative*. Watching network news also had one
indirect effect and that was to enhance evaluations of the news media.
Watching local news also exerted direct effects on three of the five institutions—the presidency, the news media, and the public school system. However, these effects were *all positive*, as noted in Table 6.3.

Robinson (1981) was referring to media coverage of Congress when
he wrote, "The real story may be that the hometown press still does not
behave much like Woodward and Bernstein—that beneath the new
'hardness' at the national level, the old 'softness' survives at the local

level" (p. 57). Our data suggest that his conclusion may be generalized to coverage of other democratic institutions.

We must reiterate that the effects of negativity found in our study emerged after we controlled for use of other media. In other words, the negative effects of watching network news, and the positive effects of watching local news, emerged *above and beyond citizens' use of other media*. In Chapter 7, we focus on the role of other television programming on confidence in institutions.

Appendix Table 6.1
Effects of Demographics, Party Identification, Network TV News Viewing, and Institutional Expertise on Evaluations of the Office of the Presidency

	Sex (M)	Age	Education	Income	Democrat	Republican	Network TV News	Expertise	R^2
Network TV News Viewing	--	(γ) .10**	--	(γ) -.09**	--	(γ) -.08**			.02
	--	--	--	--	--	--			
	--	.10**	--	-.09**	--	-.08**			
Expertise	(γ) .09**	(γ) .26**	(γ) .26**	--	(γ) .12**	(γ) .09**	(β) .09**		.17
	--	.01*	--	-.01*	--	-.01*	--		
	.09**	.27**	.26**	-.01*	.12**	.09**	.09**		
Global Attitude	(γ) -.07**	(γ) .10**	(γ) .05#	--	(γ) .08**	(γ) -.17**	(β) -.06*	(β) .26**	.16
	.02**	.06**	.07**	.00	.03**	.03**	.02**	--	
	-.04	.17**	.12**	.00	.12**	-.15**	-.03	.26**	
Trust-worthiness	(γ) -.05#	(γ) .12*	--	--	(γ) .07*	(γ) -.17**	--	(β) .18**	.11
	.02**	.05*	.05**	.00*	.02**	.02**	.02**	--	
	-.03	.17**	.05**	.00*	.09**	-.15**	.02**	.18**	
Confidence	(γ) .01**	--	(γ) .08**	--	(γ) .12**	(γ) -.11**	--	(β) .14**	.08
	.01**	.04**	.04**	.00*	.02**	.01**	.01**	--	
	.01**	.04**	.12**	.00*	.14**	-.10**	.01**	.14**	

Notes: This appendix table condenses three models, each of which includes sociodemographics, party identification, media use, institutional expertise, and *one* of three criterion variables (shown in the last three rows: global attitude, trustworthiness, or confidence). Entries in each cell are standardized direct, indirect, and total effects, respectively. Direct effects and indirect effects may not add up to total effects due to rounding. The χ^2 statistic for the global attitude model is 2.72 (5, N = 1278, p = .74), 4.33 (7, N = 1278, p = .74) for trustworthiness, and 6.87 (5, N = 1278, p = .55) for confidence.

\# p < .10
* p < .05
** p < .01

Appendix Table 6.2

Effects of Demographics, Party Identification, Network TV News Viewing, and Institutional Expertise on Evaluations of Congress

	Sex (M)	Age	Education	Income	Democrat	Republican	Network TV News	Expertise	R^2
Network TV News Viewing	—	(γ) .10**	—	(γ) -.09**	—	(γ) -.08**			.02
	—	-	—	-	—	-			
	—	.10**	—	-.09**	—	-.08**			
Expertise	.14**	(γ) .23**	(γ) .27**	—	(γ) .07*	(γ) .08**	—		.16
	-	-	-	—	-	-	—		
	.14**	.23**	.27**	—	.07*	.08**	—		
Global Attitude	(γ) -.06*	(γ) -.09**	(γ) -.06*	-	-	(γ) .08**	(β) -.08**	(β) .31**	.10
	.04**	.07**	.08**	.01*	.02*	.03**	-	-	
	-.02	-.02	.03	.01*	.02*	.11**	-.08**	.31**	
Trust-worthiness	-	-	(γ) -.06*	-	-	(γ) .06*	(β) -.08**	(β) .19**	.04
	.03**	.04**	.05**	.01*	.01*	.02**	-	-	
	.03**	.04**	-.01	.01*	.01*	.08**	-.08*	.19*	
Confidence	(γ) -.07**	(γ) -.07*	-	-	-	(γ) .12**	-	(β) .17**	.05
	.02**	.04**	.05**	-	.01*	.01**	-	-	
	-.05#	-.02	.05**	-	.01*	.14**	-	.17**	

Notes: This appendix table condenses three models, each of which includes sociodemographics, party identification, media use, institutional expertise, and *one* of three criterion variables (shown in the last three rows: global attitude, trustworthiness, or confidence). Entries in each cell are standardized direct, indirect, and total effects, respectively. Direct effects and indirect effects may not add up to total effects due to rounding. The χ^2 statistic for the global attitude model is 6.74 (7, N = 1278, p = .46), 8.61 (9, N = 1278, p = .47) for trustworthiness, and 10.24 (9, N = 1278, p = .33) for confidence.

\# p < .10
* p < .05
** p < .01

Appendix Table 6.3
Effects of Demographics, Party Identification, Network TV News Viewing, and Institutional Expertise on Evaluations of the Court System

	Sex (M)	Age	Education	Income	Democrat	Republican	Network TV News	Expertise	R²
Network TV News Viewing	--	(γ).10**	--	(γ)-.09**	--	(γ)-.08**			.02
	--	--	--	--	--	--			
		.10**	--	-.09**	--	-.08**			
Expertise	--	(γ).07*	(γ).10**	(γ).08**	--	--	--		.03
	--	--	--	--	--	--	--		
	--	.07*	.10**	.08**	--	--	--		
Global Attitude	--	--	(γ).09**	(γ).10**	(γ).08**	--	(β)-.06*	(β).13**	.06
	--	.00	.01**	.02**	--	.00#	--	--	
		.00	.10**	.11**	.08**	.00#	-.06*	.13**	
Trust-worthiness	(γ).05#	(γ).07*	(γ).11**	(γ).09**	(γ).05#	--	(β)-.07*	(β).07**	.04
	--	.00	.01*	.01**	--	.01#	--	--	
	.05#	.07*	.12**	.10**	.05#	.01#	-.07*	.07**	
Confidence	--	--	(γ).13**	(γ).08**	(γ).07*	--	--	(β).06**	.05
	--	.00	.01#	.00#	--	--	--	--	
	--	.00	.14**	.09**	.07*	--	--	.06**	

Notes: This appendix table condenses three models, each of which includes sociodemographics, party identification, media use, institutional expertise, and *one* of three criterion variables (shown in the last three rows: global attitude, trustworthiness, or confidence). Entries in each cell are standardized direct, indirect, and total effects, respectively. Direct effects and indirect effects may not add up to total effects due to rounding. The χ^2 statistic for the global attitude model is 4.61 (10, N = 1278, p = .92), 2.77 (8, N = 1278, p = .95) for trustworthiness, and 6.23 (11, N = 1278, p = .86) for confidence.

\# p < .10
* p < .05
** p < .01

126

Appendix Table 6.4
Effects of Demographics, Party Identification, Network TV News Viewing, and Institutional Expertise on Evaluations of the News Media

	Sex (M)	Age	Education	Income	Democrat	Republican	Network TV News	Expertise	R²
Network TV News Viewing	—	(γ) .10**	—	(γ) -.09**	—	(γ) -.08**			.02
	—	—	—	—	—	—			
	—	.10**	—	-.09**	—	-.08**			
Expertise	—	(γ) .15**	(γ) .14**	—	—	—	(β) .08**		.05
	—	.01*	—	-.01*	—	-.01*	—		
	—	.16**	.14**	-.01*	—	-.01*	.08**		
Global Attitude	(γ) -.05**	(γ) .05#	(γ) -.12**	—	(γ) .06*	(γ) -.07*	—	(β) .34**	.15
	—	.06**	.05**	.00*	—	.00#	.03**	—	
	-.05**	.11**	-.08**	.00*	.06*	-.07**	.03**	.34**	
Trust-worthiness	—	(γ) .10**	(γ) -.10**	—	(γ) .10**	—	—	(β) .24**	.09
	—	.04**	.03**	.00*	—	.00#	.02**	—	
	—	.14**	-.07*	.00*	.10**	.00#	.02**	.24**	
Confidence	—	—	(γ) -.09**	—	(γ) .09**	—	—	(β) .24**	.07
	—	.04**	.03**	.00*	—	.00#	.02**	—	
	—	.04**	-.06*	.00*	.09**	.00#	.02**	.24**	

Notes: This appendix table condenses three models, each of which includes sociodemographics, party identification, media use, institutional expertise, and one of th.ee criterion variables (shown in the last three rows: global attitude, trustworthiness, or confidence). Entries in each cell are standardized direct, indirect, and total effects, respectively. Direct effects and indirect effects may not add up to total effects due to rounding. The χ² statistic for the global attitude model is 2.60 (9, N = 1278, p = .98), 6.18 (11, N = 1278, p = .86) for trustworthiness, and 7.19 (12, N = 1278, p = .85) for confidence.

# p < .10
* p < .05
** p < .01

127

Appendix Table 6.5

Effects of Demographics, Party Identification, Network TV News Viewing, and Institutional Expertise on Evaluations of the Public School System

	Sex (M)	Age	Education	Income	Democrat	Republican	Network TV News	Expertise	R²
Network TV News Viewing	--	(γ) .10**	--	(γ) -.09**	--	(γ) -.08**	--		.02
	--	--	--	--	--	--	--		
	--	.10**	--	-.09**	--	-.08**	--		
Expertise	(γ) -.09**	(γ) .06*	(γ) .14**	(γ) .10**	--	--	--		.05
	--	--	--	--	--	--	--		
	-.09*	.06*	.14**	.10*	--	--	--		
Global Attitude	(γ) -.07*	--	--	--	(γ) .06*	(γ) -.09**	--	(β) .27**	.11
	-.02**	.02*	.04**	.03**	--	--	--	--	
	-.09**	.02*	.04**	.03**	.06*	-.09**	--	.27**	
Trust-worthiness	--	--	--	--	(γ) .06*	(γ) -.06#	--	(β) .22**	.07
	-.02**	.01*	.03**	.02**	--	--	--	--	
	-.02**	.01*	.03**	.03**	.06**	-.06#	--	.22**	
Confidence	--	--	--	--	(γ) .10**	--	--	(β) .22**	.06
	-.02**	.01*	.03**	.02**	--	--	--	--	
	-.02**	.01*	.03**	.02**	.10**	--	--	.22**	

Notes: This appendix table condenses three models, each of which includes sociodemographics, party identification, media use, institutional expertise, and *one* of three criterion variables (shown in the last three rows: global attitude, trustworthiness, or confidence). Entries in each cell are standardized direct, indirect, and total effects, respectively. Direct effects and indirect effects may not add up to total effects due to rounding. The χ^2 statistic for the global attitude model is 3.49 (10, N = 1278, p = .97), 5.52 (11, N = 1278, p = .90) for trustworthiness, and 7.65 (12, N = 1278, p = .81) for confidence.

\# p < .10

* p < .05

** p < .01

Appendix Table 6.6
Total Effects of Demographics, Party Identification, Local TV News Viewing, and Institutional Expertise on Evaluations of the Office of the Presidency

	Sex (M)	Age	Education	Income	Democrat	Republican	Local TV News	Expertise	R^2
Local TV News Viewing	--	(γ).09**	(γ)-.09**	(γ).05#	(γ)-.09**	--			.03
	--	--	--	--	--	--			
	--	.09**	-.09**	.05#	-.09**	--			
Expertise	(γ).09**	(γ).27**	(γ).26**	--	(γ).12**	(γ).09**	--	--	.17
	--	--	--	--	--	--	--	--	
	.09**	.27**	.26**	--	.12**	.09**	--	--	
Global Attitude	(γ)-.06*	(γ).09**	(γ).06*	--	(γ).09**	(γ)-.17**	(β).06*	(β).26**	.16
	.02**	.07**	.06**	.00	.03**	.02**	--	--	
	-.04	.17**	.12**	.00	.11**	-.15**	.06*	.26**	
Trust-worthiness	(γ)-.05#	(γ).11**	--	--	(γ).07*	(γ)-.17**	(β).06*	(β).19**	.11
	.02**	.06*	.05**	.00	.02*	.02**	--	--	
	-.03	.17**	.05**	.00	.09**	-.15**	.06*	.19*	
Confidence	--	--	(γ).09**	--	(γ).12**	(γ)-.12**	(β).07**	(β).15**	.08
	.01**	.05**	.03**	.00	.01#	.01**	--	--	
	.01**	.05**	.12**	.00	.13**	-.10**	.07**	.15**	

Notes: This appendix table condenses three models, each of which includes sociodemographics, party identification, media use, institutional expertise, and *one* of three criterion variables (shown in the last three rows: global attitude, trustworthiness, or confidence). Entries in each cell are standardized direct, indirect, and total effects, respectively. Direct effects and indirect effects may not add up to total effects due to rounding. The χ^2 statistic for the global attitude model is 6.64 (5, N = 1278, p = .25), 6.26 (6, N = 1278, p = .39) for trustworthiness, and 7.75 (7, N = 1278, p = .37) for confidence.

\# p < .10
* p < .05
** p < .01

Appendix Table 6.7

Effects of Demographics, Party Identification, Local TV News Viewing and Institutional Expertise on Evaluations of Congress

	Sex (M)	Age	Education	Income	Democrat	Republican	Local TV News	Expertise	R²
Local TV News Viewing	--	(γ) .09**	(γ) -.09**	(γ) -.05#	(γ) -.09**	--			.03
	--	--	--	--	--	--			
	--	.09*	-.09*	-.05#	-.09*	--			
Expertise	(γ) .14**	(γ) .23**	(γ) .27**	--	(γ) .07*	(γ) .08**	--		.16
	--	--	--	--	--	--	--		
	.14**	.23**	.27**	--	.07*	.08**	--		
Global Attitude	(γ) -.07*	(γ) -.10**	(γ) -.07*	(γ) -.05#	--	(γ) .08**	--	(β) .31**	.09
	.04**	.07**	.08**	--	.02*	.03**	--	--	
	-.02	-.03	.02	-.05#	.02*	.11**	--	.31**	
Trust-worthiness	.03**	--	(γ) -.06#	--	--	(γ) .06*	(β) .05#	(β) .18**	.04
	-.03**	.05**	.04**	.00	.01	.02**	--	--	
		.05**	-.01	.00	.01	.08**	.05#	.18**	
Confidence	(γ) -.07**	(γ) -.07**	--	--	--	(γ) .12**	(β) .05#	(β) .18**	.05
	.02**	.05*	.04**	.00	.01	.01**	--	--	
	-.05#	-.02	.04**	.00	.01	.13**	.05#	.18**	

Notes: This appendix table condenses three models, each of which includes sociodemographics, party identification, media use, institutional expertise, and *one* of three criterion variables (shown in the last three rows: global attitude, trustworthiness, or confidence). Entries in each cell are standardized direct, indirect, and total effects, respectively. Direct effects and indirect effects may not add up to total effects due to rounding. The χ² statistic for the global attitude model is 6.47 (6, N = 1278, p = .37), 11.21 (8, N = 1278, p = .19) for trustworthiness, and 9.96 (7, N = 1278, p = .21) for confidence.

\# p < .10
* p < .05
** p < .01

Appendix Table 6.8

Effects of Demographics, Party Identification, Local TV News Viewing, and Institutional Expertise on Evaluations of the Court System

	Sex (M)	Age	Education	Income	Democrat	Republican	Local TV News	Expertise	R^2
Local TV News Viewing	—	$(\gamma).10^{**}$	$(\gamma)-.08^{**}$	—	—	$(\gamma).07^{**}$	—		.02
	—	—	—	—	—	—	—		
	—	$.10^{**}$	$-.08^{**}$	—	—	$.07^{**}$	—		
Expertise	—	$(\gamma).07^{*}$	$(\gamma).10^{**}$	$(\gamma).08^{**}$	—	—	—		.03
	—	—	—	—	—	—	—		
	—	$.07^{*}$	$.10^{**}$	$.08^{**}$	—	—	—		
Global Attitude	—	—	$(\gamma).09^{**}$	$(\gamma).10^{**}$	$(\gamma).08^{**}$	—	—	$(\beta).13^{**}$	.06
	—	$.01^{*}$	$.01^{*}$	$.01^{*}$	—	—	—	—	
	—	$.01^{*}$	$.10^{**}$	$.11^{**}$	$.08^{**}$	—	—	$.13^{**}$	
Trust-worthiness	—	$(\gamma).06^{*}$	$(\gamma).11^{**}$	$(\gamma).10^{**}$	—	—	—	$(\beta).07^{**}$	.04
	—	$.01\#$	$.01^{*}$	$.01\#$	—	—	—	—	
	—	$.06^{*}$	$.12^{**}$	$.11^{**}$	—	—	—	$.07^{**}$	
Confidence	—	—	$(\gamma).13^{**}$	$(\gamma).08^{**}$	$(\gamma).07^{*}$	—	—	$(\beta).06^{*}$	.04
	—	$.00^{*}$	$.01\#$	$.00\#$	—	—	—	—	
	—	$.00^{*}$	$.14^{**}$	$.09^{**}$	$.07^{*}$	—	—	$.06^{*}$	

Notes: This appendix table condenses three models, each of which includes sociodemographics, party identification, media use, institutional expertise, and *one* of three criterion variables (shown in the last three rows: global attitude, trustworthiness, or confidence). Entries in each cell are standardized direct, indirect, and total effects, respectively. Direct effects and indirect effects may not add up to total effects due to rounding. The χ^2 statistic for the global attitude model is 12.42 (11, N = 1278, p = .33), 18.14 (11, N = 1278, p = .08) for trustworthiness, and 10.51 (11, N = 1278, p = .49) for confidence.

N = 1278, p = .49) for confidence.

\# p < .10
* p < .05
** p < .01

131

Appendix Table 6.9
Effects of Demographics, Party Identification, Local TV News Viewing, and Institutional Expertise on Evaluations of the News Media

	Sex (M)	Age	Education	Income	Democrat	Republican	Local TV News	Expertise	R^2
Local TV News Viewing	--	(γ) .09**	(γ) -.09**	(γ) .05#	(γ) -.09**	--			.03
	--	--	--	--	--	--			
	--	.09**	-.09**	.05#	-.09**	--			
Expertise	--	(γ) .16**	(γ) .14**	--	--	--	(β) .05#		.05
	--	.01#	.00#	.00	.00#	--	--		
	--	.16**	.14**	.00	.00#	--	.05#		
Global Attitude	(γ) -.05*	--	(γ) -.11**	--	(γ) .07*	(γ) -.07*	(β) .09**	(β) .34**	.15
	--	.06**	.04**	.01	-.01*	--	.02#	--	
	-.05*	.06**	-.08**	.01	.06*	-.07*	.11**	.34**	
Trustworthiness	--	(γ) .09**	(γ) -.09**	--	(γ) .11**	--	(β) .08**	(β) .24**	.10
	--	.05**	.03**	.00	-.01*	--	.01#	--	
	--	.13**	-.07*	.00	.10**	--	.10**	.24**	
Confidence	--	--	(γ) -.08**	--	(γ) .10**	--	(β) .08**	(β) .23**	.07
	--	.05**	.02**	.00	-.01*	--	.01#	--	
	--	.05**	-.06*	.00	.09**	--	.10**	.23**	

Notes: This appendix table condenses three models, each of which includes sociodemographics, party identification, media use, institutional expertise, and *one* of three criterion variables (shown in the last three rows: global attitude, trustworthiness, or confidence). Entries in each cell are standardized direct, indirect, and total effects, respectively. Direct effects and indirect effects may not add up to total effects due to rounding. The χ^2 statistic for the global attitude model is 7.45 (8, N = 1278, p = .49), 8.61 (9, N = 1278, p = .47) for trustworthiness, and 8.76 (10, N = 1278, p = .56) for confidence.

\# p < .10
* p < .05
** p < .01

Appendix Table 6.10
Effects of Demographics, Party Identification, Local TV News Viewing, and Institutional Expertise on Evaluations of the Public School System

	Sex (M)	Age	Education	Income	Democrat	Republican	Local TV News	Expertise	R²
Local TV News Viewing	(γ) --	(γ) .09**	(γ) -.09**	(γ) -.05#	(γ) -.09**	--			.03
	--	--	--	--	--	--			
	--	.13*	.07*	.11*	--	--			
Expertise	(γ) -.09**	(γ) .06*	(γ) .15**	(γ) .10**	--	--	(β) .05#		.05
	--	.00#	--	.00	.00	--	--		
	-.09**	.06*	.14**	.10**	.00	--	.05#		
Global Attitude	(γ) -.06*	--	--	--	(γ) .07*	(γ) -.09**	(β) .08**	(β) .28**	.11
	-.02**	.02**	.03**	.03**	-.01*	--	.01#	--	
	-.09**	.02**	.03**	.03**	.06*	-.09*	.09**	.28**	
Trust-worthiness	--	--	--	--	(γ) .07*	(γ) -.06#	(β) .06*	(β) .22**	.07
	-.02**	.02**	.03**	.03**	-.01*	--	.01#	--	
	-.02**	.02**	.03**	.03**	.06#	-.06#	.08**	.22**	
Confidence	--	--	(γ) .05#	--	(γ) .11**	--	(β) .10**	(β) .22**	.07
	-.02**	.02**	.03*	.02**	-.01*	--	.01#	--	
	-.02**	.02**	.03*	.02**	.10*	--	.11*	.22**	

Notes: This appendix table condenses three models, each of which includes sociodemographics, party identification, media use, institutional expertise, and *one* of three criterion variables (shown in the last three rows: global attitude, trustworthiness, or confidence). Entries in each cell are standardized direct, indirect, and total effects, respectively. Direct effects and indirect effects may not add up to total effects due to rounding. The χ² statistic for the global attitude model is 4.68 (7, N = 1278, p = .70), 7.02 (8, N = 1278, p = .53) for trustworthiness, and 7.61 (8, N = 1278, p = .47) for confidence.

# p < .10
* p < .05
** p < .01

133

## Chapter 7

The Effects of Television Programming

Television has become an unavoidable and unremitting factor in shaping what we are and what we will become.
Communications scholar George Comstock (1980, p. 123)

You don't change anyone's mind with these jokes. All you do is reinforce what they already believe.
Late night comic Jay Leno (in Retter, 1998, p. 269)

Once limited to newspapers, radio, and television news, Americans today find themselves faced with a multitude of sources from which to glean information about political affairs. No longer does the average American rely solely on radio news updates or wait until the morning edition of his local newspaper arrives. Nor does he have to sit down to watch the evening news in order to learn of the day's major events. Rather, citizens today have round-the-clock access to political affairs content, exemplified by the Cable News Network (CNN), which offers continuous news on both television and the Internet for viewers who seek such information. For the less politically engaged, mediated information about public affairs may come through different outlets, but it comes through nonetheless. Individuals who do not regularly watch the evening news can turn to *The Late Show with David Letterman* or *The Tonight Show* and still get a sense of what has transpired recently in Washington. Between the politically involved at one extreme and the politically apathetic at the other lies the vast proportion of citizens who care about *some* aspects of politics *some of the time*. Many of these citizens gravitate more toward television shows like *Roseanne* and *Cops* than network television news or other traditional news sources (Kurtz, 1999).

The fact remains that mediated information concerning our democratic institutions comes from a host of communication sources. In this chapter, we examine three nontraditional sources of political information: television news magazines, television entertainment talk shows, and prime-time programming.

NONTRADITIONAL MEDIA

The term "nontraditional" has been used to refer to a number of different media sources, ranging from entertainment talk shows (Meyer, 1993) to televised political talk shows (Chaffee, Zhao & Leshner, 1994; McLeod et al., 1996; Newhagen, 1994) to television tabloids (Weaver, 1994). We use the term as it relates to the role these media outlets play in imparting political information; these communication sources are nontraditional in the sense that only recently have politicians turned to them as vehicles for conveying political messages to citizens. It was during the 1992 presidential election campaign that candidates turned not only to newspaper and television news reporters, but also to nontraditional media: Ross Perot announced his candidacy for presidency on CNN's *Larry King Live,* and Bill Clinton played the saxophone on MTV in his bid to appeal to a larger, younger audience. The World Wide Web, as a nontraditional media source, already has been implicated in the 2000 presidential election, with publisher Steve Forbes announcing his candidacy on his own Web site (Swartz, 1999). Use of these nontraditional media clearly allows candidates to reach potentially larger audiences but to what effect?

Documented research on the political impact of these nontraditional media on public confidence in institutions is scarce, due in part to the novelty of these media, as well as a greater interest in primarily social effects. Research on televised talk shows is grounded in critical and cultural perspectives, and daytime talk shows, because of their sensational nature, have been examined in conjunction with audience analysis (e.g., Frisby, 1998; Livingstone, 1994), general literary analyses, and analyses of guest pathology (Greenberg et al., 1996). But examinations of the political effects of these media are virtually nonexistent.

Television News Magazines

When *60 Minutes* debuted on September 24, 1968, it featured stories and a style that would become its trademark. Americans at home watched Richard Nixon and Hubert Humphrey in their hotel rooms as they were nominated for president by their respective parties. They watched a segment dealing with the tensions between average citizens and police departments. Viewers also were treated to Art Buchwald discussing how journalists often use one another's columns as a measure of public opinion (Campbell, 1991). In its first broadcast, *60 Minutes* offered its viewers a glimpse at not only two politicians vying for the presidency but also two other American institutions—the police and the mass media.

Little did *60 Minutes* executive producer Don Hewitt know three decades ago that his brainchild would spawn dozens of similar television news magazines—programs that would employ investigative reporting, interviews, and exposés to present viewers with the "inside story" on current political, social, and economic goings-on. Today, *60 Minutes* has a baby brother, *60 Minutes II*, and the two are joined by another CBS offering, *48 Hours*. *Dateline NBC* airs several times a week, as does ABC's *20/20*. In these shows, serious affairs are presented narratively and accessibly to the average citizen. Contemporary television news magazines have adopted a version of the *60 Minutes* prototype.

With their "undercover" investigative reporting techniques, television news magazines very well may plant in viewers' minds seeds of distrust or cynicism. In 1992, Americans certainly reacted when they learned that, in a segment on problem trucks, *Dateline NBC* had rigged a General Motors truck to explode. After the incident, Rick Kaplan, executive producer of ABC's *PrimeTime Live*, a television news magazine specializing in consumer affairs stories, commented: "We used to have one terrific argument in our favor . . . that we are the networks, with established, responsible news programs. I fear [*Dateline*] may have blurred those lines" (Donlon, 1993, p. 1D). *Dateline*'s actions essentially gave viewers yet another reason not to trust the news media. However, as Mark Lorando (1995) reported, "A funny thing happened on the way to newsmagazine hell" (p. T7). In 1995, *Dateline* was the only show of this genre to fare well in the ratings. Television critics have suggested that the decline in viewership of television news magazines could be attributed not only to the steady diet of O. J. Simpson coverage, but also to the television networks' flirting with tabloid-style journalism, causing the viewing public to suffer *"a loss of trust in the validity of stories broadcast on some of the shows"* (McFarlin, 1995, p. C1, emphasis added).

News Magazines' Effects on Perceptions

We have no data linking individual viewing of *Dateline* in November 1992 to trust in the media. But our survey data showed viewing of television news magazines linked to demographic variables. As noted in Table 7.1, female and older respondents were more likely to watch programs like *60 Minutes*, *20/20*, and *Dateline*. The average for watching this

Table 7.1
Predicting Viewership of Television News Magazine Shows

	β	s.e. (β)
Sex (Male)	-.630	(.303)*
Age	.036	(.009)**
Education	-.022	(.098)
Income	.118	(.110)
Democrat	-.270	(.421)
Republican	-.242	(.466)

Note: Entries are coefficients from ordinary least squares regression with standard errors in parentheses.
* p < .05
** p < .01

Figure 7.1
Effects of Watching TV News Magazines on Evaluations of the News Media

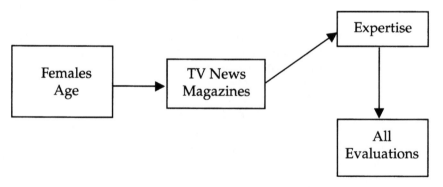

type of show stood at 4.26 out of 10, closer to print news magazines (at 3.94) than to local news, network news, or newspapers (all above 6.0).

In addition, we found viewing had an effect on perceptions of the news media. As Figure 7.1 and Appendix Table 7.4 show, watching television news magazines led to greater perceived expertise about the news media, which led to more favorable evaluations of the press. Thus, the effect of watching this particular type of program had an indirect effect on evaluations, and a positive one at that. Viewing did not have an effect on how audience members perceived any of the other institutions (see Appendix Tables 7.1 to 7.3, 7.5).

Television Entertainment Talk Shows

Talk shows run the gamut from the sensational *Jerry Springer* to the motivational *Oprah Winfrey Show* to the largely entertainment-based late-night talk shows such as *The Tonight Show* and *Late Night with David Letterman*. Shows that tend to gravitate toward the sensational—including the *Ricki Lake Show*, which has "[brought] the carnival sideshow to America's living rooms" (Oliver, 1995, p. 52)—announce to viewers that "the emotional circus really has come to town" (Zoglin, 1995, p. 77). While the content of these shows varies from day to day and from host to host, there is a general tendency toward themes dominated by sexuality and deviance and punctuated by intense moments of self-disclosure by talk show guests (Abt & Seesholtz, 1994; Greenberg et al., 1996). Obviously the content of this particular type of talk show contains fewer references to democratic institutions.

Democratic institutions, on the other hand, provide considerable fodder for monologues delivered by late-night talk show hosts such as David Letterman and Jay Leno. The *Media Monitor* (1996) logged all jokes about public affairs and political personalities from the monologues of Letterman, Leno, and Conan O'Brien in 1995. Results showed that Bill Clinton was the most popular target of late night humor and that the only other politicians ridiculed were Speaker of the House Newt Gingrich, Bob Dole, and Senator Bob Packwood—all Republicans. The *Media Monitor* cites a joke from the *Tonight Show*: "President Clinton said Newt Gingrich is not going to blackmail him with legislation. Polaroids, maybe, but not legislation" (p. 6). On February 9, 1995, David Letterman presented this Top Ten List:

Top Ten Signs Newt Gingrich Has Gone Mad with Power

10. Has beaten several Democrats to death with his gavel
 9. Now claiming he invented the Fig Newton
 8. Sending bus full of Cub Scouts to conquer Mexico
 7. U.S. map on office wall reads "Newt York" & "Newt Jersey"
 6. Insists Ed Sullivan Theater be kept freezing cold—and there's not a damn thing we can do about it!
 5. Has written new book: "Newt Gingrich's Contract with My Pants"
 4. Begins every session of Congress by singing "I Got You Babe" with Sonny Bono
 3. Actually thinks he's got as much power as Hillary
 2. He's been sportin' one of them Ito beards
 1. Two words: The crown

Our content analyses showed that, in 1995, late-night talk shows tended to be more negative toward the president and the public school

Table 7.2
Predicting Viewership of Entertainment Talk Shows

	β	s.e. (β)
Sex (Male)	-.357	(.138)**
Age	-.015	(.004)**
Education	-.303	(.046)**
Income	-.128	(.051)*
Democrat	.079	(.157)
Republican	.106	(.183)

Note: Entries are coefficients from ordinary least squares regression with standard errors in parentheses.
* p < .05
** p < .01

Figure 7.2
Effects of Watching TV Entertainment Talk Shows on Evaluations of the Presidency and Congress

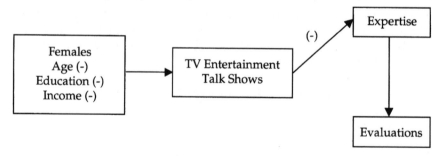

system than any of the traditional news media—newspapers, network news, and local news. Also in 1995, they were significantly more negative than other communication modalities toward Congress (or its members). But do these entertainment talk shows have any effect on confidence in our democratic institutions?

Talk Shows' Effects on Evaluations

To begin with, viewers of entertainment talk shows tended to be female (β = −.07), younger (β = −.10), with lower levels of formal schooling (β = −.19), and lower incomes (β = −.07, see Table 7.2).

Figure 7.3
**Effects of Watching TV Entertainment Talk Shows on Evaluations of the
Court System**

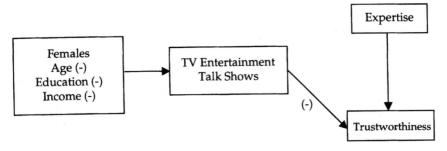

Note: Direct negative effect shown is marginally significant.

The Office of the Presidency. As reflected in Figure 7.2, watching entertainment talk shows had no direct effect on how viewers evaluated the office of the presidency. Levels of expertise were positively related to all evaluations of the presidency but watching this particular genre of programming *lowered* viewers' levels of expertise. Thus viewing had only an indirect effect on evaluations. Appendix Table 7.6 indicates that the indirect effects were small but significant ($-.01$ for global attitude and trustworthiness).

Congress. Effects of viewing on evaluations of Congress were similar to those for the executive branch (see Figure 7.2). Only an indirect effect of viewing emerged. Watching entertainment talk shows had a negative effect on expertise in Congress, but expertise itself enhanced all evaluations. Thus, as shown in Appendix Table 7.7, the indirect effects were consistently negative ($-.02$ for global attitude, and $-.01$ for trustworthiness and confidence).

Court System. Viewers' belief in the trustworthiness of the court system was the only criterion variable that was influenced directly (though of marginal significance) as a function of viewing entertainment talk shows (see Figure 7.3). Trust in the court system was negatively affected by talk shows ($\beta = -.06$, shown in Appendix Table 7.8), but positively by how much one knew about, was interested in, and was aware of the courts ($\beta = .08$). However, watching entertainment talk shows did not affect expertise in the courts.

News Media. In stark contrast to the other four democratic institutions of interest, the news media was the only one to benefit from content presented in entertainment talk shows. Watching these talk shows exerted a direct positive effect on the three evaluations of the news media (see Figure 7.4). The coefficients were somewhat similar, as noted in Appendix Table 7.4 ($\beta = .12$ for global attitude, $\beta = .10$ for trustworthiness,

Figure 7.4
Effects of Watching TV Entertainment Talk Shows on Evaluations of the News Media

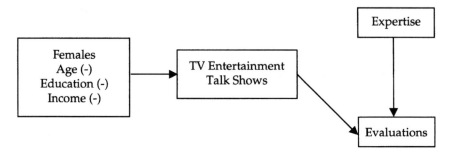

and β = .08 for confidence). However, the corresponding coefficients reflecting the impact of expertise on evaluations of the news media were two to three times greater and watching entertainment talk shows did not affect expertise.

Public School System. Our data indicate no effect of watching entertainment talk shows on how viewers felt about the public school system (see Appendix Table 7.10). This is despite the negativity found in our content analyses, shown in Chapter 4.

Prime-time Programming and the Federal Government

Because our goal in this study is to determine the degree to which confidence in democratic institutions was a function of the use of traditional and nontraditional media by individuals, we have concerned ourselves with newspapers, television news programs, television talk shows, print and broadcast news magazines, and political talk radio. In a related study, we had the opportunity to examine the extent to which people watched various types of prime-time programming. This particular study did not measure people's confidence of different democratic institutions; rather, it looked at their attitudes toward various branches of the federal government.

It is clear that the erosion of confidence in the federal government is part of a broader trend of reduced confidence in democratic institutions. It is also clear that public "disenchantment" extends to "all things federal," including federal law enforcement and regulatory functions (Hull et al., 1995, p. 57). A 1995 Luntz poll reported that, in the aftermath of the Waco and Ruby Ridge incidents, 59 percent of American adults claimed to have "lost respect for federal law enforcement," and House Majority Whip Tom DeLay, in a speech on the floor of Congress, referred to Environmental Protection Agency (EPA) officials as "Gestapo" (Weisberg, 1996, p. 36).

Are these perceptions of the federal government shaped by watching prime-time programming? We believe that they are, to some extent. Despite a drop in audience share due in part to the proliferation of cable networks (Auletta, 1991), prime-time network programs are so pervasive that they "constitute a potentially powerful source of shared images" for people (Pfau et al., 1995a, p. 308). They communicate through stories, influencing much of what we know or think we know (Morgan & Shanahan, 1997; Signorielli, 1987). Television's stories communicate values about institutions and, through repetition over time, prime-time network series exert an influence on people's perceptions of reality (Gitlin, 1977).

Because prime-time programming commands a sizable viewing audience and because these programs communicate values, prime-time series possess the potential to influence public perceptions about institutions. Richard Heffner calls prime time television "profoundly influential" because of the values it portrays (Chesebro & Hamsher, 1976, p. 7).

Heavier overall viewing of prime-time programming *may*, in fact, cultivate negative perceptions of the federal government. In recent years, prime-time program depictions of the federal government have grown increasingly negative. S. Robert Lichter, Linda Lichter, and Stanley Rothman (1994) claim that prime-time characterizations of corrupt government officials have increased in recent years. They conclude: "A majority of politicians wear black hats . . . The tube takes a dim view of the whole political process" (p. 411). This led Lawrence Grossman (1995) and others to argue that television promotes public cynicism toward government.

However, it is unreasonable to assume that all prime-time content genres are comparable in the quantity or tone of their depictions of the federal government. Programming genres vary tremendously, from crime dramas and situation comedies to science fiction (Rose, 1985). Depictions of the federal government in modern crime dramas continue to cultivate positive perceptions of the national government, especially of its law enforcement arm, including the Federal Bureau of Investigation, the Bureau of Firearms, Tobacco, and Alcohol, and other agencies. Clearly, this was the case of the crime drama *The FBI*, which aired from the mid-1960s to the mid-1970s. The program glamorized the FBI and functioned as a public relations vehicle for the agency, portraying it as "infallible" and "omniscient" (Gibson, 1997, p. 24). Today's resurgence in prime-time crime dramas (Murphy, 1993–94), such as *NYPD Blue*, *Feds*, *Law and Order*, *EZ Streets*, and others, continue to depict America's law enforcement institutions in a positive light (Oliver & Armstrong, 1995); this includes the law enforcement arm of the federal government (Nelson, 1989).

By contrast, programming genres such as science fiction are more apt to portray the federal government in a much different light. Contemporary science fiction television shows, such as *The X-Files*, feature heroic agents of the FBI who find themselves "thwarted" in their investigations by a mysterious and powerful underworld of government officials who will stop at nothing to conceal and manipulate the truth. The central plot of *The X-Files* centers on agents Fox Mulder and Dana Scully as they risk everything in pursuit of this truth. Their investigations typically lead them to discover conspiracies in the military, the CIA, and the FBI. What *The X-Files* communicates is that the "there is no end to the possible military and political schemes spawned in the seats of power" (Rapping, 1995, p. 36). Contemporary science fiction shows such as *The X-Files* have invited viewers into what Erving Goffman (1973) would characterize as "the back regions" of the federal government, which, though fictional, are sinister in their depictions and therefore cultivate "a deep and abiding distrust of our government" (Rosen, 1997, p. B7).

The Study

To empirically test the relationship between viewing of particular genres of prime-time programming and how people felt about the federal government, we conducted a telephone survey with a probability sample of 318 respondents from Dane County, Wisconsin, from March 10 to April 14, 1997. The study differed from that described in Chapter 3 in two respects.

First, respondents were not asked how they felt about the presidency, Congress, the court system, the news media, and the public school system. Rather, we asked them to evaluate four branches of the federal government; *the executive branch* (the president, vice-president, and cabinet), *the legislative branch* (the House of Representatives and the Senate), *the domestic law enforcement arm* (e.g., Attorney General, Federal Bureau of Investigation, Bureau of Alcohol, Tobacco, and Firearms), and *the regulatory arm* (e.g., Environmental Protection Agency, Federal Trade Commission, Securities and Exchange Commission, National Highway Traffic Safety Administration, Federal Election Commission).

Second, the criterion variables for the four branches of federal government differed somewhat. Respondents were asked to respond to those questions tapping global attitude and confidence in each branch of the federal government (as discussed in Chapter 4). However, they also were asked their perceptions of the *competence* and *character* of each branch. Competence and character were assessed using three semantic differentials developed and refined in previous factor analytic research by James McCroskey and colleagues (e.g., McCroskey, Jenson, & Valencia, 1973). McCroskey's measure focuses on five dimensions of source credibility, of which competence and character typically account for the greatest variance. The measure has been employed extensively in past research on political candidates, political institutions, and political advertising (e.g., Garramone, 1985; Pfau & Burgoon, 1988; Pfau, Diedrich, et al., 1993, 1995). The items used to assess perceptions of competence were unqualified/qualified, unintelligent/intelligent, and incompetent/competent.

Table 7.3
Evaluations of the Executive Branch of the Federal Government

	Global Attitude	Competence	Character	Confidence
Demographics				
Sex	-.17**	-.16**	-.12*	-.11#
Age	.08	.02	.10#	.04
Education	.00	-.02	-.04	.10#
Income	.08	.05	.06	-.02
Democrat	.14*	.16*	.19**	.03
Republican	-.31**	-.26**	-.21**	-.10
R² (%)	21.38**	17.11**	15.92**	4.24#
Expertise	.03	.09	.03	-.00
Incr. R² (%)	.00	.70	.05	.00
Prime-time viewing				
Action adventure	-.02	.00	-.01	.02
Crime	.01	-.00	-.06	.03
Dramas	.10#	.13*	.12*	.02
News magazines	.05	.07	.13*	.10#
Medical shows	.07	.12*	.14*	.07
Sitcoms	.03	.01	-.04	.01
Science fiction	-.01	-.03	-.06	-.01
Incr. R² (%)	1.59	3.17	4.59*	1.27
Total R² (%)	23.04**	20.98**	20.56**	5.51

Note: Entries are standardized coefficients from hierarchical ordinary least squares regression equations. Coefficients for the prime-time viewing block are before-entry betas and control only for demographics and expertise of the executive branch of the federal government.

\# p < .10

* p < .05

** p < .01

Items measuring character included dishonest/honest, unselfish/selfish, and unsympathetic/sympathetic. Cronbach's α for the competence scale were executive branch, .97; legislative branch, .85; law enforcement arm, .92; and regulatory arm, .93. The same reliability coefficients for the character scale were executive branch, .78; legislative branch, .86; law enforcement arm, .89; and regulatory arm, .88.

Prime-Time Programming's Effects on Confidence in the Federal Government

The results emerging from this study indicate an extremely limited influence of prime-time programs on respondents' evaluations of the federal government (see Tables 7.3 to 7.6). Broadly speaking, prime-time viewing had a significant impact on a quarter of the 16 criterion var-

Table 7.4

Evaluations of the Legislative Branch of the Federal Government

	Global Attitude	Competence	Character	Confidence
Demographics				
Sex	-.15**	-.13*	-.11*	-.07
Age	.20**	.14*	.25**	.09
Education	-.01	-.05	-.09	-.05
Income	-.03	-.04	-.01	.10#
Democrat	.03	.06	.09	-.07
Republican	.16*	.12#	.21**	-.06
R^2 (%)	8.85**	5.50*	12.34**	4.15#
Expertise	.07	.06	.04	-.07
Incr. R^2 (%)	.41	.34	.14	.44
Prime-time viewing				
Action adventure	-.03	-.06	-.13*	.01
Crime	-.06	-.06	-.06	.05
Dramas	-.07	.06	.05	.03
News magazines	-.04	-.04	-.02	.06
Medical shows	-.05	-.04	-.04	.04
Sitcoms	-.00	-.01	.06	-.04
Science fiction	-.03	-.04	.00	.12#
Incr. R^2 (%)	1.26	1.22	3.14	2.52
Total R^2 (%)	10.51**	7.05	15.62**	7.11

Note: Entries are standardized coefficients from hierarchical ordinary least squares regression equations. Coefficients for the prime-time viewing block are before-entry betas and control only for demographics and expertise of the legislative branch of the federal government.
# $p < .10$
* $p < .05$
** $p < .01$

iables studied. Three of these four criterion variables were evaluations of the regulatory arm—global attitude, competence, and character. The other criterion variable was the perceived character of the executive branch. All these broad effects were positive.

Above that, the effects of specific prime-time genres were nearly all positive. Watching crime shows such as *NYPD Blue* and *Law & Order* enhanced perceptions of the character of the executive branch, as did watching general dramas such as *Party of Five* and *Dr. Quinn, Medicine Woman*, and medical shows such as *Chicago Hope* and *ER*.

Situation comedy viewing exerted a positive impact consistently on evaluations of the regulatory arm: The more sitcoms one viewed, the more favorable the evaluations tended to be. The same trend was found for watching prime-time dramas, but results for this particular genre reached only levels of marginal significance ($p < .10$). Crime show view-

Table 7.5
Evaluations of the Law Enforcement Arm of the Federal Government

	Global Attitude	Competence	Character	Confidence
Demographics				
Sex	-.13*	-.09	-.10	-.07
Age	.14*	.08	.25**	.11#
Education	.08	.06	.07	.12*
Income	-.03	-.08	-.10#	.11#
Democrat	.07	.08	.09	.02
Republican	.01	.01	.06	-.02
R² (%)	4.94*	2.85	7.81**	5.03*
Expertise	.28**	.29**	.28**	.17**
Incr. R² (%)	7.75**	8.39**	7.45**	2.75**
Prime-time viewing				
Action adventure	.03	.02	-.01	-.03
Crime	-.01	.05	.03	.06
Dramas	.02	.01	.00	-.01
News magazines	.07	.04	.03	.08
Medical shows	.07	.08	.06	.07
Sitcoms	.01	.02	.02	-.01
Science fiction	.00	.01	-.01	.08
Incr. R² (%)	.69	.85	.59	1.37
Total R² (%)	13.38**	12.09**	15.84**	9.16*

Note: Entries are standardized coefficients from hierarchical ordinary least squares regression equations. Coefficients for the prime-time viewing block are before-entry betas and control only for demographics and expertise of the law enforcement arm of the federal government.

\# p < .10
* p < .05
** p < .01

ing also worked in favor of how this branch was perceived: Greater viewing led to more favorable evaluations, though to varying degrees of statistical significance. The only negative impact of viewing prime-time programming came from watching action adventure shows. The more one watched shows such as *The Pretender* or *Lois and Clark*, the less favorably they considered the regulatory arm.

OVERVIEW OF EFFECTS

We began this chapter with a discussion of how television programming other than network or local news could have an impact on public confidence in democratic institutions. Our data indicate that television news magazines and talk shows, which have proliferated over the last decade or so, have mixed effects.

Table 7.6
Evaluations of the Regulatory Arm of the Federal Government

	Global Attitude	Competence	Character	Confidence
Demographics				
Sex	-.09	-.10	-.06	-.12#
Age	.09	.07	.14*	.04
Education	.07	.05	.06	-.02
Income	.08	.06	.02	.13*
Democrat	.12#	.16*	.17*	-.02
Republican	.04	.06	.06	.01
R^2 (%)	4.26#	4.54*	4.81*	3.97#
Expertise	.23**	.16**	.15*	-.03
Incr. R^2 (%)	4.94**	2.31**	2.08*	.07
Prime-time viewing				
Action adventure	-.09	-.12*	-.08	-.05
Crime	.08	.11#	.12*	-.01
Dramas	.10#	.10#	.11#	.01
News magazines	.03	-.01	-.01	.02
Medical shows	.03	.00	-.00	.00
Sitcoms	.17**	.13*	.14*	.02
Science fiction	-.07	-.07	-.08	.00
Incr. R^2 (%)	5.41*	5.68*	5.57*	.46
Total R^2 (%)	14.61**	12.53**	12.46**	4.50

Note: Entries are standardized coefficients from hierarchical ordinary least squares regression equations. Coefficients for the prime-time viewing block are before-entry betas and control only for demographics and expertise of the regulatory arm of the federal government.
\# $p < .10$
* $p < .05$
** $p < .01$

As Table 7.7 shows, watching television news magazines such as *60 Minutes* and *Dateline* ultimately affects only one democratic institution—the news media, and this effect was indirect, working through expertise. In stark contrast, watching entertainment talk shows had a *direct positive effect* on confidence in the news media (see Table 7.8). There were *consistent negative effects* of this particular genre on how people viewed the presidency and Congress. The effects shown earlier in Tables 7.3 to 7.6 indicate that prime-time television genres may be telling powerful stories to their viewers, but these stories have little bearing on how viewers feel about the federal government.

Of the nontraditional media sources, only talk shows appeared to have a detrimental impact on confidence in institutions. In Chapter 8, we discuss how political talk radio has transformed American politics and potentially the views of its listeners.

Table 7.7
Effects of Watching Television News Magazines on Evaluations of Democratic Institutions: Summary Table

	Presidency	Congress	Court System	News Media	Public Schools
Global Attitude	None	None	None	Indirect effect only	None
Trustworthiness	None	None	None	Indirect effect only	None
Confidence	None	None	None	Indirect effect only	None

Note: Effects are noted based on probability levels set at p = .05.

Table 7.8
Effects of Watching Entertainment Talk Shows on Evaluations of Democratic Institutions: Summary Table

	Presidency	Congress	Court System	News Media	Public Schools
Global Attitude	Indirect effect only (negative)	Indirect effect only (negative)	None	Direct effect only	None
Trustworthiness	Indirect effect only (negative)	Indirect effect only (negative)	None	Direct effect only	None
Confidence	Indirect effect only	Indirect effect only (negative)	Indirect effect only	Direct effect only	None

Note: Effects are noted based on probability levels set at p = .05.

Appendix Table 7.1

Effects of Demographics, Party Identification, Television News Magazine Viewing, and Institutional Expertise on Evaluations of the Office of the Presidency

	Sex (M)	Age	Education	Income	Democrat	Republican	TV News Magazines	Expertise	R²
TV News Magazine Viewing	--	--	--	--	--	--	--		
	--	--	--	--	--	--	--		
	--	--	--	--	--	--	--		
Expertise	--	(γ).26**	(γ).27**	--	--	--	--		.15
	--	-	-	--	--	--	--		
	--	.26**	.27*	--	--	--	--		
Global Attitude	--	(γ).10*	-	--	(γ).10#	(γ)-.17**	--	(β).26**	.15
	--	.07**	.07**	--	-	-	--	-	
	--	.17**	.07**	--	.10#	-.17**	--	.26**	
Trustworthiness	--	(γ).13*	-	--	--	(γ)-.20**	--	(β).19**	.11
	-	.05**	.05**	--	--	-	--	-	
	.02	.18**	.05**	--	--	-.20**	--	.19**	
Confidence	--	.04*	-	--	(γ).12*	(γ)-.12*	--	(β).17**	.07
	--	-	.05*	--	-	-	--	-	
	--	.04*	.05*	--	.12*	-.12*	--	.17**	

Notes: This appendix table condenses three models, each of which includes sociodemographics, party identification, media use, institutional expertise, and *one* of three criterion variables (shown in the last three rows: global attitude, trustworthiness, or confidence). Entries in each cell are standardized direct, indirect, and total effects, respectively. Direct effects and indirect effects may not add up to total effects due to rounding. The χ^2 statistic for the global attitude model is 15.21 (15, N = 365, p = .44), 15.33 (16, N = 365, p = .50) for trustworthiness, and 16.19 (16, N = 365, p = .44) for confidence.

\# p < .10
* p < .05
** p < .01

Appendix Table 7.2

Effects of Demographics, Party Identification, Television News Magazine Viewing, and Institutional Expertise on Evaluations of Congress

	Sex (M)	Age	Education	Income	Democrat	Republican	TV News Magazines	Expertise	R^2
TV News Magazine Viewing	--	--	--	--	--	--	--		
	--	--	--	--	--	--	--		
	--	--	--	--	--	--	--		
Expertise	(γ) .14**	(γ) .23**	(γ) .27**	--	--	--	--		.15
	--	--	--	--	--	--	--		
	.14**	.23**	.27**	--	--	--	--		
Global Attitude	--	--	--	--	--	(γ) .08#	--	(β) .27**	.08
	.04*	.06**	.07**	--	--	--	--	--	
	.04*	.06**	.07**	--	--	.08#	--	.27**	
Trustworthiness	--	--	--	--	--	--	--	(β) .17**	.03
	.02*	.04**	.05**	--	--	--	--	--	
	.02*	.04**	.05**	--	--	--	--	.17**	
Confidence	--	--	--	--	--	(γ) .12*	--	(β) .15**	.04
	.02*	.03*	.04*	--	--	--	--	--	
	.02*	.03*	.04*	--	--	.12*	--	.15**	

Notes: This appendix table condenses three models, each of which includes sociodemographics, party identification, media use, institutional expertise, and *one* of three criterion variables (shown in the last three rows: global attitude, trustworthiness, or confidence). Entries in each cell are standardized direct, indirect, and total effects, respectively. Direct effects and indirect effects may not add up to total effects due to rounding. The χ^2 statistic for the global attitude model is 12.58 (16, N = 365, p = .70), 13.02 (17, N = 365, p = .73) for trustworthiness, and 10.85 (16, N = 365, p = .82) for confidence.

\# p < .10

* p < .05

** p < .01

Effects of Demographics, Party Identification, Television News Magazine Viewing, and Institutional Expertise on Evaluations of the Court System

	Sex (M)	Age	Education	Income	Democrat	Republican	TV News Magazines	Expertise	R^2
TV News Magazine Viewing	--	--	--	--	--	--	--	--	
	--	--	--	--	--	--	--	--	
	--	--	--	--	--	--	--	--	
Expertise	--	--	(γ).10#	(γ).10#	--	--	--	--	.02
	--	--	--	--	--	--	--	--	
	--	--	.10#	.10#	--	--	--	--	
Global Attitude	--	--	(γ).09#	(γ).11*	--	--	--	(β).13*	.05
	--	--	.01	.01	--	--	--	--	
	--	--	.11*	.12*	--	--	--	.13*	
Trust-worthiness	--	--	(γ).12*	(γ).12*	--	--	--	--	.04
	--	--	--	--	--	--	--	--	
	--	--	.12*	.12*	--	--	--	--	
Confidence	--	--	(γ).14*	(γ).09#	--	--	--	--	.04
	--	--	--	--	--	--	--	--	
	--	--	.14*	.09#	--	--	--	--	

Notes: This appendix table condenses three models, each of which includes sociodemographics, party identification, media use, institutional expertise, and *one* of three criterion variables (shown in the last three rows: global attitude, trustworthiness, or confidence). Entries in each cell are standardized direct, indirect, and total effects, respectively. Direct effects and indirect effects may not add up to total effects due to rounding. The χ^2 statistic for the global attitude model is 8.40 (16, N = 365, p = .94), 10.69 (17, N = 365, p = .89) for trustworthiness, and 9.06 (17, N = 365, p = .94) for confidence.

# p < .10
* p < .05
** p < .01

Appendix Table 7.4

Effects of Demographics, Party Identification, Television News Magazine Viewing, and Institutional Expertise on Evaluations of the News Media

	Sex (M)	Age	Education	Income	Democrat	Republican	TV News Magazines	Expertise	R^2
TV News Magazine Viewing	--	--	--	--	--	--			
	--	--	--	--	--	--			
	--	--	--	--	--	--			
Expertise	--	(γ) .15**	(γ) .14**	--	--	--	(β) .13**		.06
	--	-	-	--	--	--	-		
	--	.15**	.14**	--	--	--	.13*		
Global Attitude	--	-	(γ) -.13*	--	(γ) .10*	--	-	(β) .35**	.13
	--	.05**	.05**	--	-	--	.05*	-	
	--	.05**	-.08*	--	.10*	--	.05*	.35**	
Trust-worthiness	--	-	(γ) -.10#	--	(γ) .10*	--	-	(β) .26**	.08
	--	.04*	.04*	--	-	--	.04*	-	
	--	.04*	-.06	--	.10*	--	.04*	.26**	
Confidence	--	-	(γ) -.09#	--	(γ) .09#	--	-	(β) .24**	.07
	--	.04*	.03*	--	-	--	.03*	-	
	--	.04*	-.06	--	.09#	--	.03*	.24**	

Notes: This appendix table condenses three models, each of which includes sociodemographics, party identification, media use, institutional expertise, and *one* of three criterion variables (shown in the last three rows: global attitude, trustworthiness, or confidence). Entries in each cell are standardized direct, indirect, and total effects, respectively. Direct effects and indirect effects may not add up to total effects due to rounding. The χ^2 statistic for the global attitude model is 8.06 (15, N = 365, p = .92), 8.58 (15, N = 365, p = .90) for trustworthiness, and 4.55 (15, N = 365, p = 1.00) for confidence.

\# p < .10
* p < .05
** p < .01

Appendix Table 7.5
Effects of Demographics, Party Identification, Television News Magazine Viewing, and Institutional Expertise on Evaluations of the Public School System

	Sex (M)	Age	Education	Income	Democrat	Republican	TV News Magazines	Expertise	R²
TV News Magazine Viewing	--	--	--	--	--	--	--		
	--	--	--	--	--	--	--		
	--	--	--	--	--	--	--		
Expertise	(γ) -.09#	--	(γ) .14**	(γ) .12*	--	--	--		.05
	-	--	-	-	--	--	--		
	-.09#	--	.14**	.12*	--	--	--		
Global Attitude	-.03#	--	.04*	.03*	--	(γ) -.12*	--	(β) .29**	.10
	-	--	-	-	--	-	--	-	
	-.03#	--	.04*	.03*	--	-.12*	--	.29**	
Trust-worthiness	-.02#	--	.03*	.03*	--	(γ) -.08#	--	(β) .24**	.06
	-	--	-	-	--	-	--	-	
	-.02#	--	.03*	.03*	--	-.08#	--	.24**	
Confidence	-.02	--	.03*	.03*	(γ) .10*	--	--	(β) .23**	.06
	-	--	-	-	-	--	--	-	
	-.02	--	.03*	.03*	.10*	--	--	.23**	

Notes: This appendix table condenses three models, each of which includes sociodemographics, party identification, media use, institutional expertise, and *one* of three criterion variables (shown in the last three rows: global attitude, trustworthiness, or confidence). Entries in each cell are standardized direct, indirect, and total effects, respectively. Direct effects and indirect effects may not add up to total effects due to rounding. The χ^2 statistic for the global attitude model is 10.96 (16, N = 365, p = .81), 9.85 (16, N = 365, p = .87) for trustworthiness, and 8.50 (16, N = 365, p = .93) for confidence.

# p < .10
* p < .05
** p < .01

154

Appendix Table 7.6
Effects of Demographics, Party Identification, Entertainment Talk Show Viewing, and Institutional Expertise on Evaluations of the Office of the Presidency

	Sex (M)	Age	Education	Income	Democrat	Republican	Entertainment Talk Shows	Expertise	R²
Entertainment Talk Show Viewing	(γ) -.07*	(γ) -.17**	(γ) -.17**	(γ) .07*	–	–			.08
	–	–	–	–	–	–			
	-.07*	-.17**	-.17**	.07*	–	–			
Expertise	(γ) .09**	(γ) .26**	(γ) .25**	–	(γ) .12**	(γ) .09**	(β) -.05*		.17
	.00	.01#	.01#	.00	–	–	–		
	.09**	.27**	.26**	.00	.12**	.09**	-.05*		
Global Attitude	(γ) -.07*	(γ) .10**	(γ) .05*	–	(γ) .09**	(γ) -.17**	–	(β) .25**	.15
	.02**	.07**	.07**	.00	.03**	.02**	-.01*	–	
	-.04	.17**	.12**	.00	.12**	-.15**	-.01*	.25**	
Trust-worthiness	(γ) -.05#	(γ) .12**	–	–	(γ) .07**	(γ) -.17**	–	(β) .19**	.11
	.02**	.05**	.05**	.00	.02**	.02**	-.01*	–	
	-.03	.17**	.05**	.00	.09**	-.15**	-.01*	.19**	
Confidence	–	–	(γ) .08**	–	(γ) .12**	(γ) -.11**	–	(β) .14**	.08
	.01**	.04**	.04**	.00	.02**	.01**	.02#	–	
	.01**	.04**	.12**	.00	.14**	-.10**	.02#	.14**	

Notes: This appendix table condenses three models, each of which includes sociodemographics, party identification, media use, institutional expertise, and *one* of three criterion variables (shown in the last three rows: global attitude, trustworthiness, or confidence). Entries in each cell are standardized direct, indirect, and total effects, respectively. Direct effects and indirect effects may not add up to total effects due to rounding. The χ^2 statistic for the global attitude model is 2.41 (5, N = 1278, p = .79), 2.25 (6, N = 1278, p = .90) for trustworthiness, and 3.72 (7, N = 1278, p = .81) for confidence.

\# $p < .10$
* $p < .05$
** $p < .01$

Appendix Table 7.7

Effects of Demographics, Party Identification, Entertainment Talk Show Viewing, and Institutional Expertise on Evaluations of Congress

	Sex (M)	Age	Education	Income	Democrat	Republican	Entertainment Talk Shows	Expertise	R^2
Entertainment Talk Show Viewing	(γ) -.07*	(γ) -.17**	(γ) -.17**	(γ) -.07*	--	--			.08
	-	-	-	-	--	--			
	-.07*	-.17**	-.17**	-.07*	--	--			
Expertise	(γ) .14**	(γ) .22**	(γ) .25**	-	(γ) .07*	(γ) .08**	(β) -.08**		.16
	.01#	.01**	.01**	.01#	-	-	-		
	.14**	.23**	.27**	.01#	.07*	.08**	-.08**		
Global Attitude	(γ) -.07*	(γ) -.10**	(γ) -.07*	(γ) .05#	-	(γ) .08**	-	(β) .31**	.10
	.04**	.07**	.08**	.00#	.02*	.03**	-.02**	-	
	-.02	-.03	.02	.05#	.02*	.11**	-.02**	.31**	
Trust-worthiness	-	-	(γ) -.06*	-	-	(γ) .07*	-	(β) .18**	.04
	.03**	.04**	.05**	.00#	.01*	.02**	-.01**	-	
	.03**	.04**	-.01	.00#	.01*	.08**	-.01**	.18**	
Confidence	(γ) -.07**	(γ) -.07*	-	-	-	(γ) .12**	-	(β) .17**	.05
	.02**	.04**	.05**	.00#	.01*	.01**	-.01**	-	
	-.05#	-.03	.05**	.00#	.01*	.14**	-.01**	.17**	

Notes: This appendix table condenses three models, each of which includes sociodemographics, party identification, media use, institutional expertise, and *one* of three criterion variables (shown in the last three rows: global attitude, trustworthiness, or confidence). Entries in each cell are standardized direct, indirect, and total effects, respectively. Direct effects and indirect effects may not add up to total effects due to rounding. The χ^2 statistic for the global attitude model is 3.08 (5, N = 1278, p = .69), 7.12 (8, N = 1278, p = .52) for trustworthiness, and 5.34 (7, N = 1278, p = .62) for confidence.

\# p < .10

* p < .05

** p < .01

Appendix Table 7.8

Effects of Demographics, Party Identification, Entertainment Talk Show Viewing, and Institutional Expertise on Evaluations of the Court System

	Sex (M)	Age	Education	Income	Democrat	Republican	Entertainment Talk Shows	Expertise	R^2
Entertainment Talk Show Viewing	(γ) -.07* -- -.07*	(γ) -.17** -- -.17**	(γ) -.17** -- -.17**	(γ) -.07* -- .07*	-- -- --	-- -- --			.08
Expertise	-- -- --	(γ) .07* -- .07*	(γ) .10** -- .10**	(γ) .08** -- .08**	-- -- --	-- -- --	-- -- --		.03
Global Attitude	-- --	-- .01* .01*	(γ) .09** .01** .10**	(γ) .10** .01* .11**	(γ) .08** -- .08**	-- -- --	-- -- --	(β) .13** -- .13**	.06
Trust-worthiness	-- .00 .00	(γ) .05# .01* .06*	(γ) .10** .02** .12**	(γ) .09** .01* .10**	(γ) .05# -- .05#	-- -- --	(β) -.06# -- -.06#	(β) .08** -- .08**	.05
Confidence	-- -- --	-- .00 .00	(γ) .13** .01# .14**	(γ) .08** .00# .09**	(γ) .07* -- .07*	-- -- --	-- .01 .01	(β) .06* -- .06*	.04

Notes: This appendix table condenses three models, each of which includes sociodemographics, party identification, media use, institutional expertise, and *one* of three criterion variables (shown in the last three rows: global attitude, trustworthiness, or confidence). Entries in each cell are standardized direct, indirect, and total effects, respectively. Direct effects and indirect effects may not add up to total effects due to rounding. The χ^2 statistic for the global attitude model is 6.54 (10, N = 1278, p = .77), 6.48 (8, N = 1278, p = .59) for trustworthiness, and 7.96 (10, N = 1278, p = .63) for confidence.

\# p < .10
* p < .05
** p < .01

Appendix Table 7.9
Effects of Demographics, Party Identification, Entertainment Talk Show Viewing, and Institutional Expertise on Evaluations of the News Media

	Sex (M)	Age	Education	Income	Democrat	Republican	Entertainment Talk Shows	Expertise	R^2
Entertainment Talk Show Viewing	(γ) -.07#	(γ) -.17**	(γ) -.17**	(γ) -.07*	--	--			.08
	-	-	-	-	--	--			
	-.07	-.17**	-.17**	-.07*	--	--			
Expertise	--	(γ) .16**	(γ) .14**	--	--	--	--		.05
	--	-	-	--	--	--	--		
	--	.16*	.14*	--	--	--	--		
Global Attitude	(γ) -.04#	(γ) .07**	(γ) -.10**	-	(γ) .06*	(γ) -.07*	(β) .11**	(β) .34**	.15
	-.01*	.04**	.03*	-.01*	-	-	-	-	
	-.05*	.11**	-.07*	-.01*	.06*	-.07*	.12**	.34**	
Trust-worthiness	-	(γ) .11**	(γ) -.08**	-	(γ) .10**	--	(β) .10**	(β) .24**	.10
	-.01*	.02*	.02#	-.01*	-	--	-	-	
	-.01*	.14**	-.06*	-.01*	.10**	--	.10**	.24**	
Confidence	-	-	(γ) -.08**	-	(γ) .09**	--	(β) .08**	(β) .24**	.07
	-.01#	.03**	.02*	-.01#	-	--	-	-	
	-.01#	.03**	-.06*	.01#	.09**	--	.08**	.24**	

Notes: This appendix table condenses three models, each of which includes sociodemographics, party identification, media use, institutional expertise, and *one* of three criterion variables (shown in the last three rows: global attitude, trustworthiness, or confidence). Entries in each cell are standardized direct, indirect, and total effects, respectively. Direct effects and indirect effects may not add up to total effects due to rounding. The χ^2 statistic for the global attitude model is 3.25 (8, N = 1278, p = .92), 5.93 (10, N = 1278, p = .82) for trustworthiness, and 6.50 (11, N = 1278, p = .84) for confidence.

\# p < .10
* p < .05
** p < .01

Appendix Table 7.10

Effects of Demographics, Party Identification, Entertainment Talk Show Viewing, and Institutional Expertise on Evaluations of the Public School System

	Sex (M)	Age	Education	Income	Democrat	Republican	Entertainment Talk Shows	Expertise	R^2
Entertainment Talk Show Viewing	(γ) -.07*	(γ) -.17**	(γ) -.17*	(γ) -.07*	–	–			.08
	–	–	–	–	–	–			
	–	(γ) -.17**	-.17**	-.07*	–	–			
Expertise	(γ) -.09**	(γ) .06*	(γ) .14**	(γ) .10**	–	–	–		.05
	–	–	–	–	–	–	–		
	-.09**	.06*	.14**	.10**	–	–	–		
Global Attitude	(γ) -.07*	–	–	–	(γ) .06*	(γ) -.09**	–	(β) .28**	.11
	-.02**	.02*	.04**	.03**	–	–	–	–	
	-.09**	.02*	.04**	.03**	.06*	-.09**	–	.28**	
Trust-worthiness	–	–	–	–	(γ) .09**	–	–	(β) .23**	.06
	-.02**	.01*	.03**	.02**	–	–	–	–	
	-.02**	.01*	.03**	.02**	.09**	–	–	.23**	
Confidence	–	–	–	–	(γ) .10**	–	–	(β) .23**	.06
	-.02**	.01*	.03**	.02**	–	–	–	–	
	-.02**	.01*	.03**	.02**	.10**	–	–	.23**	

Notes: This appendix table condenses three models, each of which includes sociodemographics, party identification, media use, institutional expertise, and *one* of three criterion variables (shown in the last three rows: global attitude, trustworthiness, or confidence). Entries in each cell are standardized direct, indirect, and total effects, respectively. Direct effects and indirect effects may not add up to total effects due to rounding. The χ^2 statistic for the global attitude model is 3.72 (9, N = 1278, p = .93), 8.90 (11, N = 1278, p = .63) for trustworthiness, and 8.78 (11, N = 1278, p = .64) for confidence.

# p < .10
* p < .05
** p < .01

159

## Chapter 8

The Effects of Political Talk Radio

The talk that resonates most powerfully in the talk show world is negative talk.

Media reporter Howard Kurtz (1996, p. 365)

I work in the media. My job—whether on radio, TV, or in the publishing field—is to attract as large an audience as possible and maintain it as long as I can.

Political talk radio show host Rush Limbaugh (1993, p. 1)

Of the "new" communication media we described in Chapter 4, political talk radio has generated the most attention as a force in shaping public attitudes. Political talk radio's sudden ascendancy to the national scene has been accompanied by much controversy.

The medium has been vilified by some for fostering cynicism in democratic institutions, largely as the result of conservative hosts' aggressive and unrelenting attacks on President Bill Clinton. In 1993 in the wake of the "Nannygate" scandal, Zoe Baird withdrew as Clinton's nominee for attorney general after opposition from talk show hosts and callers reached Washington (Jost, 1994). In 1994, Rush Limbaugh reinterpreted the suicide of White House lawyer Vincent Foster as a murder, asserting that the body had been moved to an apartment owned by Hillary Clinton (Kurtz, 1996). More recently, the "Zippergate" sex scandal has given hosts cause for revelry, with G. Gordon Liddy joking that President Clinton "sits in the Oral Office" (Henneberger, 1998, p. A18). However, talk radio has also been praised as a forum for ordinary citizens, in which the voices of "the little guy" are heard (Munson, 1993).

Fear of talk radio's impact is perhaps best illustrated by Clinton's reaction following the 1995 bombing of the Oklahoma City federal building. Clinton charged talk radio hosts with fueling antigovernment sentiment and giving listeners the impression that violence was an acceptable means of venting their frustrations.

Concern over talk radio's negative influence is directed mainly at conservative hosts such as Rush Limbaugh, G. Gordon Liddy, and Ken Hamblin. However, we must stress that talk radio is not a unitary phenomenon. Joseph Cappella, Joseph Turow, and Kathleen Hall Jamieson have concluded that although talk radio is "not monolithic, . . . in both number of shows and size of audience most talk radio is conservative" (1996, p. 8).

In this chapter, we review the existing corpus of literature on political talk radio, examine how institutions have been depicted on this communication modality, and summarize research on the effects of such coverage. The data from our study indicate that political talk radio, to some extent, undermines confidence levels in democratic institutions.

POLITICAL TALK RADIO

Political talk radio is by no means a recent phenomenon, dating as far back as the early twentieth century. It was a medium used then by politicians and commentators alike. While President Franklin D. Roosevelt used his fireside chats to bring about public acceptance of his New Deal, Americans were tuning in to Father Charles Coughlin, a right-wing Catholic priest who regularly criticized the New Deal in his radio broadcasts (Davis, 1997; Tull, 1965). "Radio Priest" Coughlin also voiced his support for Hitler's efforts to eliminate Jewish Communists in Germany (Chester, 1969). In addition, the 1930s marked the rise of controversial radio comedian Fred Allen in a medium that at the time tended to avoid the controversial. According to historian Alan Havig (1992), Allen used radio comedy as a vehicle for social criticism, challenging national beliefs and dominant social groups, and defending artistic autonomy.

Today's talk radio landscape resembles that of six decades ago. Just as his predecessors used radio to reach a nationwide audience, President Clinton today uses this medium for his weekly address. Sharing the medium is a group of men and women who once spent much time in the political spotlight. Notable members of this group include Ed Koch, Mario Cuomo, and Oliver North. Political figures aside, perhaps the most famous of all contemporary talk radio personalities is arch-conservative Rush Limbaugh, a man who commands an impressive weekly following of 20 million "dittoheads" (Brossard, 1996).

While today's players often adopt the same roles as those from earlier this century, characteristics of contemporary talk radio make it a new genre. Resulting in part from the rise of television talk shows, talk radio today is marked by extreme verbiage, where "the talk is frequently repetitious, inane, uninformed, unbearably shrill" (Kurtz, 1996, p. 364). At a recent panel discussion on the role of talk shows in elections, Tom Leykis (1996) of Westwood One Radio likened talk radio to advertising or Hamburger Helper: "a little bit of meat, a lot of sauce."

The number of talk radio stations has grown dramatically in the last decade to stand at over 1,000 (Jones, 1994). Talk is the second most popular format, garnering approximately 15 percent of the radio audience (Kurtz, 1996). A recent nationwide survey conducted by the Times Mirror Center for the People and the Press (1993) found that nearly half of adults tune into talk radio relatively frequently, with one in six listening "regularly." *The Rush Limbaugh Show*, the forerunner of political talk radio shows, is carried on over 650 stations (St. George, 1994).

The current popularity of talk radio may be attributed partly to technology. Satellite technology has made it possible for talk radio shows to be broadcast to a geographically wider area at relatively low costs (Edsall, 1994). Freed from the costs of linking stations by telephone wire, radio networks can use satellite transmissions to provide programming to their affiliates at considerably lower costs (Roberts, 1991). For those who want to enter the realm of talk radio, start-up costs for producing a local radio show are nominal. Gini Graham Scott (1996), former host of the San Francisco-based talk show *Changemakers*, estimates that her production costs totalled $50 a week in the early 1990s.

The growth of talk radio also may be a result of policy changes. Under the Reagan administration, the Federal Communications Commission repealed the Fairness Doctrine in 1987, deeming it unconstitutional. As a result, broadcasters were no longer obligated to present all sides of a given story (Zerbinos, 1995–1996). Because this move effectively allowed broadcasters to air whatever content they wished, various attempts were made to reinstitute the statute, none of which was successful. Some, like host Armstrong Williams, have praised the repeal, arguing that "through this free and unfettered exhange of information, millions of Americans have achieved a level of political sophistication the country hasn't known before" (The Heritage Foundation, 1993, p. 3). The National Association of Radio Talk Show Hosts has taken a more neutral stance, recognizing in October 1993 its "responsibility as guardians of the First Amendment to present balanced programming, and to seek out those ideas, thoughts and issues that may not now enjoy adequate airing" (The Heritage Foundation, 1993, p. 3).

Content as Controversy

In today's political arena, talk radio is besieged by controversy and at the heart of the matter is its content. America is entrenched in a talkathon culture and "the talk that resonates most powerfully . . . is negative talk"

(Kurtz, 1996, p. 365). This kind of offensive content ranges from Ed Koch calling former *Daily News* columnist Earl Caldwell—who is black—a "racist" (Kurtz, 1996), to Jerry Williams labeling Massachusetts governor William Weld an "orange-headed WASP" (Katz, 1991). Conservative hosts have lambasted the presidency: Bob Grant referred to Clinton as a "sleazebag in the White House," while G. Gordon Liddy heralded him as "the coward-in-chief" (Kurtz, 1996, p. 294).

Anecdotes aside, there is varied evidence that democratic institutions are often the focus of talk radio content. According to a survey conducted by *Talkers*, the talk radio industry magazine, President Clinton was the most heavily criticized of all political figures in April and May 1993, even more so than Saddam Hussein during the Persian Gulf War (Viles, 1993). If crime and violence and education rank among the top ten topics addressed on talk radio (*Talkers*, 1993), then the police and the public schools are implicated alongside the government. The results of our content analyses, presented in Chapter 4, indicate that talk radio references to major democratic institutions—the presidency, news media, public schools, and the courts—were strikingly negative. In stark contrast was its extremely positive depiction of Congress.

Talk radio has the potential to delegitimize government authority and leave "an impression of widespread distress" (Levin, 1987, p. 21). After the Oklahoma City bombing in 1995, President Clinton denounced hate speech but noted that the violent rhetoric he condemned was not limited to conservative-minded talk radio.

If people are encouraging conduct that will undermine the fabric of this country, it should be spoken against whether it comes from the left or the right, whether it comes on radio, television or in the movies. (Harris, 1995)

The link between what Clinton calls "a constant unremitting drumbeat of negativism and cynicism" (Jones, 1994) and violent behavior, however, is not one that has been established empirically. A nine-month content analysis of political talk radio led Kathleen Hall Jamieson to conclude that talk radio licenses forms of speech previously unheard over the airwaves. This does not necessarily mean that talk radio incites people to violence. If anything, she offers a plausible alternative: that people who are able to talk about violence are less likely to commit acts of violence (Fleeson, 1995). Along this line of reasoning, Zhongdang Pan and Gerald Kosicki (1997) found that exposure to call-in talk shows was associated with certain forms of political participation, namely contacting elected officials and contributing to or being affiliated with political organizations for specific causes.

There is, however, much talk about the power of talk. In 1989, when Congress attempted to give itself a 51 percent pay increase, talk radio show hosts were besieged by calls from angry listeners. These listeners, at the urging of the hosts, called and wrote their congressperson and effectively forced Congress to reject the recommended pay increase (Roberts, 1991).

On Christmas Eve 1992, Clinton announced his nomination of Zoe Baird for attorney general of the United States. Within a month's time, details of Baird's personal life became public, and the sentiment aired on talk radio was clearly against the nomination of a woman who had employed two illegal residents as household workers. The public uproar, Benjamin Page (1996) concluded, reached the innermost sanctums of the Beltway, and overturned a confirmation that once had been a sure bet. Another piece of anecdotal evidence of the power of talk radio involves Boston-based talk show host Jerry Williams, who initiated a campaign that ultimately forced state legislators to rescind a mandatory seat-belt law (Kurtz, 1996).

Perhaps the power that talk radio show hosts wield was most obviously acknowledged in September 1993 when the White House invited dozens of hosts to broadcast from the White House lawn. At this press conference concerning his health care reform proposal, President Clinton expressed his hope that talk show hosts will continue to be briefed by the administration (Davis, 1997; McAvoy, 1993). Not long thereafter, Speaker of the House Newt Gingrich allowed talk radio hosts to broadcast from the basement of the Capitol (Davis, 1997; Seelye, 1995). Others, like Howard Kurtz (1996), consider Limbaugh to be at least on equal footing with network news anchors or Larry King, especially when it comes to influencing audiences. If Limbaugh and other political talk radio hosts are indeed as influential as some believe, what are the effects of the content aired on their shows?

Effects on Perceptions

Experts have had no difficulty conferring power to political talk radio. Political commentator Richard Vatz argues that talk radio has become "a significant force in creating and molding public opinion" (St. George, 1994, p. 1). A Times Mirror Center study (1993) concludes that "American public opinion is being distorted and exaggerated by the voices that dominate the airwaves of talk radio" (p. 1). The American public, on the other hand, is less united in its views on the "power of babble" (Roberts, 1991, p. 61). According to a *Los Angeles Times* poll conducted after the Oklahoma City bombing, 62 percent of those surveyed agreed with President Clinton that "loud and angry voices" posed a problem for our society, yet 55 percent thought that conservative talk show hosts bore not much or no responsibility for creating a climate that encouraged the bombing (Brownstein, 1995).

Additional data come from a Times Mirror Center (1993) survey, which found that larger proportions of talk show hosts and listeners tend to hold unfavorable views of politicians and the news media, particularly daily newspapers and network television news. Similarly, in a 1995 nationwide survey, almost six out of ten Rush Limbaugh listeners expressed very little confidence in the news media (Brossard, 1996). Using data from the American National Election Studies, David Barker found that people's feelings of warmth toward Limbaugh were associated with greater negative feelings toward President Clinton's national health insurance proposal, an effect that was much more pronounced for Limbaugh listeners as opposed to nonlisteners. Barker concluded that his findings help to "explain the magnitude of the love/hate relationship between talk radio and the Clinton presidency" (1998, p. 94).

Underlying these conclusions about how political talk radio affects its listeners is the long-held belief that listeners are atypical: that they are older and tend to belong to lower socioeconomic strata than nonlisteners (Turow, 1974), and that they turn to talk radio for companionship (Avery, Ellis, & Glover, 1978). Indeed, research on the uses and gratifications of talk radio has revealed a number of motives for tuning in, including a desire for entertainment, relaxation, and passing time (Armstrong & Rubin, 1989). However, based on Diana Owen's (1995) data that two-thirds of talk radio listeners also read daily newspapers and 59 percent watched television news, Russell Mayer and Kimberly Gross called this depiction "a far cry from the image of the lonely disaffected listener" (1996, p. 9).

C. Richard Hofstetter and colleagues (1994), in a San Diego study, found evidence suggesting that the stereotype of talk radio listeners should be revised. Their data showed that listeners reported higher levels of interest in politics, were more likely to vote, and were less alienated than others. They conclude that "although heavier listeners may use talk radio more for entertainment than for public affairs surveillance, no strong tendencies for talk audiences to be alienated, cynical, or less politically efficacious were apparent" (p. 477).

Conclusions by Hofstetter et al. (1994) are consistent with those of John Crittenden (1971), who credited talk radio with enhancing local democracy. He found that a local "open mike" forum, to some extent, stimulated political communication, and listeners believed that they learned through this medium.

Such findings, as well as a growing body of research, suggest that talk radio, rather than undermining confidence, may do just the opposite by engaging citizens in the political process. Hofstetter (1996) concluded that exposure to talk radio may not only enhance political participation, but also heighten sensitivity to ideological and partisan cleavages in political society. This finding is echoed by Pan and Kosicki, who found that "exposure to call-in talk shows largely constitutes a form of political mobilization" by increasing people's likelihood of contacting elected officials (1997, p. 83). Mayer and Gross (1996) concluded that talk radio audience members "believe they can do something to change the situation and they act on those beliefs" (p. i.). This past research suggests that listening may affect confidence through political efficacy, yet some have disputed this link. For instance, Susan Herbst (1995) found that 57 percent of callers and 58 percent of noncallers believed that public officials did not care what they think. Barry Hollander (1996, 1997), in two studies, failed to detect an interaction between political efficacy and trust. As a result, he disputed the contention that talk radio is uniquely able to mobilize listeners who do not trust government but are high in feelings of political self-efficacy. However, these latter studies conceded that talk radio exerts considerable influence on the attitudes and behaviors of conservative listeners.

Similarly, there is no consensus on the direct effects of political talk radio on public confidence. The Times Mirror Center's (1993) data indicated more negative views of certain groups (e.g., politicians, news media) among talk radio listeners. Yet a re-analysis of these data led Owen (1997) to conclude that, after controlling for demographic characteristics and prior political orientations, the negative relationship between listening to talk radio and evaluations of President Clinton disappeared for the most part. Similarly, other research indicates that political partisanship predicted evaluations of various democratic institutions (Moy et al., 1999). Moreover, use of talk radio interacted with partisanship to influence perceptions. Specifically, talk radio reduced confidence in the criminal court system, news media, and the public school system among strongly committed Republicans, less so for the moderately committed, and not at all for non-Republicans.

NEGATIVE INFLUENCE OF POLITICAL TALK RADIO

Who's Listening?

An analysis of our data reveals that controlling for the use of all other media, listening to political talk radio can be predicted by a number of demographic characteristics. As reflected in Table 8.1, males and those with lower levels of education were much more likely to tune in to political talk radio shows. In light of the fact that such shows are mostly conservative in nature, it is not surprising that Republicans also gravitated toward this particular modality.

Such findings partly echo those of national surveys. In their recent analysis of surveys conducted by the Times Mirror Center for the People and the Press, Michael Traugott and colleagues (1996) showed that reg-

Table 8.1
Predicting Use of Political Talk Radio

	β	s.e. (β)
Sex (Male)	.198	(.054)**
Age	-.003	(.002)#
Education	-.059	(.018)**
Income	-.032	(.020)
Democrat	-.107	(.062)
Republican	.467	(.072)**

Note: Entries are coefficients from ordinary least squares regression with standard errors in parentheses.
# p < .10
** p < .01

ular listening to talk radio is predicted by being male, older, or Republican. In addition, Hollander's (1996) analyses revealed that demographic differences existed between listeners, callers, and nonlisteners. In particular, nonlisteners and callers tended to be nonwhite, while listeners tended to be white.

The Effects of Political Talk Radio

As with the analyses of print and broadcast media shown in Chapters 5 through 7, use of political talk radio was residualized for use of all other media. In other words, we control for use of all other media. This control seems particularly appropriate here given the oftentimes supplementary role of talk radio in today's media environment; Tom Leykis (1996) estimates that approximately 15 percent of Americans listen to talk radio, a relatively low figure. Research also has shown that people do not listen to talk radio at the exclusion of all other media. Owen (1997) found that only one percent of a nationwide sample relied on talk radio exclusively; this figure is lower than the 7 percent who do not rely on any media.

The Office of the Presidency. Researchers have documented a manifestly anti-liberal tone on the part of talk radio shows toward the office of the presidency (e.g., Cappella, Turow, & Jameson, 1996), and our own data presented in Chapter 4 support this finding. Yet the impact of political talk radio on *perceptions* of the office of the presidency was mixed.

Figure 8.1
Effects of Listening to Political Talk Radio on Evaluations of the Office of the Presidency

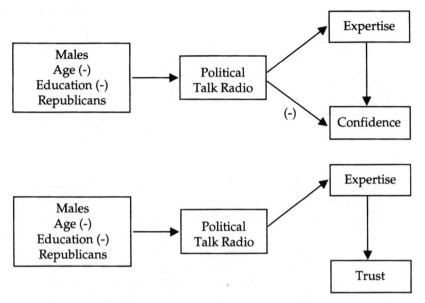

Note: Total effects of listening to political talk radio on confidence were marginally significant.

Listening to political talk radio influenced listeners' evaluations of the presidency but in different manners. Figure 8.1 illustrates the path of talk radio's influence on evaluations of the presidency. The diagram shows that use of talk radio influenced respondents' confidence levels directly and negatively so. At the same time, listening increased awareness, interest, and knowledge of the institution, which enhanced confidence, but the total effect (noted in Appendix Table 8.1) was marginally significant.

The pattern of results that emerged for talk radio and one's global attitude was similar to that of the 0–100 confidence rating, but the total effect did not even reach marginal significance. At the same time, listening to political talk radio had an indirect positive effect on trustworthiness.

In light of the negativity documented in our content analyses, we would expect use of talk radio to lead to negative perceptions of this democratic institution. However, our data reveal quite limited influences of political talk radio. The only overall negative effect did not reach statistical significance, and any positive effects were not too substantive, with total effects of .01. Given controls for use of all other media and

Figure 8.2
Effects of Listening to Political Talk Radio on Evaluations of the Court System

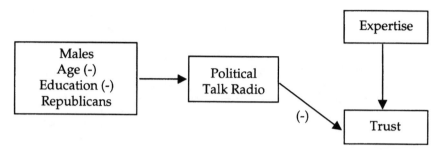

the fact that political party identification alone produced strong effects, we must question the extent to which the negativism and cynicism of talk radio contribute to the crisis of confidence.

Congress. Our content analyses showed that references to Congress on political talk radio shows were favorable. This finding was not surprising, given that the Republicans gained control of the U.S. House of Representatives after the 1994 elections, and political talk shows tend to be politically conservative in nature (Cappella, Turow, & Jamieson 1996). Yet the public opinion data collected in this investigation revealed no impact from this medium on any perceptions of Congress, as shown in Appendix Table 8.2. In addition, after controlling for use of all other media, talk radio did not affect expertise in Congress.

Not shown in either graphical or tabular form is how listening to political talk radio influenced all evaluations of Congress if use of other media was *not* taken into consideration. As with global attitude toward and trust in the presidency, the process of influence for evaluations of Congress was through expertise—positive from talk radio to expertise, and positive from expertise to each of the three criterion measures of global attitude, trust and confidence.

The finding that talk radio, after controlling for all other media, does not enhance evaluations of Congress raises a question: What does expertise or confidence in Congress entail? Congress as a whole is a complex entity, compared to specific individuals such as a respondent's congressperson or Speaker of the House Newt Gingrich. Because references on political talk radio would more likely target specific politicians, the link between talk radio and expertise or confidence in *Congress* may not be warranted.

The Court System. A similar lack of effects for political talk radio on evaluations of the court system was discernible from the data. As Figure 8.2 and Appendix Table 8.3 indicate, expertise exerted a consistently pos-

Figure 8.3
Effects of Listening to Political Talk Radio on Evaluations of the News Media and the Public Schools

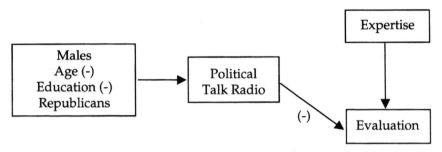

itive impact: The greater one's level of interest, awareness, and knowledge in the court system, the more positive one's global attitude (β = .13), the more trust (β = .07), and the more confidence (β = .06) expressed toward the court system.

Negative effects of political talk radio emerged from the data. Listening to political talk radio lowered trust in the court system directly (β = −.05) and lowered expertise in the institution, but only marginally.

The News Media. As shown earlier in Table 4.4, political talk radio generated considerable negativity toward the news media. The survey data revealed that such negativity may indeed translate into negative attitudes. Appendix Table 8.4 shows the numbers, and Figure 8.3 depicts the model of influence of political talk radio on perceptions of the news media.

There is a direct negative effect of this medium on all three evaluations of the news media: global attitude (β = −.11), trust (β = −.08), and confidence (β = −.07). Use of political talk radio did not affect how interested, knowledgeable, or aware one was regarding the news media. Expertise did, however, affect all three evaluation measures positively.

What accounts for the negative direct effect of talk radio on perceptions of the news media, and lack of effect on expertise in the news media? One answer may lie in the role of direct experience. It may be possible for political talk radio hosts to undermine confidence in the media directly with strong, emotionally laden words, but it is almost impossible to change our knowledge or awareness of something with which we have extensive, first-hand contact.

The Public Schools. As with the news media, political talk radio had a direct negative impact on perceptions of the public schools (β = −.08, −.07, and −.07 for global attitude, trust, and confidence, respectively). As shown in Figure 8.4 and Appendix Table 8.5, there were no direct effects of listening on expertise, but expertise did exert a strong positive

Table 8.2

Effects of Listening to Political Talk Radio on Evaluations of Democratic Institutions: Summary Table

	Presidency	Congress	Court System	News Media	Public Schools
Global Attitude	Direct and indirect effects (negative)	None	None	Direct effect only (negative)	Direct effect only (negative)
Trustworthiness	Indirect effect only	None	Direct and indirect effects (negative)	Direct effect only (negative)	Direct effect only (negative)
Confidence	Direct and indirect effects (negative)	None	None	Direct effect only (negative)	Direct effect only (negative)

Note: Effects are noted based on probability levels set at $p = .05$.

influence on the public schools (β = .28, .23, and .23 for global attitude, trust, and confidence, respectively).

Again, the logic used to explain the pattern of findings for evaluations of the news media may be used to explain the effects found for evaluations of the public school system. Similar to the agenda-setting phenomenon, in which effects are stronger for unobtrusive issues or issues not directly experienced by audience members (McCombs, Einsiedel, & Weaver, 1991), the effects of political talk radio may be considerably weaker, or nonexistent, when the content concerns an institution with which we deal directly.

CONCLUSION

Portrayals of talk radio and its role in democratic systems have grown increasingly complex over the past few decades. Although early research depicted listeners as situated on the periphery of society (Avery & Ellis, 1979), more recent studies have found that listeners are interested in politics, efficacious, and politically active (e.g., Hofstetter et al., 1994). Moreover, there has been a trend in scholarly research in this area to examine various conditions under which use of political talk radio affects its audience. When more stringent controls are applied in analyses of both local and national data, findings show that political talk radio is not exerting a great impact on evaluations of politicians or institutions (Moy et al., 1999; Owen, 1997).

Our content analyses revealed that depictions of various democratic institutions on political talk radio are markedly negative. These findings would mesh well with the growing collection of colorful phrases heard on talk radio. Limbaugh (1993) claims that his job, as a media personality, is "to attract as large an audience as possible" (p. 1). But such talk has not been without consequences. Talk radio hosts have been charged with fueling anti-government sentiment (Levin, 1987), as well as credited with mobilizing their listeners to action (e.g., Page, 1996).

Our survey data reveal very limited effects of political talk radio on various democratic institutions. After controlling for use of all other media, listening to talk radio exerted no influence on how respondents evaluated Congress (see Table 8.2). This is despite the favorable depictions of Congress.

Listening to political talk radio had a direct negative impact on evaluations of the news media and the public schools, a finding suggesting that the views broadcast are ultimately translated into negative perceptions on the part of listeners. These direct negative impacts, however, are offset by the strong positive influence of expertise—interest, awareness, and knowledge of the news media and public schools. The finding that use of political talk radio, after controlling for all other media use, does not affect expertise in these two institutions is an intuitive one. After all, these are two institutions with which we have direct experience. Most Americans have acquired some type of schooling and undoubtedly have formed much of their opinion based on their personal experience. Similarly, most Americans use the news media regularly. Consequently the lack of influence of talk radio on how much we know about these two institutions is not surprising.

Finally, the empirical relationships that emerged between use of talk radio and evaluations of the office of the presidency run contrary to popular belief. Working through expertise, use of talk radio enhances trust in the presidency. However, listening exerts a direct negative effect on confidence and global attitude, resulting in a (marginal) negative total effect. These findings move in the direction of work suggesting a limited impact of talk radio.

Thus the outcry over political talk radio needs to be qualified. Our data indicate that the negativity of talk radio toward particular institutions does get translated into negative perceptions—but not in all cases. Talk radio entertains, informs, and activates, and as David Brudnoy of Boston's WBZ-AM notes: "The popularity of talk radio reminds us that Americans still prefer talking to fighting. And though our national conversations are not always civil, talk radio helps ensure that at least we'll keep having them" (1994, p. 60).

Appendix Table 8.1

Effects of Demographics, Party Identification, Listening to Political Talk Radio, and Institutional Expertise on Evaluations of the Office of the Presidency

	Sex (M)	Age	Education	Income	Democrat	Republican	Political Talk Radio	Expertise	R²
Listening to Political Talk Radio	(γ) .10**	(γ) -.06*	(γ) -.10**	–	(γ) -.06#	(γ) .19**			.08
	–	–	–	–	–	–			
	.10**	-.06*	-.10**	–	-.06#	.19**			
Expertise	(γ) .09**	(γ) .27**	(γ) .27**	–	(γ) .12**	(γ) .08**	(β) .06*		.17
	.01#	.00	-.01#	–	.00	.01*	–		
	.09**	.27**	.26**	–	.12**	.09**	.06*		
Global Attitude	(γ) -.06*	(γ) .10**	(γ) .05#	–	(γ) .08**	(γ) -.16**	(β) -.05#	(β) .26**	.16
	.02*	.07**	.07**	–	.03**	.01	.01*	–	
	-.04	.17**	.12**	–	.12**	-.15**	-.03	.26**	
Trust-worthiness	–	(γ) .13**	–	–	(γ) .08**	(γ) -.17**	–	(β) .18**	.11
	.02**	.05**	.05**	–	.02**	.02**	.01*	–	
	.02**	.18**	.05**	–	.10**	-.15**	.01*	.18**	
Confidence	–	–	(γ) .07*	–	(γ) .11**	(γ) -.10**	(β) -.06*	(β) .14**	.08
	.01	.04**	.04**	–	.02**	.00	.01*	–	
	.01	.04**	.12**	–	.13**	-.10**	-.05#	.14**	

Notes: This appendix table condenses three models, each of which includes sociodemographics, party identification, media use, institutional expertise, and *one* of three criterion variables (shown in the last three rows: global attitude, trustworthiness, or confidence). Entries in each cell are standardized direct, indirect, and total effects, respectively. Direct effects and indirect effects may not add up to total effects due to rounding. The χ^2 statistic for the global attitude model is 4.03 (3, N = 1278, p = .26), 7.14 (6, N = 1278, p = .26) for trustworthiness, and 7.21 (5, N = 1278, p = .21) for confidence.

\# p < .10
* p < .05
** p < .01

174

Effects of Demographics, Party Identification, Listening to Political Talk Radio, and Institutional Expertise on Evaluations of Congress

	Sex (M)	Age	Education	Income	Democrat	Republican	Political Talk Radio	Expertise	R^2
Listening to Political Talk Radio	(γ) .10**	(γ) -.06*	(γ) -.10**	--	(γ) -.06#	(γ) .19**			.08
	--	--	--	--	--	--			
	.10**	-.06*	-.10**	--	-.06#	.19**			
Expertise	(γ) .14**	(γ) .23**	(γ) .27**	--	(γ) .07*	(γ) .08**	--		.16
	--	--	--	--	--	--	--		
	.14**	.23**	.27**	--	.07*	.08**	--		
Global Attitude	(γ) -.07*	(γ) -.10**	(γ) -.07*	(γ) .05#	--	(γ) .08**	--	(β) .31**	.09
	.04**	.07**	.08**	--	.02*	.03**	--	--	
	-.02	-.03	.02	.05#	.02*	.11**	--	.31**	
Trust-worthiness	--	--	(γ) -.06*	--	--	(γ) .07**	--	(β) .18*	.04
	.03**	.04**	.05**	--	.01*	.02**	--	--	
	.03**	.04**	-.01	--	.01*	.08**	--	.18**	
Confidence	(γ) -.07*	(γ) -.07*	--	--	--	(γ) .12**	--	(β) .17**	.05
	.02**	.04**	.05**	--	.01*	.01**	--	--	
	-.05#	-.02	.05**	--	.01*	.14**	--	.17**	

Notes: This appendix table condenses three models, each of which includes sociodemographics, party identification, media use, institutional expertise, and *one* of three criterion variables (shown in the last three rows: global attitude, trustworthiness, or confidence). Entries in each cell are standardized direct, indirect, and total effects, respectively. Direct effects and indirect effects may not add up to total effects due to rounding. The χ^2 statistic for the global attitude model is 4.92 (5, N = 1278, p = .43), 9.80 (8, N = 1278, p = .28) for trustworthiness, and 8.37 (7, N = 1278, p = .30) for confidence.

\# p < .10

* p < .05

** p < .01

Appendix Table 8.3
Effects of Demographics, Party Identification, Listening to Political Talk Radio, and Institutional Expertise on Evaluations of the Court System

	Sex (M)	Age	Education	Income	Democrat	Republican	Political Talk Radio	Expertise	R²
Listening to Political Talk Radio	(γ) .10**	(γ) -.06*	(γ) -.10**	--	(γ) -.06#	(γ) .19**			.08
	--	--	--	--	--	--			
	.10**	-.06*	-.10**	--	-.06#	.19**			
Expertise	--	(γ) .07*	(γ) .09**	(γ) .08**	.00	-.01#	(β) -.05#		.03
	-.01#	.00	.01#	--	.00	--	-.01		
	-.01#	.07*	.10**	.08**	.00	-.01#	-.05#		
Global Attitude	--	--	(γ) .09**	(γ) .10**	(γ) .08**	.00	--	(β) .13**	.06
	.00	.01*	.01#	.01*	.00	.00	-.01#	--	
	.00	.01*	.10**	.11**	.08**	.00	-.01#	.13**	
Trust-worthiness	(γ) .05#	(γ) .06*	(γ) .10**	(γ) .10**	.00	-.01*	(β) -.05*	(β) .07**	.05
	-.01#	.01*	.01**	.01#	.00	.00	-.00	--	
	.04	.07*	.12**	.10**	.00	-.01*	-.06*	.07**	
Confidence	--	--	(γ) .13**	(γ) .08**	(γ) .07**	.00	--	(β) .06*	.04
	.00	.00	.01#	.00#	.00	.00	.00	--	
	.00	.00	.14**	.09**	.07*	.00	.00	.06*	

Notes: This appendix table condenses three models, each of which includes sociodemographics, party identification, media use, institutional expertise, and *one* of three criterion variables (shown in the last three rows: global attitude, trustworthiness, or confidence). Entries in each cell are standardized direct, indirect, and total effects, respectively. Direct effects and indirect effects may not add up to total effects due to rounding. The χ^2 statistic for the global attitude model is 5.78 (8, N = 1278, p = .67), 5.30 (6, N = 1278, p = .51) for trustworthiness, and 5.53 (8, N = 1278, p = .70) for confidence.

# p < .10
* p < .05
** p < .01

Appendix Table 8.4
Effects of Demographics, Party Identification, Listening to Political Talk Radio, and Institutional Expertise on Evaluations of the News Media

	Sex (M)	Age	Education	Income	Democrat	Republican	Political Talk Radio	Expertise	R²
Listening to Political Talk Radio	(γ) .10**	(γ) -.06*	(γ) -.10**	--	(γ) -.06#	(γ) .19**			.08
	--	--	--	--	--	--			
	.10**	-.06*	-.10**	--	-.06#	.19**			
Expertise	--	(γ) .16**	(γ) .14**	--	--	--	--	--	.05
	--	--	--	--	--	--	--	--	
	--	.16**	.14**	--	--	--	--	--	
Global Attitude	(γ) -.04#	--	(γ) -.13**	--	(γ) .08**	--	(β) -.11**	(β) .35**	.15
	-.01**	.06**	.06**	--	.01#	-.02**	--	--	
	-.06*	.06**	-.07**	--	.09**	-.02**	-.11**	.35**	
Trustworthiness	--	(γ) .09**	(γ) -.11**	--	(γ) .09**	--	(β) -.08**	(β) .25**	.10
	-.01*	.04**	.04**	--	.00	-.01*	--	--	
	-.01*	.14**	-.07*	--	.09**	-.01*	-.08**	.25**	
Confidence	--	--	(γ) -.10**	--	(γ) .08**	--	(β) -.07*	(β) .24**	.07
	-.01*	.04**	.04**	--	.00	-.01*	--	--	
	-.01*	.04**	-.06*	--	.09**	-.01*	-.07*	.24**	

Notes: This appendix table condenses three models, each of which includes sociodemographics, party identification, media use, institutional expertise, and *one* of three criterion variables (shown in the last three rows: global attitude, trustworthiness, or confidence). Entries in each cell are standardized direct, indirect, and total effects, respectively. Direct effects and indirect effects may not add up to total effects due to rounding. The χ^2 statistic for the global attitude model is 11.51 (9, N = 1278, p = .24), 8.07 (10, N = 1278, p = .62) for trustworthiness, and 7.92 (9, N = 1278, p = .54) for confidence.

\# p < .10
* p < .05
** p < .01

Appendix Table 8.5
Effects of Demographics, Party Identification, Listening to Political Talk Radio, and Institutional Expertise on Evaluations of the Public School System

	Sex (M)	Age	Education	Income	Democrat	Republican	Political Talk Radio	Expertise	R²
Listening to Political Talk Radio	(γ) .10**	(γ) -.06*	(γ) -.10**	--	(γ) -.06#	(γ) .19**			.08
	--	--	--	--	--	--			
	.10**	-.06*	-.10**	--	-.06#	.19**			
Expertise	(γ) -.09**	(γ) .06*	(γ) .14**	(γ) .10**	--	--	--	--	.05
	--	--	--	--	--	--	--	--	
	-.09**	.06*	.14**	.10**	--	--	--	--	
Global Attitude	(γ) -.06*	--	--	--	(γ) .06#	(γ) -.07*	(β) -.08**	(β) .28**	.11
	-.03**	.02**	.05**	.03**	.00#	-.02**	--	--	
	-.09**	.02**	.05**	.03**	.06*	-.09**	-.08**	.28**	
Trust-worthiness	--	--	--	--	(γ) .08**	-.01*	(β) -.07**	(β) .23**	.07
	-.03**	.02**	.04**	.02**	.00	-.01	--	--	
	-.03**	.02**	.04**	.02**	.08**	-.01	-.07*	.23**	
Confidence	--	--	--	--	(γ) .09**	-.01*	(β) -.07*	(β) .23**	.07
	-.03**	.02**	.04**	.02**	.00	-.01	--	--	
	-.03**	.02**	.04**	.02**	.09**	-.01	-.07*	.23**	

Notes: This appendix table condenses three models, each of which includes sociodemographics, party identification, media use, institutional expertise, and *one* of three criterion variables (shown in the last three rows: global attitude, trustworthiness, or confidence). Entries in each cell are standardized direct, indirect, and total effects, respectively. Direct effects and indirect effects may not add up to total effects due to rounding. The χ² statistic for the global attitude model is 4.76 (7, N = 1278, p = .69), 8.14 (9, N = 1278, p = .52) for trustworthiness, and 7.50 (9, N = 1278, p = .59) for confidence.

\# p < .10
* p < .05
** p < .01

Chapter 9

Conclusions

Have we made it harder for the system to work?
Television journalist Cokie Roberts
(Cappella & Jamieson, 1997, p. 37)

As the fourth estate, the news media have been charged with performing several key functions in democratic societies—functions that make it easier for the system to work. At the top of the list, according to Michael Gurevitch and Jay Blumler (1990), is the news media's surveillance of the sociopolitical environment. Equal importance is placed on the media's identification of key issues, their provision of platforms for various groups, their encouragement of dialogue across various groups, and their motivation of citizens to learn and become involved in the political process. Normative standards, however, do not translate easily into reality, and the news media's ability to meet these democratic standards has been the topic of considerable research in communication, political science, and that juncture called political communication.

How well are the media doing? The jury is still deliberating. While the news media are extremely powerful in disseminating vast quantities of information across large geographical spaces and are able to reach diverse audiences, what effects do they have? Surely the media are capable of making audiences aware of important issues. Certainly they transmit a greater number of perspectives on an issue than what many citizens may be accustomed to in their daily interactions. It is no wonder then that Leo Bogart (1998, p. 4) wrote: "Representative democracy is inconceivable without forms of mass communication."

At the same time, experts and laypersons alike have questioned the extent to which audience members can learn about public issues from the media. More recently, they have placed the burden of responsibility of America's decline in trust squarely on the news media. Early accusations of fault targeted the *news* media—newspapers and television news—for lowering levels of trust. With the expansion of news sources, these accusations quickly encompass nontraditional sources of political news. These sources, which include various forms of "softer" news on television, prime-time programming, and political talk radio, are nontraditional because their goal is not necessarily to disseminate political information, yet they provide a large proportion of Americans with information about current public affairs. This information, many claim, has lowered Americans' trust in their democratic institutions. The media have, in fact, become a whipping boy for many.

This certainly was the case in the late 1990s, when the media brought to their audiences events that highlighted the shortcomings of various institutions. One major event concerned a murder case that tied race, sex, and domestic conflict together: The O. J. Simpson case was a drawn-out spectacle that kept Americans glued to their television sets watching the trial. In the end, one had to question the impact of media coverage on the justice system and on the news media. Those who craved sex and intrigue—from either the trial or from daytime soap operas—did not have to wait long. Soon thereafter, the news media were delivering romance and intrigue straight from the White House. The Monica Lewinsky scandal showed Americans how the personal really could become the political and that the White House may not be as pristine as many had thought. These two events kept news reporters busy and citizens captivated for the past several years. Regardless of how public opinion stood on Simpson and Clinton, there was general concern over how the media covered them.

Do the media then deserve this role as whipping boy? According to our study, the answer is yes, but a qualified yes. The data we present in Chapters 4 through 8 show that people's use of various media sources is indeed related to their trust in democratic institutions—some of the time. Use of *some* communication modalities is related to lower levels of trust in *some* democratic institutions. In this final chapter, we elaborate on the patterns of effects that emerged from our study and discuss the implications of our findings.

As we noted at the outset of the book, the relationship between media use and evaluations of democratic institutions is not clear-cut. We mentioned in Chapter 2 a host of other factors that may potentially confound the relationship between media use and trust in institutions. Therefore, our study controlled for demographics, political ideology, and institutional expertise.

PATTERNS OF EFFECTS

Effects of Sociodemographics

Sociodemographic factors oftentimes determine how an individual stands on public policy issues. For example, an individual's race influences his or her attitudes toward policies dealing with equal opportunity, affirmative action, and the like, according to analyses conducted by Donald Kinder and Lynn Sanders (1996). Benjamin Page and Robert Shapiro (1992), in their portrait of how the policy preferences of Americans have changed over time, show that gender makes a difference in attitudes toward gun control: females generally tend to support gun control more than males. Similarly, older Americans typically are more supportive of traditional values than are younger Americans, resisting legalizing marijuana and favoring prayers in school. In the realm of foreign policy, better-educated individuals were more likely to support the Vietnam War (Mueller, 1973).

The story is similar when it comes to confidence in democratic institutions. Our data indicate that demographic variables have an effect on the media sources to which one turns, how much one knows about a given institution, and how favorably one views that institution. The effects of sociodemographics on confidence are sometimes direct and, at other times, indirect, working through other variables.

This study revealed trends in media use among certain subgroups. After taking into account all other variables, we found that females were more frequent viewers of entertainment talk shows and television news magazines, but males were more frequent listeners of political talk radio. Age predicted use of all modalities: older people read the newspaper more often, but younger people were more likely to read news magazines. Older individuals also tended to watch local and network television news as well as television news magazines (this last relationship, however, emerged before controlling for other variables). Younger individuals were more likely to gravitate toward entertainment talk shows and political talk radio. Education worked in favor of consuming information from the print media, while lower levels of education were associated with viewing of local television news and entertainment talk shows, as well as listening to political talk radio. The effect of income on media use was similar to that of education: It was positively related to reading of news magazines and newspapers but negatively to watching network television news and entertainment talk shows. Political partisanship had slight effects as well, with Democrats more likely to watch local news, and Republicans less likely to watch network news. Republican affiliation, however, was associated with listening to political talk radio. In short, mass media may pervade our lives, but they are not appealing equally to all segments of society.

Sociodemographic variables also played a role in affecting how much people were aware of, believed they knew about, and were interested in specific democratic institutions. We used the term "institutional expertise" as a rubric for these cognitions. Age and education were positively related to expertise in all five democratic institutions. But gender, income, and political affiliation did not have across-the-board effects. Males reported greater expertise in the presidency and Congress, as did the politically partisan. Individuals with higher levels of income had greater expertise in the court system and the public school system; females had higher levels of awareness, interest, and knowledge in the public school system.

In Chapter 2, we reported some mixed findings indicating that certain demographics may have an effect on confidence in democratic institutions. The results of our study show that demographics (and ideology) do indeed influence evaluations of institutions. In addition, these results are both direct and indirect. The indirect effects sometimes work through use of a particular communication modality, and other times through institutional expertise.

Not shown in the figures in Chapters 5 through 8, but noted in the corresponding appendices, demographics had direct effects on evaluations of democratic institutions. The patterns of direct effects show that gender had a direct effect on four of the five institutions: Controlling for all other variables, females had more positive evaluations of the presidency, Congress, the news media, and the public school system. Older people felt more favorably toward the presidency and the news media, but less favorably toward Congress. Age also had indirect positive effects on evaluations of the court system and the public school system. In other words, older individuals tended to read the newspaper more often ($\gamma = .13$), newspaper use led greater expertise in the public school system ($\beta = .08$), and expertise enhanced one's global attitude ($\beta = .27$), trustworthiness ($\beta = .22$), and confidence ($\beta = .22$) in the institution (see Appendix Table 5.5). Education had direct positive effects on evaluations of two institutions and direct negative effects on evaluations of two. Higher levels of education led to more favorable ratings of the office of the presidency and the court system; these positive direct effects, coupled with positive indirect effects, indicate that education has an overall positive (total) effect in determining how people feel about these two institutions.

Congress and the news media, in contrast, did not fare as well. Education had a direct negative effect on one's global attitude and trustworthiness ratings of Congress, but these negative effects were offset by positive indirect effects (working through expertise and media use, specifically newspapers and weekly news magazines) to produce nonsignificant total effects. Our third criterion variable related to Congress, confidence, was influenced only indirectly by education: Education worked through use of various media and expertise to enhance confidence in Congress.

Similarly, while the overall impact of education on evaluations of the public school system was positive, this effect stemmed only from indirect effects through media use and institutional expertise.

The effects of income on evaluations of democratic institutions were relatively consistent. For four of the five institutions we studied—the presidency, Congress, the news media, and the public schools—income exerted a negligible yet statistically significant positive indirect effect. There were no direct effects of income on the criterion variables, hence the total effects were the same as the indirect effects—small and positive. The only institution for which income made a difference was the court system. Greater income meant a more favorable global attitude, greater trustworthiness, and higher levels of confidence in the court system. This relationship was both direct and indirect through media use and expertise in the court system.

Political party identification affected ratings of institutions as well, but more consistently for Democrats than for Republicans. Being Democrat meant more positive evaluations for all institutions, but the process of effects differed across institutions. The effects were direct only for the news media, the court system, and the public school system, direct and indirect for the presidency, and indirect only for Congress.

The effects of Republican partisanship were more mixed. It exerted a strong negative direct effect on evaluations of the office of the presidency and was offset slightly by positive indirect effects; the total effects remained strong and negative. Republican partisanship, as expected, had the opposite relationship with evaluations of Congress: Strong positive direct effects were bolstered by positive indirect effects, for strong positive total effects. Where the public school system was concerned, Republican partisanship exerted a consistent negative influence on global attitude. This was the only direct effect to emerge from all the models involving evaluations of the school system. Partisanship also affected evaluations of the news media, although the effects were more sporadic. The only consistent effect to emerge was that of Republicans expressing a less favorable global attitude toward the news media. Finally, there was essentially no effect (1 out of 21) of Republican partisanship on how people viewed the court system.

These findings illustrate that sociodemographics do make a difference when we talk about public confidence in demographic institutions. Certain groups of individuals tend to use certain media more often. Similarly, certain groups tend to have more favorable perceptions of democratic institutions, all else being equal. The effects are both direct and indirect.

Role of Institutional Expertise

Institutional expertise has been, by far, the strongest predictor of how one feels about various democratic institutions. This concept was operationalized by respondents' reports of awareness, interest, and knowledge in an institution, and in our model, is situated between media use and confidence in that institution. We placed the concept here since its dimensions often are influenced by the media. Media use results in learning of important political issues, and it can generate interest and awareness in a particular issue.

Of the 105 models run for this study (7 modalities × 3 criterion variables × 5 democratic institutions), expertise was a significant predictor of the criterion variable (global attitude, trustworthiness, or confidence) 102 times. The greater one's expertise in a given institution, the more favorable one's evaluation was in general.

Pattern of Media Effects

In our everyday lives, the term "media" is bandied about and used relatively loosely in conversation, and little attention is paid to what constitutes the media. Fortunately, scholarly research in the area is more stringent and examines the concepts of media use and trust more systematically. The body of research that relates the two, however, has tended to use different metrics to gauge the impact of media use on trust in institutions. These measures differ not only across studies examining the same media and institutions (e.g., two studies investigating how television news affects perceptions of Congress), but also across studies of different media (e.g., one study looking at the effects of newspapers only and another examining the effects of television news).

One strength of our study lies in the use of identical items to measure not only negativity toward institutions on the part of various communication sources, but also the negativity of individual respondents toward these same institutions. The link between the two, of course, is media use. If a particular communication modality portrays the court system in a negative light, and someone uses this modality, then will he or she tend to perceive the court system in that same light?

What then are the effects of media use on public confidence in democratic institutions? Have the media really made it harder for the system to work? We reiterate our qualified yes and summarize the media effects here.

Echoing the results of numerous studies, our study found that the print media are better than broadcast news in bolstering levels of public confidence in democratic institutions. Relative to television news, newspapers and news magazines were more effective in enhancing evaluations of the five institutions we studied. For each print medium, all 15 criterion variables (3 criterion variables × 5 institutions) were influenced positively by use of that medium. Moreover, reading newspapers and news magazines increased respondents' expertise in the five institutions.

This finding stands in stark contrast to the effects that emerged for local and network television news. The relationship between local television news viewing and evaluations of democratic institutions was positive for only three of the five institutions—the presidency, the news media, and the public school system. Viewing was marginally related to evaluations of Congress and not at all related to ratings of the court system. Network television news had somewhat deleterious effects on evaluations: positive effects on the news media, negative effects on Congress and the court system, mixed for the office of the presidency, and no effects on the public school system. Even more interesting is that while use of the print media increased expertise in all institutions, watching news on television did not have a similar effect. Watching network news increased viewers' expertise in the office of the presidency and the news media only, and watching local news did not have an effect on institutional expertise whatsoever.

Our study went beyond traditional news sources to address the impact of nontraditional sources of political information on public confidence in institutions. Specifically, we examined how watching television news magazines such as *Dateline* and *60 Minutes* as well as entertainment talk shows such as *Late Night with David Letterman* and *The Tonight Show* affected perceptions of these institutions. Similarly, we were interested in how political talk radio would affect evaluations.

Watching television news magazines did not affect evaluations of any institution except the news media and that effect was positive, working through institutional expertise. The relationship between viewing of entertainment talk shows and the news media was positive as well, but the effects were purely direct. In addition, talk show viewing decreased confidence in the presidency and Congress, and these effects were indirect. Listening to political talk radio had consistently negative (direct and indirect) influences on evaluations of the court system, the news media, and the public school system. The effects of listening on evaluations of the office of the presidency were mixed.

The effects of these nontraditional sources on institutional expertise were slight. Only respondents' reports of how much they knew about and were interested in or aware of the news media increased with viewing of television news magazines. Expertise in the office of the presidency and Congress *decreased* with the watching of entertainment talk shows, although expertise in the presidency was positively related to listening to political talk radio.

The effects of nontraditional communication sources, where there were any, were essentially negative. The only institution to benefit from coverage by these sources was the news media. Furthermore, with the exception of the news media and the presidency, use of nontraditional media does not appear to be improving levels of expertise in these institutions.

DISCUSSION

We began this book by painting a picture of how levels of trust in American institutions have dropped steadily for the past few decades. The causes of this decline in public confidence are many, and our focus on the mass media does not imply that there is no merit to other perspectives. Rather, the mass media must be viewed as one part of the larger picture.

While citizens use the term "confidence" loosely, scientific approaches to the study of the concept have examined different referents and, therefore, have employed different measures. As we noted in Chapter 3, we adopted—and adapted—various measures used in previous studies of confidence and trust. Discriminant validity and construct validity were borne out by the patterns of relationships between the antecedents and the three measures of confidence.

We posed a question on the cover of this book: Is there malice on the part of the mass media toward all? The answer clearly is no. The results of our content analyses, presented in Chapter 4, show that media coverage of democratic institutions is not indiscriminately negative. The evidence is embodied in findings that include political talk radio as tending to be the most negative toward the presidency and the court system, and entertainment talk shows as depicting Congress in a most unfavorable light. Both these modalities were the most negative toward the public schools as well, while local television news covered the news media most harshly. Coverage of institutions not only differs across modalities, but also fluctuates from year to year.

For many, it is tempting to speak of "the mass media" as a broad, overarching term. It is easier to cast aspersions on—or applaud—a single entity than to discriminate among specific media. But to draw conclusions about the "mass media" as a whole simply would be inappropriate. Therefore, while the term is incorporated into the subtitle of this book, we must note again the differences between specific communication modalities. Use of broadcast media—particularly the more established network news, entertainment talk shows, and political talk radio—is generally associated with lower levels of confidence and trust in institutions. On the other hand, the relationship between use of the print media and evaluations is a positive one.

These relationships emerged in a macro-level study, one in which the focus was on how the media covered democratic institutions, how citizens used these media, and how these media use patterns affected their attitudes toward institutions sitting at the core of society. Our study was not geared toward establishing individual-level relationships under relatively controlled conditions; rather, it plots broader, aggregate relationships in media coverage of democratic institutions and trust in these institutions. While the strength of experiments, relative to surveys, lies in their ability to argue causality, our study provides an opportunity to examine how these relationships hold outside a controlled setting. Few would maintain that the relationship between media use and confidence in institutions is entirely unidirectional, but rather confidence levels can drive media use, and over time, the potential for each to enforce the other arises. It would behoove scholars, then, to undertake research employing multiple methods to examine how macro-level political, economic, and social factors operate *in conjunction* with the media to affect public confidence. Or, as Jack Citrin and Samantha Luks (1998) noted regarding trust in government, "Is it party, policy, performance, or personality?" (p. 5). Obviously all of these—and the mass media—account for fluctuations in confidence in democratic institutions.

What can others do about media coverage and declining levels of trust in democratic institutions? Some would argue that nothing needs to be done. According to this line of reasoning, too much of a good thing is bad. It may not be healthy to have 95 percent of Americans expressing great confidence in their government and other democratic institutions, and demagoguery may be only a few steps behind such extreme levels of compliance. But a healthy dose of distrust—however "healthy" may be defined and quantified—demands an assessment of the status quo and the extent to which the populace's interests are being served and provides an impetus for change.

How then can public confidence be reinvigorated? According to the findings presented here, expertise plays a crucial role. In 102 of 105 models, institutional expertise increased public confidence. Citizens' perceptions of their government, their schools, and the news media have their origins in what they know about these institutions. How do citizens come to learn of politics? The most rudimentary facts related to the political process and the functioning of our system are disseminated early on in one's life. Social studies, history, government, and civics classes arm schoolchildren and high schoolers alike with the tools they need to realize their full potential as citizens. But these courses are not required in many institutions of higher learning, and regardless of where on the educational spectrum one stops, civics skills should be made an integral part of one's life, and as early on as possible. This is not a call for public schools across the country to overhaul their curricula, but we do argue that greater emphasis needs to be placed on instilling and involving younger citizens into the political process. In this sense, we applaud the efforts of such nonpartisan, nonprofit organizations as Kids Voting USA, aimed at educating and involving schoolchildren in the election process today. Experiential learning of civic skills provides an opportunity for children to practice democracy, and this type of socialization enhances political participation in one's adult life.

Even more important than how one acquires civics skills is *who* acquires these skills. This is where the public school system must take responsibility. Perhaps political theorist Benjamin Barber (1998) put it most passionately when he wrote:

It is the glory and the burden of public schools that they cater to *all* of our children, whether delinquent or obedient, drug damaged or clean, brilliant or handicapped, privileged or scarred. This is what makes them *public* schools. (p. 227)

Thus, education can play a key role in offsetting distrust in democratic institutions, by providing citizens from all strata with basic knowledge of the political process and helping them understand the citizen's role in a democratic society.

Beyond schooling, the finding that expertise increases confidence charges the media with raising citizens' awareness, interest, and knowledge of their institutions. This is no small feat, and in a time when efforts to print (or broadcast) "all the news that's fit to print" have fallen victim to commercial pressures, the media's responsibility to disseminate substantive political information has become increasingly burdensome.

Critics cannot deny the fourth estate's role as a political educator. After all, television and, more recently, the Internet have made politics accessible to a greater number of citizens. They have brought the Beltway and its personalities into millions of Americans' homes. But to what end? Television viewing suppresses public confidence in some democratic institutions. It also has a long, albeit somewhat contested, history of falling short of the print media in educating the public.

Can the media stimulate awareness, interest, and knowledge of political affairs? Yes, according to the founders of the public journalism movement (e.g., Black, 1997; Charity, 1995; Rosen, 1996). Given declining membership in civic associations (Putnam, 1995a, b) and steadily falling levels of political participation (Verba, Schlozman, & Brady, 1995), public journalism was designed to combat citizens' discontent with politics and to revive civic life. Where traditional or "conventional" journalists see the people who purchase their newspapers as readers, public—or civic—journalists view them as readers who *want* to be citizens, hampered only by time, money, access, and expertise (Charity, 1995). Hence the public journalist takes it upon himself or herself to link the citizen with the system, or as movement founder and chief spokesman Jay Rosen (1991) noted:

If politics has lost its hold on citizens, the solution is to start with what does have a hold on citizens. The political reporter needs to be redefined as someone who enters in to the common life of the community in search of politics. (p. 18)

As such, successful public journalism projects stimulate discussion among citizens, promote political participation, and reconstitute the public (Carey, 1987). The content of public journalism then has the potential to increase awareness, interest, and knowledge of public affairs, and ultimately trust in our democratic institutions. However, this cannot be accomplished if the assumption of public journalism—that the individual media consumer wants to be a citizen—is not met.

To return to the question posed at the beginning of this chapter, the mass media system *in its entirety* has not made it harder for the system to work. The news media have a responsibility to inform the public and, in doing so fairly, may convey information that, in the short- or long-term, hurts the system. But if *parts* of the mass media consistently undermine citizens' confidence in the system, then they are making it more difficult for a democracy to function properly. Change can occur only if the media reach within to meet the standards they have set for themselves as a democratic institution.

References

Abramson, P. R. (1983). *Political attitudes in America: Formation and change.* San Francisco: W. H. Freeman and Company.

Abt, V., & Seesholtz, M. (1994). The shameless world of Phil, Sally and Oprah: Television talk shows and the deconstructing of society. *Journal of Popular Culture, 28,* 195–215.

Alvarez, L. (1998, January 27). Some optimistic words break democratic silence on Clinton. *New York Times,* p. A16.

Alwin, D., & Hauser, R. M. (1975). The decomposition of effects in path analysis. *American Sociological Review, 40,* 37–47.

Ansolabehere, S., Behr, R., & Iyengar, S. (1993). *The media game: American politics in the television age.* New York: Macmillan.

Ansolabehere, S., & Iyengar, S. (1995). *Going negative: How attack ads shrink and polarize the electorate.* New York: The Free Press.

Arbitron. (1994, Spring). *Radio market report: Audience estimates in the metropolitan statistical area and TSA for: Madison, WI.* New York: The Arbitron Company.

———. (1996, Spring). *Quarterly radio local market report for the general listening audience, twelve and over.* New York: The Arbitron Company.

Arendt, H. (1958). *The human condition.* Chicago: University of Chicago Press.

———. (1961). *Between past and future: Eight exercises in political thought.* New York: Viking Press.

Armstrong, C. B., & Rubin, A. M. (1989). Talk radio as interpersonal communication. *Journal of Communication, 39,* 84–91.

Asher, H. B. (1983). *Causal modeling* (2nd ed.). Beverly Hills, CA: Sage.

———. (1984). Regression analysis. In H. B. Asher, H. F. Weisberg, J. H. Kessel, & W. P. Shively (Eds.), *Theory-building and data analysis in the social sciences* (pp. 237–261). Knoxville, TN: University of Tennessee Press.

———. (1988). *Polling and the public: What every citizen should know.* Washington, D.C.: Congressional Quarterly Press.

Audience Research & Development. (1997, February). *A study of newspaper reader attitudes*. Dallas, TX: Audience Research & Development.

Audit Report. (1995). Schaumburg: Audit Bureau of Circulations.

———. (1996). Schaumburg: Audit Bureau of Circulations.

Auletta, K. (1991). *Three blind mice: How the TV networks lost their way*. New York: Random House.

Avery, R. K., & Ellis, D. G. (1979). Talk radio as an interpersonal phenomenon. In G. Gumpert & R. Cathcart (Eds.), *Inter/media: Interpersonal communication in a media world* (pp. 108–115). New York: Oxford University Press.

Avery, R. K., Ellis, D. G., & Glover, T. W. (1978). Patterns of communication on talk radio. *Journal of Broadcasting, 22*, 5–17.

Baldwin, T. F., Barrett, M., & Bates, B. (1992). Influence of cable on television news audiences. *Journalism Quarterly, 69*, 651–658.

Barber, B. (1983). *The logic and limits of trust*. New Brunswick, NJ: Rutgers University Press.

Barber, B. R. (1998). *A passion for democracy: American essays*. Princeton, NJ: Princeton University Press.

Barker, D. C. (1998). Rush to action: Political talk radio and health care (un)reform. *Political Communication, 15*, 85–99.

Becker, L. B., Sobowale, I. A., & Casey, W. E., Jr. (1979). Newspaper and television dependencies: Effects on evaluations of public officials. *Journal of Broadcasting, 23*, 465–475.

Becker, L. B., & Whitney, D. C. (1980). Effects of media dependencies: Audience assessment of government. *Communication Research, 7*, 95–120.

Bennett, S. E. (1986). *Apathy in America 1960–1984: Causes & consequences of citizen political indifference*. Dobbs Ferry, NY: Transnational Publishers.

Berger, P. L., & Luckmann, T. (1967). *The social construction of reality: A treatise in the sociology of knowledge*. Garden City, NY: Anchor.

Bielby, W. T., & Hauser, R. M. (1977). Structural equation models. *Annual Review of Sociology, 3*, 137–161.

Black, G. S., & Black, B. D. (1994). *The politics of American discontent: How a new party can make democracy work again*. New York: John Wiley & Sons.

Black, J. (1997). *Mixed news: The public/civic/communitarian journalism debate*. Mahwah, NJ: Erlbaum.

Blackman, A., Bonfante, J., Dahir, M., Drummond, T., Graff, J. L., & Rivera, E. (1996, October 21). Read all about it. *Time*, pp. 66–69.

Blackman, A., Cohen, A., Jackson, D. S., & Tynan, W. (1996, October 21). The news wars. *Time*, pp. 58–64.

Blendon, R. J., Benson, J. M., Morin, R., Altman, D. E., Brodie, M., Brossard, M., & James, M. (1997). Changing attitudes in America. In J. S. Nye, Jr., P. D. Zelikow, & D. C. King (Eds.), *Why people don't trust government* (pp. 205–216). Cambridge: Harvard University Press.

Blumler, J. G. (1997). Origins of the crisis of communication for citizenship. *Political Communication, 14*, 395–404.

Bogart, L. (1998). Media and democracy. In E. E. Dennis & R. W. Snyder (Eds.), *Media & democracy* (pp. 3–11). New Brunswick, NJ: Transaction Publishers.

Bok, D. (1997). Measuring the performance of government. In J. S. Nye, Jr., P. D. Zelikow, & D. C. King (Eds.), *Why people don't trust government* (pp. 55–75). Cambridge: Harvard University Press.

Bok, S. (1978). *Lying: Moral choice in public and private life*. New York: Pantheon Books.

Borrell, A. J., & Schwenk, M. M. (1997, May). Political talk radio: Giving America something to talk about. Paper presented at the annual meeting of the International Communication Association, Montreal, Canada.

Braun, G. (1994, October 23). Voters a weary, wary lot. *San Diego Union-Tribune*, p. A1.

Brossard, M. (1996, January 29). Audience participation in radio land: Limbaugh listeners most likely to vote. *Washington Post*, p. A7.

Brownstein, R. (1995, April 30). The Time Poll: Public fears the price of security may be liberty. *Los Angeles Times*, p. A1.

Brudnoy, D. (1994, Summer). Gurus of gab: Talk radio stars are changing America. *Policy Review, 69*, 60–67.

Budiansky, S. (1995, January 9). The media's message: The public thinks the national press is elitist, insensitive, and arrogant. *U.S. News & World Report*, pp. 45–47.

Caldeira, G. A. (1986). Neither the purse nor the sword: Dynamics of public confidence in the Supreme Court. *American Political Science Review, 80*, 1211–1226.

Campbell, D., & Stanley, J. (1963). *Experimental and quasi-experimental designs for research*. Chicago: Rand McNally.

Campbell, R. (1991). *60 Minutes and the news: A mythology for middle America*. Urbana, IL: University of Illinois Press.

Cannon, C. L., & Barham, F. E. (1993). Are you and your public polls apart? What those national poll results really mean. *Executive Educator, 15*, 41–42.

Cappella, J. N., & Jamieson, K. H. (1996). News frames, political cynicism, and media cynicism. *Annals of the American Academy of Political and Social Science, 546*, 71–84.

———. (1997). *Spiral of cynicism: The press and the public good*. New York: Oxford University Press.

Cappella, J. N., Turow, J., & Jamieson, K. H. (1996). *Call-in political talk radio: Background, content, audiences, portrayal in mainstream media* (Rep. No. 5). Philadelphia: University of Pennsylvania, Annenberg Public Policy Center.

Carey, J. W. (1987, March/April). The press and public discourse. *The Center Magazine, 20*, 4–16.

Center for Media and Public Affairs. (1994, July/August). They're no friends of Bill: TV news coverage of the Clinton administration. *Media Monitor, 8*, 1–7.

Center for Political Studies. (1996). *1996 American National Election Study*. Ann Arbor, MI: Institute for Social Research, University of Michigan.

Chaffee, S. H., & Schleuder, J. (1986). Measurement and effects of attention to media news. *Human Communication Research, 13*, 76–107.

Chaffee, S. H., Zhao, X., & Leshner, G. (1994). Political knowledge and the campaign media of 1992. *Communication Research, 21*, 305–324.

Chaiken, S. (1987). The heuristic model of persuasion. In M. P. Zanna, J. M. Olson, & C. P. Herman (Eds.), *Social influence: The Ontario symposium* (Vol. 5, pp. 3–39). Hillsdale, NJ: Lawrence Erlbaum.

Chanley, V., & Rahn, W. M. (1996). A time series perspective on Americans' views of government and the nation. Paper presented at the annual meeting of the American Political Science Association, San Francisco, California.

Charity, A. (1995). *Doing public journalism*. New York: Guilford.

Chesebro, J. W., & Bertelsen, D. A. (1996). *Analyzing media: Communication technologies as symbolic and cognitive systems*. New York: Guilford Press.

Chesebro, J. W., & Hamsher, C. D. (1976). Communication, values, and popular television series. In H. Newcomb (Ed.), *Television: The critical view* (pp. 6–25). New York: Oxford University Press.

Chester, E. W. (1969). *Radio, television, and American politics*. New York: Sheed and Ward.

Chua-Eoan, H., & Gleick, E. (1995, October 16). Making the case. *Time*, pp. 48–64.

Citrin, J. (1974). Comment: The political relevance of trust in government. *American Political Science Review, 68*, 973–988.

Citrin, J., & Green, D. P. (1986). Presidential leadership and the resurgence of trust in government. *British Journal of Political Science, 16*, 431–453.

Citrin, J., Green, D., & Reingold, B. (1987, November/December). The soundness of our structure: Confidence in the Reagan years. *Public Opinion*, pp. 18–19, 59–60.

Citrin, J., & Luks, S. (1998, October). Political trust revisited: Déjà vu all over again? Paper presented at the Hendrick Symposium on Public Dissatisfaction with Government, Lincoln, Nebraska.

Clines, F. X. (1998, January 27). Mrs. Clinton in Harlem: A portrait of resilience. *New York Times*, p. A16.

Clines, F. X., & Gerth, G. (1998, January 22). Subpoenas sent as Clinton denies reports of an affair with aide at White House. *New York Times*, p. A1, A24.

Cohen, A. (1998, Winter). Lessons from the Timothy McVeigh trial. *Media Studies Journal, 12*, 14–17.

Comstock, G. (1980). *Television in America*. Beverly Hills, CA: Sage.

Converse, P. E. (1972). Change in the American electorate. In A. Campbell & P. E. Converse (Eds.), *The human meaning of social change* (pp. 263–337). New York: Russell Sage Foundation.

Craig, S. C. (1993). *The malevolent leaders: Popular discontent in America*. Boulder, CO: Westview.

———. (1996). The angry voter: Politics and popular discontent in the 1990s. In S. C. Craig (Ed.), *Broken contract? Changing relationships between Americans and their government* (pp. 46–60). Boulder, CO: Westview Press.

Crittenden, J. (1971). Democratic functions of the open mike radio program. *Public Opinion Quarterly, 35*, 200–210.

Cronbach, L. J. (1951). Coefficient alpha and the internal structure of tests. *Psychometrika, 16*, 297–334.

Crotty, W. J., & Jacobson, G. C. (1980). *American parties in decline*. Boston: Little, Brown and Company.

Culbertson, H. M., & Stempel H., III. (1985). "Media malaise": Explaining personal optimism and societal pessimism about health care. *Journal of Communication, 43*, 180–190.

Davidson, R. H., Kovenock, D. M., & O'Leary, M. K. (1966). *Congress in crisis: Politics and congressional reform*. Belmont, CA: Wadsworth.

Davidson, R. H., & Parker, G. R. (1972). Positive support for political institutions: The case of Congress. *The Western Political Quarterly, 25*, 600–612.

Davis, R. (1997). Understanding broadcast political talk. *Political Communication, 14*, 323–332.

DeFleur, M. L., & Dennis, E. E. (1998). *Understanding mass communication: A liberal arts perspective (6th ed.)*. Boston: Houghton Mifflin.

Delli Carpini, M. X., & Keeter, S. (1996). *What Americans know about politics and why it matters*. New Haven, CT: Yale University Press.

Denton, F. (1995, August 27). City's schools need guidance from the people. *Wisconsin State Journal*, p. 1B.

Dionne, E. J., Jr. (1991). *Why Americans hate politics*. New York: Simon & Schuster.

Donlon, B. (1993, February 11). After the blowup: The long-term impact is often slight; NBC begins to regroup after apology. *USA Today*, p. 1D.

Dowling, R. E. (1989). Print journalism as political communication: The Iran hostage crisis. *Political Communication and Persuasion 6*, 129–150.

Eagly, A. H., & Chaiken, S. (1993). *The psychology of attitudes*. Orlando, FL: Harcourt Brace Jovanovich.

Editor and Publisher International Year Book (1995) *Top one hundred daily newspapers in the United States according to circulation Sep 30, 1994*. New York: Editor and Publisher.

———. (1996). *Top one hundred daily newspapers in the United States according to circulation Sep. 30, 1995*. New York: Editor and Publisher.

Edsall, T. (1994, October 6). America's sweetheart. *The New York Review of Books*, pp. 6–10.

Edwards, E. (1995, February 22). O. J.'s supporting role: Trial lifts TV crime coverage to new high. *Washington Post*, p. D1.

Elam, S. M. (1984). *The Phi Delta Kappa/Gallup Polls of attitudes toward education, 1969–1984*. Bloomington, IN: Phi Delta Kappa Educational Foundation.

Elam, S. M., & Rose, L. C., & Gallup, A. M. (1995). The twenty-seventh annual Phi Delta Kappa/Gallup Poll of the public's attitudes toward the public schools. *Phi Delta Kappan, 77*, 41–56.

Electronic Media. (1995, September 4). Viewers give local media high mark, pp. 1 & 29.

Elshtain, J. B. (1995). *Democracy on trial*. New York: Basic Books.

Erber, R., & Lau, R. R. (1990). Political cynicism revisited: An information-processing reconciliation of policy-based and incumbency-based interpretations of changes in trust in government. *American Journal of Political Science, 34*, 236–253.

Fallows, J. (1996). *Breaking the news: How the media undermine American democracy*. New York: Pantheon Books.

Fedler, F., Meeske, M., & Hall, J. (1979). *Time* magazine revisited: Presidential stereotypes persist. *Journalism Quarterly, 56*, 353–359.

Feldman, S. (1983). The measurement and meaning of trust in government. *Political Methodology, 9*, 341–354.

Finifter, A. W. (1970). Dimensions of political alienation. *American Political Science Review, 64*, 389–410.

Fiske, S. T., Lau, R. R., & Smith, R. A. (1990). On the varieties and utilities of political expertise. *Social Cognition, 8*, 31–48.

Fleeson, L. (1995, April 24). Talk radio hosts blast attacks on "Debate of Ideas." *The Philadelphia Inquirer*, p. 1.

Fowles, J. (1992). *Why viewers watch: A reappraisal of television's effects (rev. ed.).* Newbury Park, CA: Sage.

Frisby, C. M. (1998, August). Can social comparison theory explain fascination with TV talk shows? Paper presented at the annual meeting of the Association for Education in Journalism and Mass Communication, Baltimore, Maryland.

Frisby, C. M., & Weigold, M. (1994, August). *Gratifications of talk: Esteem and affect-related consequences of viewing television talk shows.* Paper presented at the annual meeting of the Association for Education in Journalism and Mass Communication, Atlanta, Georgia.

Gallup Organization. (1987). *Confidence in institutions: Religion regains public confidence after declining last year* (Survey 278-G, Q.). New York: The Gallup Organization.

———. (1995). American confidence in public institutions on the rise. *The Gallup Poll News Service* (vol. 60, no. 1), pp. 1–4.

———. (1996). *Public confidence in major institutions little changed from 1995.* New York: The Gallup Organization.

Gallup/Phi Delta Kappa. (1981–1997). *Gallup/Phi Delta Kappan poll of the public's attitudes toward the public schools.* New York: The Gallup Organization.

Gamson, W. A. (1968). *Power and discontent.* Homewood, IL: Dorsey.

Garramone, G. M. (1983). Issue versus image orientation and effects in political advertising. *Communication Research, 10*, 59–76.

———. (1985). Effects of negative political advertising: The roles of sponsor and rebuttal. *Journal of Broadcasting & Electronic Media, 29*, 147–159.

Gebotys, R. J., Roberts, J. V., & DasGupta, B. (1988). News media use and public perceptions of crime seriousness. *Canadian Journal of Criminology, 30*, 3–16.

Gerbner, G., & Gross, L. (1976). Living with television: The violence profile. *Journal of Communication, 26*, 173–199.

Gerbner, G., Gross, L., Morgan, M., & Signorielli, N. (1980). The "mainstreaming" of America: Violence profile no. 11. *Journal of Communication, 30*, 10–29.

———. (1986). Living with television: The dynamics of the cultivation process. In J. Bryant & D. Zillmann (Eds.), *Perspectives on media effects* (pp. 17–40). Hillsdale, NJ: Lawrence Erlbaum.

———. (1994). Growing up with television: The cultivation perspective. In J. Bryant & D. Zillmann (Eds.), *Media effects: Advances in theory and research* (pp. 17–41), Hillsdale, NJ: Lawrence Erlbaum.

Gibson, D. C. (1997). A quantitative description of FBI public relations. *Public Relations Review, 23*, 11–30

Giddens, A. (1990). *The consequences of modernity.* Stanford, CA: Stanford University Press.

———. (1991). *Modernity and self-identity: Self and society in the late modern age.* Cambridge: Polity Press.

Gitlin, T. (1977). The televised professional. *Social Policy, 8*, 94–99.

Goel, M. L. (1980). Conventional political participation. In D. H. Smith & J. Macaulay (Eds.), *Participation in social and political activities* (pp. 108–132). San Francisco: Jossey-Bass.

Goffman, E. (1973). *The presentation of self in everyday life.* Woodstock, NY: Overlook.

Graber, D. A. (1980). *Mass media and American politics.* Washington, D.C.: Congressional Quarterly Press.

———. (1993). *Mass media and American politics (4th ed.).* Washington, D.C.: Congressional Quarterly Press.

———. (1996). Say it with pictures. *The Annals of the American Academy of Political and Social Science, 546,* 86–96.

Greenberg, B. S., Sherry, J. S., Busselle, R. W., & Rampoldi-Hnilo, L. (1996, August). Daytime television talk shows: Tops, guests and reactions. Paper presented at the annual meeting of the Association for Education in Journalism and Mass Communication, Anaheim, California.

Grossman, L. K. (1995). *The electronic republic: Reshaping democracy in the information age.* New York: Penguin.

GSS News. (1997, August). Trendlets: Confidence in government, p. 3. Storrs, CT: Roper Center, University of Connecticut.

Guo, Z., & Moy, P. (1998). Medium or message? Predicting dimensions of political sophistication. *International Journal of Public Opinion Research, 10,* 25–50.

Gurevitch, M., & Blumler, J. G. (1990). Political communication systems and democratic values. In J. Lichtenberg (Ed.), *Democracy and the mass media* (pp. 269–289). Cambridge: Cambridge University Press.

Hagerty, R. (1995). *The crisis of confidence in American education: A blueprint for fixing what is wrong and restoring America's confidence in the public schools.* Springfield, IL: Charles C. Thomas.

Hallin, D. C. (1986). We keep America on top of the world. In T. Gitlin (Ed.), *Watching television* (pp. 9–41). New York: Pantheon Books.

———. (1992). Sound bite news: Television coverage of elections, 1968–1988. *Journal of Communication, 42,* 5–24.

Harris, J. F. (1995, April 26) Clinton says talk shows not his only target. *Washington Post,* p. A14.

Hart, P. D., & Teeter, R. M. (1995, March). *A national public opinion survey conducted for the council for excellence in government* (Study #4356B). Washington, D.C.: Council for Excellence in Government.

Hart, R. P., Smith-Howell, D., & Llewellyn, J. (1990). Evolution of presidential news coverage. *Political Communication and Persuasion, 7,* 213–230.

Hart, V. (1978). *Distrust and democracy: Political distrust in Britain and America.* New York: Cambridge University Press.

Harwood, R. (1996, February 5). The messenger shouldn't bear all the blame. *Washington Post,* p. A21.

Havig, A. (1992). Fred Allen and radio comedy as a vehicle of social criticism. *Journal of Radio Studies, 1,* 97–103.

Hawkins, R. P., & Pingree, S. (1981). Uniform messages and habitual viewing: Unnecessary assumptions in social reality effects. *Human Communication Research, 7,* 291–301.

———. (1982). Television's influence on social reality. In D. Pearl, L. Bouthilet, & J. Lazar (Eds.), *Television and behavior: Ten years of scientific progress and implications for the eighties* (pp. 224–247). Washington, D.C.: Government Printing Office.

Henneberger, M. (1998, January 25). Tense home life before moving to capital. *New York Times*, p. A17.

Herbst, S. (1995). On electronic public space: Talk shows in theoretical perspective. *Political Communication, 12,* 263–274.

The Heritage Foundation. (1993). *The "Fairness Doctrine": Pulling the plug on talk radio.* Washington, D.C.: The Heritage Foundation.

Hess, S. (1996). *News & newsmaking.* Washington, D.C.: The Brookings Institution.

Hibbing, J. R., & Theiss-Morse, E. (1995). *Congress as public enemy: Public attitudes toward American political institutions.* New York: Cambridge University Press.

Hill, D. B. (1981). Attitude generalization and the measurement of trust in American leadership. *Political Behavior, 3,* 257–270.

Hirsch, P. (1980). The "scary world" of the nonviewer and other anomalies: Reanalysis of Gerbner et al.'s finding on cultivation analysis: Part I. *Communication Research, 7,* 403–456.

———. (1981). On not learning from one's own mistakes: A reanalysis of Gerbner et al.'s findings on cultivation analysis: Part II. *Communication Research, 8,* 3–37.

Hochschild, J., & Scott, B. (1998). The polls—trends: Governance and reform of public education in the United States. *Public Opinion Quarterly, 62,* 79–120.

Hofstetter, C. R. (1996, April). Situational involvement and political mobilization: Political talk radio and public action. Paper presented at the annual meeting of the Midwest Political Science Association, Chicago, Illinois.

Hofstetter, C. R., Donovan, M. C., Klauber, M. R., Cole, A., Huie, C. J., & Yuasa, T. (1994). Political talk radio: A stereotype reconsidered. *Political Research Quarterly, 47,* 467–479.

Hollander, B. A. (1995). The new news and the 1992 presidential campaign: Perceived versus actual political knowledge. *Journalism & Mass Communication Quarterly, 72,* 786–798.

———. (1996). Talk radio: Predictors of use and effects on attitudes about government. *Journalism and Mass Communication Quarterly, 73,* 102–113.

———. (1997). Fuel to the fire: Talk radio and the Gamson hypothesis. *Political Communication, 14,* 355–369.

Horowitz, D. L. (1987, Summer). Is the presidency failing? *The Public Interest,* pp. 3–27.

Hulin-Salikin, B. (1987, July 20). Stretching to deliver readers' needs. *Advertising Age,* pp. S-1, S-2, S-4, S-6.

Hull, J. D., Rothchild, J., Shannon, E., & Gleick, E. (1995, January 30). The state of the union: As Clinton reports to the Congress, citizens are busy remaking America. *Time,* pp. 52–75.

Huntington, S. P. (1975). The United States. In M. Crozier, S. P. Huntington, & J. Watanuki (Eds.), *The crisis of democracy: Report on the governability of democracies to the Trilateral Commission.* (pp. 59–118) New York: New York University Press.

Inglehart, R. (1997). Postmaterialist values and the erosion of institutional authority. In J. S. Nye, Jr., P. D. Zelikow, & D. C. King (Eds.), *Why people don't trust government* (pp. 217–236). Cambridge: Harvard University Press.

International Demographics (1996). *The Media Audit*. Houston, TX: International Demographics, Inc.

Iyengar, S. (1991). *Is anyone responsible?* Chicago: University of Chicago Press.

Iyengar, S., & Kinder, D. (1987). *News that matters: Television and American opinion*. Chicago: University of Chicago Press.

Izard, R. S. (1985). Public confidence in the news media. *Journalism Quarterly, 62*, 247–255.

Jaffe, E. A. (1994, July). Antipolitics as an American given, gift to the world, and the Trojan Horse. Paper presented at the Vienna Dialogue on Democracy Conference on "The Politics of Antipolitics," Vienna, Austria.

Johnson, A. P., & Shields, S. (1995, May). George Bush and "that vision thing": Newsmagazine coverage and public opinion during the 1992 presidential campaign. Paper presented at the annual meeting of the International Communication Association, Albuquerque, New Mexico.

Johnson, K. S. (1986). The portrayal of lame-duck presidents by the national print media. *Presidential Studies Quarterly, 16*, 50–65.

Jones, T. (1994, July 17). Hot air on the air: Talk is not only cheap, it's calling out to more and more listeners, radio stations are discovering. *Chicago Tribune*, p. 1.

Jöreskog, K. G. (1993). Testing structural equation models. In K. A. Bollen & J. S. Long (Eds.), *Testing structural equation models* (pp. 294–316). Newbury Park, CA: Sage.

Jost, K. (1994, April 29). Talk show democracy: The issues. *The CQ Researcher*, 363–383.

Just, M. R., Crigler, A. N., Alger, D. E., Cook, T. E., Kern, M., & West, D. M. (1996). *Crosstalk: Citizens, candidates and the media in a presidential campaign*. Chicago: University of Chicago Press.

Kaid, L. L., & Sanders, K. R. (1978). Political television commercials: An experimental study of type and length. *Communication Research, 5*, 57–70.

Kaniss, P. (1991). *Making local news*. Chicago: University of Chicago Press.

Katz, J. L. (1991, March). The power of talk. *Governing*, pp. 38–42.

Kaye, J. S. (1998, Winter). The third branch and the fourth estate. *Media Studies Journal, 12*, 74–79.

Kedrowski, K. M. (1988). Elite press perceptions of Congress: The Iran-Contra investigations. Paper presented at the annual meeting of the Southern Political Science Association, Atlanta, Georgia.

Kern, M., Just, M., & Crigler, A. (1997, November). Citizen use of world wide web sites in the 1996 presidential election. Paper presented an the annual meeting of the National Communication Association, Chicago, Illinois.

Kernall, S. (1978). Explaining presidential popularity. *American Political Science Review, 72*, 506–522.

Kettering Foundation. (1991). *Citizens and politics: A view from Main Street America*. Dayton, OH: Kettering Foundation.

Kinder, D. R. (1981). Presidents, prosperity, and public opinion. *Public Opinion Quarterly, 45*, 1–21.

Kinder, D. R., & Sanders, L. M. (1996). *Divided by color: Racial politics and democratic ideals.* Chicago: University of Chicago Press.

King, D. C. (1997). The polarization of American parties and mistrust of government. In J. S. Nye, Jr., P. D. Zelikow, & D. C. King (Eds.), *Why people don't trust government* (pp. 155–178). Cambridge: Harvard University Press.

Klein, J. (1995, September 25). Stalking the radical middle. *Newsweek,* pp. 32–36.

Kohut, A., & Toth, R. C. (1998). The central conundrum: How can the people like what they distrust? *Press/Politics, 3,* 110–117.

Kraft, J. (1981, January 18). Ramshackle legacy. . . . *Washington Post,* p. C7.

Kurtz, H. (1996). *Hot air: All talk, all the time.* New York: Times Books.

———. (1999). Tuning out traditional news. In R. E. Hiebert (Ed.), *Impact of mass media: Current issues (4th ed.)* (pp. 72–77). New York: Longman.

Ladd, E. C., Jr. (1981, June/July). 205 and going strong. *Public Opinion,* pp. 7–12.

Lane, R. E. (1959). *Political life: How and why people get involved in politics.* New York: Free Press.

Lau, R. R., & Erber, R. (1985). Political sophistication: An information-processing perspective. In S. Kraus & R. M. Perloff (Eds.), *Mass media and political thought* (pp. 37–64). Beverly Hills, CA: Sage.

Lawrence, R. Z. (1997). Is it really the economy, stupid? In J. S. Nye, Jr., P. D. Zelikow, & D. C. King (Eds.), *Why people don't trust government* (pp. 111–132). Cambridge: Harvard University Press.

Levin, M. B. (1987). *Talk radio and the American dream.* Lexington, MA: Lexington Books.

Leykis, T. (1996, August). The talk shows in an election year: Bypassing journalists? Annual meeting of the Association for Education in Journalism & Mass Communication, Anaheim, California.

Lichter, S. R., & Amundson, D. R. (1994). Less news is worse news: Television news coverage of Congress, 1972–92. In T. E. Mann & N. J. Ornstein (Eds.), *Congress, the press, and the public* (pp. 131–140). Washington, D.C.: American Enterprise Institute and the Brookings Institution.

Lichter, S. R., Lichter, L. S., & Rothman, S. (1994). *Prime time: How TV portrays American culture.* Washington, DC: Regency Publishing Inc.

Limbaugh, R. (1993). *See, I told you so.* New York: Pocket Books.

Lippmann, W. (1922). *Public opinion.* New York: Free Press.

Lipset, S. M., & Schneider, W. (1983, August/September). Confidence in confidence measures. *Public Opinion,* pp. 42–44.

———. (1987). *The confidence gap: Business, labor, and government in the public mind* (rev. ed.). Baltimore, MD: Johns Hopkins University Press.

Livingstone, S. (1994). Watching talk: Gender and engagement in the viewing of audience discussion programmes. *Media, Culture & Society, 16,* 429–447.

Lorando, M. (1995, April 2). NBC news show hotter than ever. *The Times-Picayune,* T7.

Loveless, T. (1997). The structure of public confidence in education. *American Journal of Education, 105,* 127–159.

Luntz, F., & Dermer, R. (1994, September/October). A farewell to the American dream? *The Public Perspective,* pp. 12–14.

MacCallum, R. C. (1995). Model specification: Procedures, strategies, and related issues. In R. H. Hoyle (Ed.), *Structural equation modeling: Concepts, issues, and applications* (pp. 16–36). Thousand Oaks, CA: Sage.

Macke, A. S. (1979). Trends in aggregate-level political alienation. *The Sociological Quarterly, 20,* 77–87.

Magleby, D. B., & Patterson, K. D. (1994). The polls—trends: Congressional reform. *Public Opinion Quarterly, 58,* 419–427.

Mann, T. E., & Ornstein, N. J. (1994). *Congress, the press, and the public.* Washington, D.C.: American Enterprise Institute and the Brookings Institution.

Mansbridge, J. (1997). Social and cultural causes of dissatisfaction with U.S. government. In J. S. Nye, Jr., P. D. Zelikow, & D. C. King (Eds.), *Why people don't trust government* (pp. 133–153). Cambridge: Harvard University Press.

Markus, G. B. (1979). The political environment and the dynamics of public attitudes: A panel study. *American Journal of Political Science, 23,* 338–359.

Mayer, R., & Gross, K. (1996, April). The empowering effects of talk radio. Paper presented at the annual meeting of the Midwest Political Science Association, Chicago, Illinois.

McAnery, L. (1996). *Public confidence in major institutions little changed from 1995.* www.gallup.com.news/960606.html.

McAnery, L., & Moore, D. W. (1995, May 6). American confidence in public institutions on the rise. *The Gallup Poll News Service,* Vol. 60, No. 1, pp. 3–4.

McAvoy, K. (1993, September 27). White House woos local news outlets. *Broadcasting and Cable,* p. 54.

McCombs, M. E., Einsiedel, E., & Weaver, D. (1991). *Contemporary public opinion: Issues and the news.* Hillsdale, NJ: Lawrence Erlbaum.

McCroskey, J. C., Jenson, T. A., & Valencia, C. (1973, April). *Measurement of the credibility of peers and spouses.* Paper presented at the annual meeting of the International Communication Association, Montreal, Canada.

McFarlin, J. (1995, June 14). Networks cut back on magazines as credibility and ratings go south. *The Detroit News,* p. C1.

McLeod, J. M., Brown, J. D., Becker, L. B., & Ziemke, D. A. (1977). Decline and fall at the White House: A longitudinal analysis of communication effects. *Communication Research, 4,* 3–22.

McLeod, J. M., Daily, K., Eveland, W., Guo, Z., Culver, K., Kurpius, D., Moy, P., Horowitz, E., & Zhong, M. (1995). The synthetic crisis: Media influences on perceptions of crime. Paper presented at the annual meeting of the Association for Education in Journalism and Mass Communication, Washington, D.C.

McLeod, J. M., Guo, Z., Daily, K., Steele, C. A., Huang, H., Horowitz, E. & Chen, H. (1996). The impact of traditional and nontraditional media forms in the 1992 presidential election. *Journalism & Mass Communication Quarterly, 73,* 401–416.

McLeod, J. M., & McDonald, D. G. (1985). Beyond simple exposure: Media orientations and their impact on political processes. *Communication Research, 12,* 3–33.

McLeod, J., Ward, S., & Tancill, K. (1965–1966). Alienation and uses of the mass media. *Public Opinion Quarterly, 29,* 583–594.

Media Monitor. (1996, January/February). *1995 year in review.* www.cmpa.com/html/janfeb96.htlm#laughter.

Mediamark Research (1993). *Television audience report* (T-1). New York: Mediamark Research, Inc.

Merkle, D. M. (1996). The polls—review: The National Issues Convention deliberative poll. *Public Opinion Quarterly, 60,* 588–619.

Merrill, J. C. (1965). How *Time* stereotyped three U.S. presidents. *Journalism Quarterly, 42,* 563–570.

Meyer, P. (1993). The media reformation: Giving the agenda back to the people. In M. Nelson (Ed.), *The elections of 1992* (pp. 89–108). Washington, D.C.: Congressional Quarterly Press.

Meyer, T. (1996, October 29). Ex-bomb suspect lashes FBI, media. *Wisconsin State Journal,* p. 2A.

Meyrowitz, J. (1985). *No sense of place: The impact of electronic media on social behavior.* New York: Oxford University Press.

Miller, A. H. (1974a). Political issues and trust in government: 1964–1970. *American Political Science Review, 68,* 951–972.

———. (1974b). Rejoinder to "comment" by Jack Citrin: Political discontent or ritualism. *American Political Science Review, 68,* 989–1001.

Miller, A. H., & Borrelli, S. A. (1991). Confidence in government during the 1980s. *American Politics Quarterly, 19,* 147–173.

Miller, A. H., Goldenberg, E. N., & Erbring, L. (1979). Type-set politics: Impact of newspapers on public confidence. *The American Political Science Review, 73,* 67–84.

Miller, M. D., & Burgoon, M. (1979). The relationship between violations of expectations and induction of resistance to persuasion. *Human Communication Research, 5,* 301–313.

Miller, M. M., & Reese, S. D. (1982). Media dependency as interaction: Effects of exposure and reliance on political activity and efficacy. *Communication Research, 9,* 227–248.

Mondak, J. M. (1996). *Nothing to read: Newspapers and elections in a social experiment.* Ann Arbor, MI: University of Michigan Press.

Moore, D. W., & Newport, F. (1993, April 1). *High public confidence in police, military.* Los Angeles: Times Syndicate.

Moore, M. (1998, January 30). Americans say they're drowning in the deluge. *USA Today,* p. 7A.

Morgan, M., & Shanahan, J. (1997). Two decades of cultivation research: An appraisal and meta-analysis. In B. R. Burelson & A. W. Kunkel (Eds.), *Communication yearbook 20* (pp. 1–45). Thousand Oaks, CA: Sage.

Morgan, M., & Signorielli, N. (1990). Cultivation analysis: Conceptualization and methodology. In N. Signorielli & M. Morgan (Eds.), *Cultivation analysis: New directions in media effects research* (pp. 13–34). Newbury Park, CA: Sage.

Morin, R., & Balz, D. (1996, January 28). Americans losing trust in each other and institutions: Suspicion of strangers breeds widespread cynicism. *Washington Post,* p. A1.

Moy, P., Pfau, M., & Kahlor, L. (1999). Media use and public confidence in democratic institutions. *Journal of Broadcasting & Electronic Media, 43,* 137–158.

Mueller, J. (1973). *War, presidents, and public opinion.* New York: Wiley.

Munson, W. (1993). *All talk: The talk show in media culture.* Philadelphia: Temple University Press.

Murphy, J. W. (1993–94). Cinema verité and the criminal element: A perspective. *Et cetera, 50,* 501–502.

Mutz, D. C. (1994). Contextualizing personal experience: The role of mass media. *Journal of Politics, 56,* 689–714.

Myers, L. (1995, August 1). Americans distrust leaders, opening door for new party. *Wisconsin State Journal,* p. 4A.

Nelson, S. A. (1989). Crime-time television. *FBI Law Enforcement Bulletin, 58* (8), 1–9.

Neuendorf, K., Jeffres, L., & Atkin, D. (1995). Cultivation and the influence of media in public opinion homogenization. Paper presented at the annual meeting of the Association for Education in Journalism and Mass Communication, Washington, D.C.

Neuman, W. R. (1986). *The paradox of mass politics: Knowledge and opinion in the mass electorate.* Cambridge: Harvard University Press.

Neustadt, R. E. (1997). The politics of mistrust. In J. S. Nye, Jr., P. D. Zelikow, & D. C. King (Eds.), *Why people don't trust government* (pp. 179–201). Cambridge: Harvard University Press.

The New York Times. (1974, July 14). Impeachable offenses. Section 4, p. 16.

Newhagen, J. E. (1994). Self-efficacy and call-in political television talk show use. *Communication Research, 21,* 366–379.

Newspaper Association of America. (1997, June). *Leveraging newspaper assets.* New York: Clark, Martire, & Bartolomeo, Inc.

Nie, N. H., Junn, J., & Stehlik-Barry, K. (1996). *Education and democratic citizenship in America.* Chicago: University of Chicago Press.

Nielsen. (1993). *Nielsen station index for television and radio, Madison, WI.* New York: Nielsen Media Research.

———. (1995). *Nielsen station index for television and radio, Madison, WI.* New York: Nielsen Media Research.

———. (1996). *Nielsen station index for television and radio, Madison, WI.* New York: Nielsen Media Research.

National Opinion Research Center (1993, November/December). Public opinion and demographic report: Confidence in institutions. *The American Enterprise,* pp. 94–96.

Nye, J. S., Jr. (1997). Introduction: The decline of confidence in government. In J. S. Nye, Jr., P. D. Zelikow, & D. C. King (Eds.), *Why people don't trust government* (pp. 1–18). Cambridge: Harvard University Press.

Nye, J. S., Jr., & Zelikow, P. D. (1997). Conclusion: Reflections, conjectures, and puzzles. In J. S. Nye, Jr., P. D. Zelikow, & D. C. King (Eds.), *Why people don't trust government* (pp. 253–281). Cambridge: Harvard University Press.

Nye, J. S., Jr., Zelikow, P. D., & King, D. C. (Eds.) (1997). *Why people don't trust government.* Cambridge: Harvard University Press.

O'Connor, A.-M. (1995, April 1). Clinton hears Haitian cheers. *Wisconsin State Journal,* p. 1A.

O'Keefe, G. J. (1980). Political malaise and reliance on media. *Journalism Quarterly, 57,* 122–128.

———. (1984). Television exposure, credibility, and public views on crime. In R. Bostrom (Ed.), *Communication yearbook 8* (pp. 513–536). Newbury Park, CA: Sage.

O'Keefe, G. J., & Mendelsohn, H. (1978). Nonvoting: The media's role. In C. Winick (Ed.), *Deviance and the mass media* (pp. 263–286). Beverly Hills, CA: Sage.

O'Keefe, G. J., & Reid-Nash, K. (1987). Crime news and real-world blues: The effects of the media on social reality. *Communication Research, 14,* 147–163.

Oliver, C. (1995, April). Freak parade. *Reason,* pp. 52–54.

Orren, G. (1997). Fall from grace: The public's loss of faith in government. In J. S. Nye, Jr., P. D. Zelikow, & D. C. King (Eds.), *Why people don't trust government* (pp. 77–107). Cambridge: Harvard University Press.

Owen, D. (1995, September). *Old media, new media, and evaluations of President Clinton.* Paper presented at the annual meeting of the American Political Science Association, Chicago, IL.

———. (1996). Who's talking? Who's listening? The new politics of radio talk shows. In S. C. Craig (Ed.), *Broken contract: Changing relationships between Americans and their government* (pp. 127–145). Boulder, CO: Westview Press.

———. (1997). Talk radio and evaluations of President Clinton. *Political Communication, 14,* 333–353.

Page, B. I. (1996). *Who deliberates? Mass media in modern democracy.* Chicago: University of Chicago Press.

Page, B. I., & Shapiro, R. Y. (1992). *The rational public: Fifty years of trends in Americans' policy preferences.* Chicago: University of Chicago Press.

Pan, Z., & Kosicki, G. M. (1997). Talk show exposure as an opinion activity. *Political Communication, 14,* 371–388.

Parisot, L. (1988, January/February). Attitudes about the media: A five country comparison. *Public Opinion,* pp. 18–19.

Parker, G. R. (1977). Some themes in congressional unpopularity. *American Journal of Political Science, 21,* 93–110.

Patterson, S. C., & Caldeira, G. A. (1990). Standing up for Congress: Variations in public esteem since the 1960s. *Legislative Studies Quarterly, 15,* 25–47.

Patterson, T. E. (1991). More style than substance: Television news in U.S. national elections. *Political Communication and Persuasion, 8,* 145–161.

———. (1993). *Out of order.* New York: Alfred A. Knopf.

Pedhazur, E. J. (1982). *Multiple regression in behavioral research: Explanation and prediction (2nd ed.).* New York: Holt, Rinehart and Winston.

Perse, E. M. (1990). Cultivation and involvement with local television news. In N. Signorielli & M. Morgan (Eds.), *Cultivation analysis: New directions in media effects research* (pp. 51–69). Newbury Park, CA: Sage.

Petty, R. E., & Cacioppo, J. T. (1986). The elaboration likelihood model of persuasion. *Advances in Experimental Social Psychology, 19,* 123–205.

Pew Research Center for the People and the Press. (1996, May 13). *TV news viewership declines.* Washington, D.C.: Pew.

———. (1998). *Deconstructing distrust: How Americans view government.* Washington, D.C.: Pew.

Pfau, M., & Burgoon, M. (1988). Inoculation in political campaign communication. *Human Communication Research, 15,* 91–111.

Pfau, M., Diedrich, T., Larson, K. M., & Van Winkle, K. M. (1993). Relational and competence perceptions of presidential candidates during primary election campaigns. *Journal of Broadcasting & Electronic Media, 37,* 275–292.

Pfau, M., Diedrich, T., Larson, K. M., & Van Winkle, K. M. (1995). Influence of communication modalities on voters' perceptions of candidates during presidential primary campaigns. *Journal of Communication, 45* (1), 122–133.

Pfau, M., & Eveland, W. P., Jr. (1996). The influence of traditional and nontraditional news media in the 1992 election campaign. *Western Journal of Communication, 60,* 214–232.

Pfau, M., Kenski, H., Nitz, M., & Sorenson, J. (1990). Efficacy of inoculation strategies in promoting resistance to political attack messages: Application to direct mail. *Communication Monographs, 57,* 1–12.

Pfau, M., Moy, P., Holbert, R. L., Szabo, E. A., Lin, W.-K., & Zhang, W. (1999). Use of political talk radio versus other media and public confidence in democratic institutions. *Journalism & Mass Communication Quarterly, 75,* 730–745.

Pfau, M., Moy, P., Radler, B., & Bridgeman, M. K. (1998). The influence of individual communication media on public confidence in democratic institutions. *The Southern Communication Journal, 63,* 91–112.

Pfau, M., Mullen, L. J., Diedrich, T., & Garrow, K. (1995). Television viewing and public perceptions of attorneys. *Human Communication Research, 21,* 307–330.

Pfau, M., Mullen, L. J., & Garrow, K. (1995). The influence of television viewing on public perceptions of physicians. *Journal of Broadcasting & Electronic Media, 39,* 441–458.

Phillips, K. (1994). *Arrogant capital: Washington, Wall Street, and the frustration of American politics.* Boston: Little, Brown and Company.

Pinkleton, B. E., Austin, E. W., & Fortman, K. K. J. (1998). Relationships of media use and political disaffection to political efficacy and voting behavior. *Journal of Broadcasting & Electronic Media, 42,* 34–49.

Potter, W. J. (1986). Perceived reality and the cultivation hypothesis. *Journal of Broadcasting & Electronic Media, 30,* 159–174.

———. (1988). Three strategies for elaborating the cultivation hypothesis. *Journalism Quarterly, 65,* 930–939.

———. (1993). Cultivation theory and research: A conceptual critique. *Human Communication Research, 19,* 564–601.

Potter, W. J., & Chang, I. C. (1990). Television exposure measures and the cultivation hypothesis. *Journal of Broadcasting & Electronic Media, 34,* 335–350.

Price, V., & Zaller, J. (1993). Who gets the news? Alternative measures of news reception and their implications for research. *Public Opinion Quarterly, 57,* 133–164.

Priest, P. J., & Dominick, J. R. (1994). Pulp pulpits: Self-disclosure on "Donahue." *Journal of Communication, 44,* 74–97.

Putnam, R. (1995a). Bowling alone: America's declining social capital. *Journal of Democracy, 6,* 65–78.

Putnam, R. D. (1995b). Tuning in, tuning out: The strange disappearance of social capital in America. *PS: Political Science & Politics, 28,* 664–683.

Raftery, A. E. (1993). Bayesian model selection in structural equation models. In K. A. Bollen & J. S. Long (Eds.), *Testing structural equation models* (pp. 163–180). Newbury Park, CA: Sage.

———. (1995). Bayesian model selection in social research. In P. V. Marsden

(Ed.), *Sociological methodology 1995, Volume 2* (pp. 111–183). Cambridge, MA: Blackwell.

Rapping, E. (1995, January). Cult tv with a twist. *The Progressive,* pp. 34–36.

Rehm, D. (1996). A tower of Babel: Talk shows and politics. *Press/Politics, 1,* 138–142.

Retter, J. D. (1998). *Anatomy of a scandal: An investigation into the campaign to undermine the Clinton presidency.* Los Angeles: General Publishing Group.

Roberts, J. C. (1991, May/June). The power of talk radio. *The American Enterprise,* pp. 57–61.

Robinson, J. P., & Davis, D. K. (1990). Television news and the informed public: An information-processing approach. *Journal of Communication, 40,* 106–119.

Robinson, J. P., & Levy, M. R. (1986). *The main source: Learning from television news.* Beverly Hills, CA: Sage.

―――. (1996). News media use and the informed public: A 1990s update. *Journal of Communication, 46,* 129–135.

Robinson, M. (1974). The impact of the televised Watergate hearings. *Journal of Communication, 24,* 17–30.

―――. (1975). American political legitimacy in an era of electronic journalism. In D. Cater & R. Adler (Eds.), *Television as a social force: New approaches to TV criticism* (pp. 97–141). New York: Praeger.

―――. (1976). Public affairs television and the growth of political malaise: The case of "The Selling of the Pentagon." *American Political Science Review, 70,* 409–432.

―――. (1977). Television and American politics: 1956–1976. *Public Interest, 48,* 3–39.

―――. (1981). Three faces of Congressional media. In T. E. Mann & N. J. Ornstein (Eds.), *The New Congress* (pp. 55–96). Washington, D.C.: American Enterprise Institute.

Robinson, M. J., & Appel, K. R. (1979). Network news coverage of Congress. *Political Science Quarterly, 94,* 407–48.

Robinson, M. J., & Sheehan, M. (1983). *Over the wire and on TV.* New York: Russell Sage Foundation.

Roeder, P. W. (1994). *Public opinion and policy leadership in the American states.* Tuscaloosa, AL: University of Alabama Press.

Roper Organization. (1981). *Evolving public attitudes toward television and other mass media 1959–1980.* New York: Television Information Office.

Roper Starch Worldwide. (1997, May 28). TV remains dominant news and product information source, new poll reveals. www.roper.com.

Rose, B. G. (Ed.) (1985). *TV genres: A handbook and reference guide.* Westport, CT: Greenwood Press.

Rosen, J. (1991, October). To be or not to be? *ASNE Bulletin, 735,* 16–19.

―――. (1996). *Getting the connections right: Public journalism and the troubles in the press.* New York: The Twentieth Century Fund Press.

Rosen, R. (1997, July 11). The sinister images of "The X-Files." *The Chronicle of Higher Education,* p. B7.

Rosenstone, S. J., & Hansen, J. M. (1993). *Mobilization, participation, and democracy in America.* New York: Macmillan.

Rosenthal, R. (1984). *Meta-analytic procedures for social research.* Beverly Hills, CA: Sage.

————. (1987). *Judgment studies: Design, analysis, and meta-analysis.* Cambridge: Cambridge University Press.

Rozell, M. J. (1994). Press coverage of Congress, 1946–92. In T. E. Mann & N. J. Ornstein (Eds.), *Congress, the press, and the public* (pp. 59–129). Washington, D.C.: American Enterprise Institute and The Brookings Institution.

Rubin, A. M., Perse, E. M., & Taylor, D. S. (1988). A methodological investigation of cultivation. *Communication Research, 15,* 107–134.

Sabato, L. J. (1991). *Feeding frenzy: How attack journalism has transformed American politics.* New York: The Free Press.

Sanchez, R. (1995, June 15). Survey finds maturity, cynicism among high-achieving teens. *Washington Post,* p. A3.

Sargent, L. W., & Stempel, G. H., III. (1968). Poverty, alienation and media use. *Journalism Quarterly, 45,* 324–326.

Schaefer, R. J., & Avery, R. K. (1993). Audience conceptualizations of "Late Night with David Letterman." *Journal of Broadcasting & Electronic Media, 37,* 253–273.

Schiesel, S. (1998, January 26). Cyberspace is on alert for more scandal news. *New York Times,* p. A14.

Schönbach, K., Lauf, E., McLeod, J. M., & Scheufele, D. A. (1999). Distinction and integration: Sociodemographic determinants of newspaper reading in the USA and Germany, 1974–96. *European Journal of Communication, 14,* 225–239.

Schramm, W., & White, D. M. (1949). Age, education, economic status: Factors in newspaper reading. *Journalism Quarterly, 26,* 149–159.

Scott, G. G. (1996). *Can we talk? The power and influence of talk shows.* New York: Insight Books.

Seelye, K. (1995, January 3). GOP starts expanding TV coverage. *New York Times,* p. A17.

Semple, R. B., Jr. (1969, January 19). Now Nixon: He comes to office cautiously and largely uncommitted. *New York Times,* p. E1.

Seter, J., Ito, T. M., & Bennefield, R. M. (1995, October 16). Simpson trial & trivia. *U.S. News & World Report,* pp. 42–43.

Shabecoff, P. (1976, December 8). Ford staff loses sense of momentum. *New York Times,* p. A1, B8.

Shaffer, S. D. (1981). A multivariate explanation of decreasing turnout in presidential elections, 1960–1976. *American Journal of Political Science, 25,* 68–95.

Shannon, E. (1995, January 30). Crime: Safer streets yet greater fear. *Time,* p. 63.

Shrum, L. J., O'Guinn, T. C., & Faber, R. J. (1993). Television and the social reality of consumption. Paper presented at the annual meeting of the International Communication Association, Washington, D.C.

Signorielli, N. (1987). Drinking, sex, and violence on television: The cultural indicators perspective. *Journal of Drug Education, 17,* 245–260.

Signorielli, N., & Morgan, M. (1996). Cultivation analysis: Research and practice. In M. B. Salwen & D. W. Stacks (Eds.), *An integrated approach to communication theory and research* (pp. 111–126). Mahwah, NJ: Lawrence Erlbaum.

Simmons Study of Media and Markets. (1994). *Technical guide.* New York: Simmons Market Research Bureau, Inc.

———. (1996). *Technical guide.* New York: Simmons Market Research Bureau, Inc.

Smoller, F. (1986). The six o'clock presidency: Patterns of network news coverage of the president. *Presidential Studies Quarterly, 16,* 31–49.

Smoller, F. T. (1990). *The six o'clock presidency: A theory of presidential press relations in the age of television.* New York: Praeger.

Sniderman, P. M. (1981). *A question of loyalty.* Berkeley, CA: University of California Press.

Solomon, J. (1996, November 8). Money equaled votes in congressional race. *Wisconsin State Journal,* p. 1A, 4A.

Sörbom, D., & Jöreskog, K. G. (1981). The use of LISREL in sociological model building. In D. J. Jackson & E. F. Borgatta (Eds.), *Factor analysis and measurement in sociological research: A multidimensional perspective* (pp. 179–199). Beverly Hills, CA: Sage.

Spayd, L. (1995, July 23). Welcome to the state of paranoia: Why America wallows in Waco and Whitewater. *Washington Post,* p. C1.

SRDS. (1995). *SRDS circulation report, 1995.* Des Plains, IL: SRDS Audit Bureau of Circulations.

———. (1996). *SRDS circulation report, 1996.* Des Plains, IL: SRDS Audit Bureau of Circulations.

Srull, T., & Wyer, R. (1979). The role of category accessibility in the interpretation of information about persons: Some determinants and implications. *Journal of Personality and Social Psychology, 37,* 1660–1672.

St. George, D. (1994, October 27). America's rush to judgment. Knight-Ridder Washington Bureau, p. 1.

Stokes, D. E. (1962). Popular evaluations of government: An empirical assessment. In H. Cleveland & H. D. Lasswell (Eds.), *Ethics and bigness: Scientific, academic, religious, political and military* (pp. 61–72). New York: Harper & Brothers.

Stone, G. (1987). *Examining newspapers: What research reveals about America's newspapers.* Beverly Hills, CA: Sage.

Supplemental Data Report (1994). *Paid circulation analysis by counties.* Schaumburg, IL: Audit Bureau of Circulation.

Swartz, J. (1999, March 27). Electronic engineering: Presidential wannabes take their campaigns to the Internet. *The San Francisco Chronicle,* p. D1.

Tanaka, J. S. (1993). Multifaceted conceptions of fit in structural equation models. In K. A. Bollen & J. S. Long (Eds.), *Testing structural equation models* (pp. 10–39). Newbury Park, CA: Sage.

Tapper, J. (1995). The ecology of cultivation: A conceptual model for cultivation research. *Communication Theory, 5,* 36–57.

Taylor, H. (1992, July/August). The American angst of 1992. *The Public Perspective,* pp. 3–5.

———. (1993, January 4). *Harris alienation index virtually unchanged from last year's all-time high.* New York: Louis Harris & Associates.

———. (1993, March). Confidence in military leadership climbs to highest point in 27 years; Confidence in medical leadership falls again. *The Harris Poll,* Number 11 (p. 3). New York: Louis Harris & Associates.

Taylor, P. (1996, February 1). Fading American dream haunts WWII generation. *Washington Post*, pp. A1, A10–11.

Thaler, P. (1997). *The spectacle: Media and the making of the O. J. Simpson story.* Westport, CT: Praeger.

Tidmarch, C. M., & Pitney, J. J., Jr., (1985). Covering Congress. *Polity, 17,* 463–483.

Time. (1995, May 22). The budget revolution. Cover story.

———. (1996, November 11). Clinton fund-raising scandal. Cover story.

———. (1998, February 2). Monica and Bill: The sordid tale that imperils the president. Cover story.

Times Mirror Center for the People and the Press. (1993, July 16). *The vocal minority in American politics.* Washington, D.C.: Times Mirror Center.

———. (1995). *The people, the press, and their leaders.* Washington, D.C.: Times Mirror Center.

Toch, T. with Bennefield, R. M. & Bernstein, A. (1996, April 1). The case for tough standards. *U.S. News & World Report,* pp. 52–56.

Tocqueville, A. de (1848/1969). *Democracy in America.* New York: Harper & Row.

Toedtman, J. (1995, May 22). Jaundiced view seen in poll; Says U.S. distrusts polls, business. *Newsday,* pp. 2–4.

Toner, R. (1991, January 13). Mindful of history, Congress agonizes over going to war. *New York Times,* Sec. 1, p. 12.

Traugott, M., Berinsky, A., Cramer, K., Howard, M., Mayer, R., Schuckman, H. P., Tewksbury, D., & Young, M. (1996, April). The impact of talk radio on its audience. Paper presented at the annual meeting of the Midwest Political Science Association, Chicago, Illinois.

Trumbo, C. (1995). Longitudinal modeling of public issues: An application of the agenda-setting process to the issue of global warming. *Journalism & Mass Communication Monographs, 152,* 1–57.

Tull, C. J. (1965). *Father Coughlin and the New Deal.* Syracuse, NY: Syracuse University Press.

Turow, J. (1974). Talk show radio as interpersonal communication. *Journal of Broadcasting, 18,* 171–179.

Tyndall, A. (1998, Winter). What gets on the networks? *Media Studies Journal, 12,* 54–59.

Verba, S., Schlozman, K. L., & Brady, H. E. (1995). *Voice and equality: Civic voluntarism in American politics.* Cambridge: Harvard University Press.

Viles, P. (1993, July 12). Hosts, callers trash Clinton on talk radio. *Broadcasting & Cable,* p. 43.

Walsh, E. (1981, January 18). A flawed presidency of good intentions. *New York Times,* p. C1, C4.

Wamsley, G. L., & Pride, R. A. (1972). Television network news: Re-thinking the iceberg problem. *The Western Political Quarterly, 25,* 434–450.

Weatherford, M. S. (1987). How does government performance influence political support? *Political Behavior, 9,* 5–28.

Weaver, D. (1994). Media agenda setting and elections: Voter involvement or alienation? *Political Communication, 11,* 347–356.

Weaver, P. (1972). Is television news biased? *Public Interest, 26,* 57–74.

Weisberg, J. (1996). *In defense of government: The fall and rise of public trust.* New York: Scribner.

Wicker, T. (1969, January 19). The last post for LBJ. *New York Times,* p. E23.

Wisconsin State Journal. (1995, April 18). Simpson trial degenerates. p. 7A.

———. (1995, November 14). Schoolchildren against segregation. p. 1C.

Woodward, G. C. (1997). *Perspectives on American political media.* Boston: Allyn & Bacon.

Wright, J. D. (1976). *The dissent of the governed: Alienation and democracy in America.* New York: Academic Press.

Zerbinos, E. (1995–1996). The talk radio phenomenon: An update. *Journal of Radio Studies, 3,* 10–22.

Zoglin, R. (1995, January 30). Talking trash. *Time,* pp. 77–78.

Index

About the Authors

PATRICIA MOY is Assistant Professor, School of Communications, University of Washington. Professor Moy has published numerous articles in journals dealing with communication and journalism issues.

MICHAEL PFAU is Professor and Director of Graduate Studies, School of Journalism and Mass Communication, University of Wisconsin–Madison. Professor Pfau has published five earlier books and numerous journal articles dealing with the media and public perceptions.